Multimedia Projects in Education

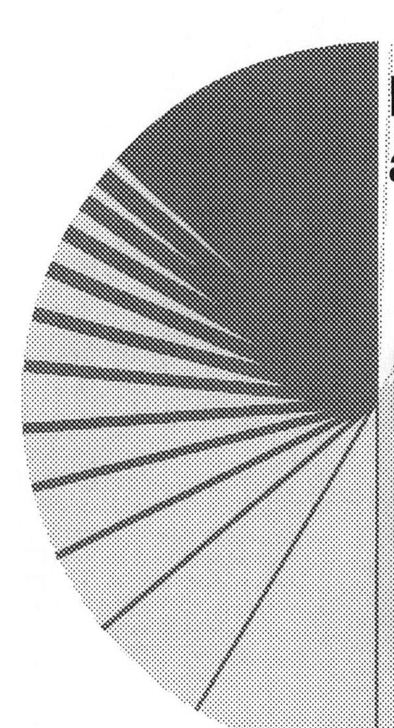

Designing, Producing, and Assessing Multimedia Projects in Education

Karen S. Ivers and Ann E. Barron

1998
Libraries Unlimited, Inc.
and Its Division
Teacher Ideas Press
Englewood, Colorado

LIBRARIES UNLIMITED, INC.
and Its Division
Teacher Ideas Press
P.O. Box 6633
Englewood, CO 80155-6633
1-800-237-6124
www.lu.com

Library of Congress Cataloging-in-Publication Data

Ivers, Karen S.
Multimedia projects in education : designing, producing, and assessing / Karen S. Ivers and Ann E. Barron.
xviii, 201 p. 22×28 cm.
Includes bibliographical references and index.
ISBN 1-56308-572-0
1. Media programs (Education) 2. Interactive multimedia.
3. Instructional systems--Design. I. Barron, Ann E. II. Title.
LB1028.4.I95 1998
371.33--dc21 97-28332
CIP

CONTENTS

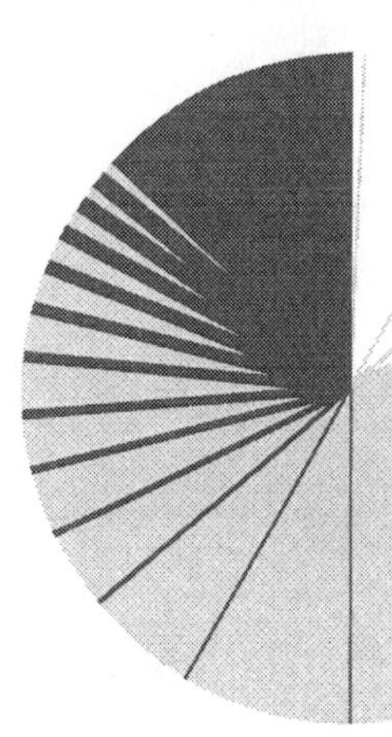

FIGURES

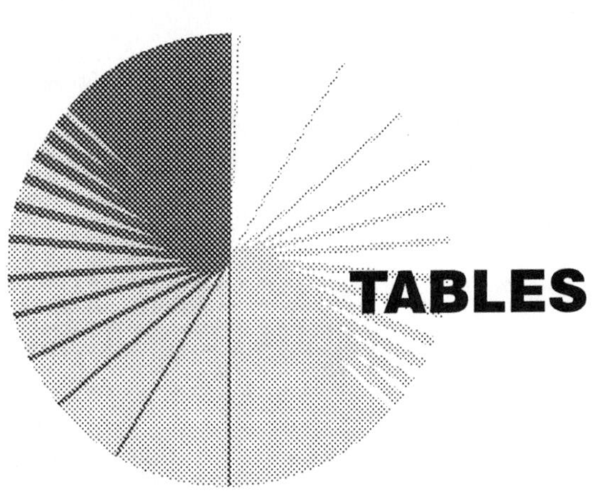

TABLES

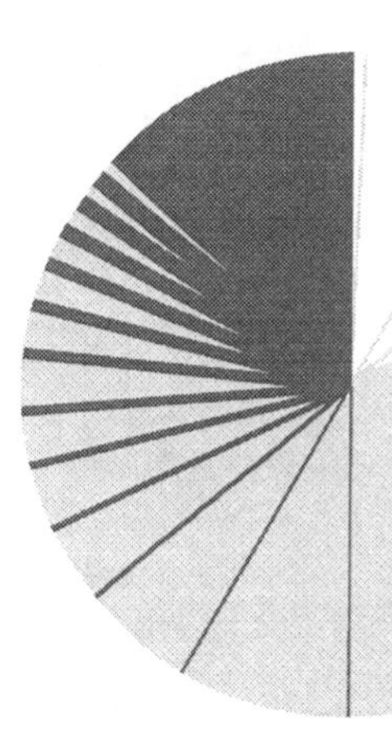

PREFACE

There is nothing more rewarding for an educator than to experience the enthusiasm and joy created by students actively engaged in and enthralled by a learning activity. Students *willingly* seek knowledge, spend extra time on their projects, and take pride in their work. Both the teacher and the students enjoy coming to school!

Although there are no magic potions to guarantee positive student outcomes, teachers can use a variety of strategies to ensure that learning is an active, personally relevant, meaningful process. These strategies include cooperative learning, constructivism, identifying each individual student's needs and talents, and using a variety of alternative assessment techniques. *Multimedia Projects in Education: Designing, Producing, and Assessing* provides educators with strategies and ideas for incorporating multimedia projects into the curriculum, taking advantage of the many benefits associated with the development of multimedia projects.

Multimedia Projects in Education: Designing, Producing, and Assessing begins by describing research in the areas of cooperative learning, multiple intelligences, and constructivism. It provides practical ideas as to how these theories can be applied to the development of multimedia projects. Chapter 2 introduces a model (DECIDE, DESIGN, DEVELOP, and EVALUATE) that is used to guide the reader throughout the rest of the book. Chapter 3 (DECIDE) discusses classroom management issues, grouping alternatives, computer scheduling options, and other issues related to deciding on a project. Chapter 4 (DESIGN) introduces the reader to the planning stages of multimedia development, including flowcharts, storyboards, and basic design issues. DEVELOP is divided into two chapters. Chapter 5 (DEVELOP: Media Components) addresses and defines the various media components that are available for multimedia projects. Chapter 6 (DEVELOP: Authoring Multimedia Projects) describes and teaches readers the basics of three development tools: HyperStudio®, HTML, and Microsoft® PowerPoint®. Chapter 7 (EVALUATE) discusses alternative assessment techniques, assessment strategies, and how to design a rubric.

Following the chapters on DECIDE, DESIGN, DEVELOP, and EVALUATE, activity chapters provide the reader with multimedia project ideas for authoring tools, Web pages, and presentation tools. The activities focus on several content areas and levels of research for a variety of grade levels. Chapters contain detailed graphics, charts, and tables. In addition, blackline masters are included that can be copied for educational purposes.

Throughout the book, emphasis is placed on managing the development of multimedia projects and on student learning outcomes. Each chapter begins with a scenario illustrating the implementation of multimedia projects in an educational setting. Teachers, media specialists, and administrators will find this book an invaluable resource for producing, designing, and assessing multimedia projects.

This book is designed from the educator's perspective and can be used to facilitate classroom instruction as well as in-service workshops on strategies for developing multimedia projects. It is appropriate for classroom teachers and for educational technology courses at both the undergraduate and graduate levels.

CHAPTER 1

Impact of Multimedia on Student Learning

A Scenario

Ms. Othmar's classroom was anything but still and quiet. Her students were engaged in small group discussions, intent on completing their storyboards for their multimedia projects. Student teams consisted of four members. Team members worked with each other to create wording for the storyboards, decide whether still pictures or animations should be used, and find possible audio segments. Each team was responsible for developing a multimedia project on a selected state. Ms. Othmar's fifth graders had previously brainstormed and voted on topics for research about their state, in addition to those assigned by Ms. Othmar. The class had also decided on a standard layout for the projects, because each project would eventually be linked to a main menu. After the students had an opportunity to view several examples of multimedia projects, they agreed that consistency made certain projects easier to understand and follow. As Ms. Othmar observed and interacted with each group, she noticed that all of her students were on task and felt as though they had something to contribute. She reflected on the amount of planning that she had put into developing this year's unit on state reports, but she already knew her time was well spent. Her students were engaged in higher level processing skills and *wanted* to learn! Unlike previous assignments, Ms. Othmar's students were working together and displaying a sense of ownership and pride in their learning. What more could a teacher want?

Recess came quickly, but many of the students wanted to stay in the classroom to continue working on their projects or to get a head start on finding clip art on the computer. The students' desire to use the classroom computers added to the attraction of the multimedia projects. Students adapted to the technology quickly, unlike Ms. Othmar and several of her colleagues. Ms. Othmar was determined, however, to keep abreast of the latest tools in teaching and learning. Following several workshops and a class at her local university, Ms. Othmar jumped at the opportunity to integrate computers as a tool into her curriculum. As with other instructional units, she learned that effective technology integration requires planning, flexibility, and a means to assess and evaluate students' learning.

Overview

Multimedia projects allow students to exhibit their understanding of a topic in a variety of ways, and they provide students with the opportunity to explain their work and ideas to others. Bennett (1996, 16) notes that students "know that they have learned something when they can explain their work and ideas to others or when they can successfully teach others difficult concepts or content." Multimedia provides students with a powerful medium of communication and offers students new insights into organizing, synthesizing, and evaluating information. Multimedia has the potential to change the roles of teacher and learner and the interaction between them by allowing students to create their own interpretations of information.

In addition to content knowledge and skill development, developing multimedia projects offers students the opportunity to work collaboratively, engage in multimodalities of learning and reflective thinking, and use a constructivist approach to learning. This chapter defines multimedia and examines research addressing the benefits of developing multimedia projects. Topics include:

- Definition of multimedia
- Why use multimedia?
- Research on multimedia and student learning
  - —Howard Gardner's Theory of Multiple Intelligences
  - —Cooperative learning
  - —Constructivism

Definition of Multimedia

In general terms, *multimedia* is the use of several media to present information. Combinations may include text, graphics, animation, pictures, video, and sound. Educators have been using multimedia for years. For example, it is not uncommon for teachers to support a unit on Spain with videotapes, audio cassettes, pictures, text, and artifacts. Today's technologies, however, allow educators and students to integrate, combine, and interact with media far beyond what was previously possible.

"Hyper" environments, such as hypertext and hypermedia, have added to the complexity and sophistication of multimedia's definition by providing electronic, nonlinear approaches to moving through a body of information. Hypertext facilitates interaction between readers and texts by organizing and linking information through text chunks. This is used to create associations, definitions, examples, and other relationships between the text passages (Rouet, Levon, Dillion, and Spiro 1996). Hypermedia adds video clips, graphics, or audio files to hypertext. The combination of these elements results in greater comprehension, recall, and inference (Large, Beheshti, Breuleux, and Renaud 1995). These multimodal approaches to education are effective for accommodating students with diverse learning and cognitive styles (Chun and Plass 1995; Frey and Simonson 1993; Jones and Berger 1995). In addition, hypermedia applications are better suited to transmit knowledge that is not easily conveyed through print or verbal explanations (Ayersman 1996).

Both hypertext and hypermedia can be considered subsets of multimedia. Combining the traditional elements of multimedia with hyper environments, Gayeski (1993, 4) defines *computer-based* multimedia as "a class of computer-driven interactive communications systems which create, store, transmit, and retrieve textual, graphical and auditory networks of information." In other words, computer-based multimedia involves the computer presentation of multiple media formats (e.g., text, pictures, sounds, video, etc.) to convey information in a linear or nonlinear format. This book is based on this definition.

Why Use Multimedia?

Multimedia projects encourage students to work in groups, express their knowledge in multiple ways, solve problems, revise their own work, and construct knowledge. Students have the opportunity to learn and apply real-world skills. They learn the value of teamwork; the impact and importance of different media, including design issues, media appropriateness, and copyright laws; the challenges of communicating to different audiences; the importance of research, planning, and organization skills; the significance of presentation and speaking skills; and how to accept and provide constructive feedback. Creating multimedia projects helps to reinforce students' technology skills and to prepare students for the demands of future job options.

Research on Multimedia and Student Learning

Within the last decade, advancements in technology have made it possible for teachers and students to develop elaborate multimedia programs in the classroom. Using Macintosh and PC-based computers, students are able to express themselves through a variety of media—text, audio, video, graphics, animation, and sound—in linear and nonlinear formats. Although limited, research in the area of multimedia is promising, demonstrating that the use of multimedia can be effective for teaching and learning (Ayersman 1996; Najjar 1996) with all levels of students, including those with special needs (Hearne and Stone 1995; Hoerr 1992; Moeller and Jeffers 1996; Rieber 1995).

Viewing the learner as an active participant in the process of acquiring and using knowledge, educators are reexamining ways to activate appropriate learning strategies during the instructional process. These include a renewed interest in cooperative learning (Slavin 1990), a shift from behavioral theories of learning to cognitive theories of learning (Toffler 1990), and an investigation into the theory of multiple intelligences (Armstrong 1994). This section examines these theories and their relationship to the design and development of multimedia projects.

Howard Gardner's Theory of Multiple Intelligences

Several researchers have developed theories on various ways of knowing, suggesting that students possess several different intelligences (Gardner 1983; Samples 1992; Sternberg 1994). Perhaps the most recognized theory of multiple ways of knowing is Howard Gardner's Theory of Multiple Intelligences (Gardner 1983). In his book, *Frames of the Mind: The Theory of Multiple Intelligences*, Gardner identifies at least seven different dimensions of human intellectual functioning.

Gardner defines *intelligence* as the ability to resolve problems and to create an effective product that is valued in society. He also notes that intelligence "must also entail the potential for finding or creating problems, thereby laying the groundwork for the acquisition of new knowledge" (Gardner 1983, 61). Gardner's proposed seven areas of intelligence include:

1. Linguistic Intelligence—the ability to use words effectively, whether orally or in writing.
2. Logical-Mathematical Intelligence—the capacity to use numbers effectively and to reason well.
3. Spatial Intelligence—the ability to perceive the visual-spatial world accurately and to perform transformations upon those perceptions.
4. Bodily-Kinesthetic Intelligence—expertise in using one's body to express ideas and feelings and facility in using one's hands to produce or transform things.
5. Musical Intelligence—the ability to perceive, discriminate, transform, and express musical forms.
6. Interpersonal Intelligence—the ability to perceive and make distinctions in the moods, intentions, motivations, and feelings of other people.
7. Intrapersonal Intelligence—self-knowledge and the ability to act on the basis of that knowledge.

Gardner identified these intelligences based on a series of tests that included eight different criteria. Additional intelligences have been proposed—including spirituality, moral sensibility, sexuality, humor, intuition, and creativity—but it remains to be seen whether these proposed intelligences meet the required criteria (Armstrong 1994).

There are several important elements to remember about Gardner's Theory of Multiple Intelligences. In his book, *Multiple Intelligences in the Classroom*, Armstrong (1994) states that:

- Each person possesses all seven intelligences
- Most people can develop each intelligence to an adequate level of competency
- Intelligences usually work together in complex ways
- There are many ways to be intelligent within each category

Many educators have successfully implemented Gardner's Theory of Multiple Intelligences into their classrooms and have found these statements to be true (Blythe and Gardner 1990; Bolanos 1994; Ellison 1992; Fowler 1990; Hoerr 1992). The application of Gardner's Theory of Multiple Intelligences can benefit all learners, including learning-disabled students (Hearne and Stone 1995), gifted students (Hoerr 1994), and students from diverse cultural backgrounds (Gray and Viens 1994).

Commercial multimedia applications and the development of multimedia projects encourage a multimodal approach to learning. Well-designed multimedia applications present content in a variety of media formats and allow students to use their own individual learning styles.

Intelligence	Observed Student Behaviors	Roles in Multimedia Projects
Linguistic	Loves to read books, write, and tell stories; good memory for names, dates, and trivia; communicates well	Gather and develop text for project; provide narration; keep journal of group progress
Logical–Mathematical	Excels in math; has strong problem-solving skills; enjoys playing strategy games and working on logic puzzles	Design flowchart; write scripting and programming code; develop navigation routes
Spatial	Needs a mental or physical picture to best understand things; draws figures that are advanced for age; doodles a lot	Create graphics, animation, and other visual media for project; design layout
Bodily–Kinesthetic	Excels in one or more sports; good fine motor skills; tendency to move around, touch things, gesture	Keyboard information; manipulate objects with mouse; operate multimedia equipment
Musical	Remembers melodies; recognizes when music is off-key; has a good singing voice; plays an instrument; hums a lot	Identify works for content integration; create musical score for project; input audio/sound effects
Interpersonal	Enjoys socializing with peers; has leadership skills; has a good sense of empathy and concern for others	Coordinate group efforts; help set group goals; help solve group disputes
Intrapersonal	Has strong sense of self; is confident; prefers working alone; has high self-esteem; displays independence	Conduct independent research to share with teammates; pilot test multimedia projects; lead multimedia project presentations

Table 1.1 Roles of multiple intelligences in the creation of multimedia projects

Although multimedia applications can effectively teach content, student-based multimedia projects allow students to gain skills beyond content-area knowledge. These skills include finding and interpreting information, articulating and communicating knowledge, and using the computer as a cognitive tool (Ayersman 1996).

Applying the Theory of Multiple Intelligences to Multimedia Projects

One of the many benefits of developing multimedia projects is that it allows students to construct and communicate knowledge in various ways. Multimedia projects also encourage group work and social interaction, but they do not require a uniform experience for all students. According to Levin (1994), group work and social interaction are necessary for a multiple intelligences approach, but a uniform experience for all children is not.

When assigning multimedia design teams, students should be placed in groups that provide them with the opportunity to take advantage of their strengths, as well as nurture their weaknesses. For example, students who are observed as or identify themselves as spatial intelligent might be responsible for the graphic content and layout of a multimedia project. Students who are observed as or identify themselves as logical-mathematical intelligent might be responsible for designing the structure/flowchart of the project and the scripting or programming requirements. Table 1.1 identifies an intelligence, observed student behaviors, and a recommended role in the development of a multimedia project.

It is important to note that all students have all intelligences, though one or more may be stronger than others. Placing students in design teams that capture the diversity of their intellectual profiles can provide them with the motivation, skills, and support necessary to learn. Armstrong (1994) comments that most students have strengths in several areas; hence, students may contribute to projects in multiple ways. For example, one student may lead the group in developing the text and music for the project, another student may lead the group in creating the graphics and flowcharts for the project, and so on.

Intellectual profiles can change over time as intelligences develop in strength. Gray and Viens (1994, 24) note that "the differences among individual intellectual profiles are the result of personal and local factors as well as cultural influences." Working in diverse groups allows students to nurture their weaknesses and capitalize on their strengths. Students are able to make valuable contributions to group projects as well as augment their intellectual profiles.

Cooperative Learning

Cooperative learning takes place when students work together to accomplish shared goals. Most cooperative conditions use small groups "so that individuals work together to maximize their own and each other's productivity and achievement" (Johnson and Johnson 1991, 6). Johnson, Johnson, and Holubec (1994) suggest that a cooperative learning group has five defining characteristics:

1. There is a group goal to maximize all members' learning beyond their individual abilities.
2. Group members hold themselves and each other accountable for high-quality work.
3. Group members work face-to-face to produce joint products, providing both academic and personal support.
4. Group members are taught social skills and are expected to use them to coordinate their efforts; teamwork and taskwork are emphasized.
5. Groups analyze how well they are achieving their goals, working together, and learning.

As a result, Johnson, Johnson, and Holubec (1994) state that a cooperative group is more than the sum of its parts; students perform better academically than they would if they worked by themselves.

There are a variety of cooperative group techniques, including Student Teams Achievement Divisions, Teams Games Tournament, Team Assisted Individualization, Jigsaw, Group Investigation, and Learning Together (Slavin 1987; 1990):

- *Student Teams Achievement Divisions (STAD)*—students learn something as a team, contribute to the team by improving their own past performance, and earn team rewards based on their improvements. Students are usually heterogeneously mixed by ability and take individual weekly quizzes. For example, student teams may study about the Westward Movement and take weekly quizzes on the content. Teams earn points based on each student's improvement from previous quizzes. For example, if a student scores 5 out of 10 points on the first quiz and 8 out of 10 on the second quiz, he may earn 8 points for his team, plus 2 bonus points for improving. If a student scores 7 out of 10 points on the first quiz and 5 out of 10 on the second quiz, he may earn 5 points for his team, but no bonus points. If a student scores 10 points on both quizzes, she may earn a total of 12 points (10 points for the second quiz plus 2 bonus points for the perfect score) for her team.

- *Teams Games Tournament (TGT)*—similar to STAD except that weekly tournaments replace weekly quizzes. Homogeneous, three-member teams are formed from the existing heterogeneous groups and compete against similar ability groups to earn points for their regular, heterogeneous group. As with STAD, high-performing teams earn group rewards. For example, existing heterogeneous groups may contain one each low-, average-, and high-ability student. During weekly tournaments (e.g., a game of Jeopardy), low-ability students form groups of three, average-ability students form groups of three, and high-ability students form groups of three. Low-ability groups compete against each other, average-ability groups compete against each other, and high-ability groups compete against each other. The winning homogeneous groups earn points for their heterogeneous teams.
- *Team Assisted Individualization (TAI)*—combines cooperative learning with individualized instruction. Students are placed into groups but work at their own pace and level. Team members check each other's work and help one another with problems. Teams earn points based on the individual performance of each member in the group. Slavin (1990, 5) notes that "[s]tudents encourage and help one another to succeed because they want their teams to succeed." For example, students at different spelling levels may be placed into heterogeneous groups. The group may consist of one low speller, two average spellers, and one advanced speller. Students are responsible for learning their assigned spelling words, but they have their team members to assist and encourage them. Groups earn points based on their team members' performance on weekly spelling tests. Members take responsibility for each other's learning as well as their own.
- *Jigsaw*—a method of cooperative group learning that assigns each of its members a particular learning task. For example, learning about the Civil War may include famous men and women, battles, economic factors, and issues of slavery. Each member chooses a topic and is responsible for teaching his or her team members "all that there is to know" about that topic. Team members meet with other members of other groups to form "expert groups" to discuss and research their topic. For example, the team members of the cooperative groups who chose famous women would meet together in a separate cooperative group focused on learning only about famous women of the Civil War. Following research and discussion, the students return to their own teams and take

turns teaching their teammates about their topic. Afterward, students take individual quizzes and earn a team score.

- *Group Investigation*—similar to the Jigsaw method except that students do not form expert groups. Student teams give class presentations of findings rather than taking tests.
- *Learning Together*—incorporates heterogeneous student groups that work on a single assignment and receive rewards based on their group product. For example, student groups may be assigned to draw and label the human skeletal system. Each student would receive the same final grade for the group product.

Cooperative learning groups differ from traditional learning groups in that most support positive interdependence, individual accountability, group processing, peer responsibility, and heterogeneous membership (Johnson and Johnson 1991). General findings conclude that:

- Cooperative groups are appropriate for any instructional task.
- Cooperative groups do just as well or better on achievement than competitive and individualistic learning conditions.
- Cooperative conditions appear to work best when students are heterogeneously grouped, although high-ability students do just as well or better in homogeneous groups.
- Group discussion promotes higher achievement.
- Cooperative learning is more likely to have an effect on student outcomes when cooperation is well defined.
- Stereotypes are likely to be reduced when using cooperative groups.
- Using cooperative groups promotes equality among perceived ability and leadership roles among males and females.
- Cooperative learning can reduce anxiety and create more interesting learning.
- Cooperative groups can be more cost-effective than individualistic learning conditions.
- Cooperative learning appears to be effective at all primary and secondary grade levels and with groups of two to five.
- Cooperative conditions can benefit all ability levels.
- Cooperative groups support achievement-oriented behavior and healthy social development.
- Cooperative grouping can increase student self-esteem and foster higher-order thinking skills.

Although researchers report many positive outcomes of using cooperative learning (Adams and Hamm 1990; Johnson and Johnson 1991; Sharan 1990; Slavin 1990), others note that there are pitfalls (Johnson and Johnson 1991; Slavin 1990). Pitfalls include the "free-rider effect" (members let the more capable members do all the work) and the "sucker effect" (more able members have the less able members

Cooperative Group Method	Multimedia Project Example and Evaluation	Student Roles and Responsibilities in Multimedia Projects
Student Teams Achievement Divisions (STAD)	Groups are provided with specific questions for research and content information on the Westward Movement. They display their knowledge through group multimedia projects. Announced weekly quizzes check individual content learning. A rubric can be used to evaluate final projects for a group grade.	Students learn about the Westward Movement as a team, helping each other understand the content. Groups may alternate project responsibilities to ensure that everyone has a chance to encounter the content in different ways.
Teams Games Tournament (TGT)	Same as STAD, except weekly tournaments replace weekly quizzes. Responsibilities remain the same.	
Team Assisted Individualization (TAI)	Groups create projects on a select genre, such as mystery stories. Groups display information about several books. The project is evaluated based on each student's book report.	Each student is responsible for reading a select book (at the appropriate level) and reporting on it through multimedia. The team project introduces and links each report.
Jigsaw	Groups create projects on the Civil War. Students are evaluated on their group's final project and their individual knowledge of all the content areas researched for the Civil War.	Each member is assigned a particular content area of the Civil War, such as famous men and women, battles, economic factors, issues of slavery, and so on. Members meet with other groups' members assigned to the same content area. For example, members researching famous battles meet together and help each other become "expert" on the topic. Members return to their original groups and share what they have learned. Students design their portion of the group's multimedia project. (This approach may also be used to learn about different skills, such as creating animation, scanning, and the like.)
Group Investigation	Similar to the Jigsaw method, except that students do not form expert groups. Student teams give class presentations of their findings instead of taking tests.	
Learning Together	Groups decide on a multimedia project of interest (e.g., a project about volcanoes) and present their final project to the class. Each student receives the same final grade for the group product.	After deciding on the project, students determine each other's roles and responsibilities based on their interests. Responsibilities and roles may change during the project. (Individual accountability may be weak.)

Table 1.2 Cooperative group settings and responsibilities in multimedia projects

do all the work). Individual accountability and grades based on the average of the team's individual scores can help to avoid these pitfalls (Johnson and Johnson 1991; Slavin 1990).

Applying the Theory of Cooperative Learning to Multimedia Projects

Benefits of using cooperative groups in multimedia design and development include collaborative help-seeking and help-giving, increased use of metacognitive and elaboration strategies, the accommodation of individual differences, self-reflection, increased motivation and positive attitudes toward learning, and increased performance (Ayersman 1996; Milone 1994; Schroeder and Zarinnia 1994). The teacher's role is to guide and facilitate the cooperative groups' efforts. Table 1.2 provides examples of students' roles and responsibilities in different cooperative group settings. Cooperative group methods that require individual accountability and assign grades based on the average of the team's individual scores are recommended (see ch. 7).

Cooperative group multimedia projects support small group interactions and the development of original projects reflective of the groups' collaboration (Wilson and Tally 1991). In addition, cooperative groups can reduce the complexity and time commitment of creating multimedia projects by assigning students to specific design roles and responsibilities. Each student contributes to the project as a whole and has the opportunity to share his or her expertise with, as well as learn from, others. Techniques for establishing, monitoring, and assessing group projects are included in chapters 3 and 7.

Constructivism

Cognitive psychologists believe in the process of learning through the construction of knowledge. They assert that "people learn by actively constructing knowledge, weighing new information against their previous understanding, thinking about and working through discrepancies (on their own and with others), and coming to a new understanding" (Association for Supervision and Curriculum Development 1992, 2). These ideas, combined with social learning, are not new. Kilpatrick (1918) expressed the need to base education on purposeful acts and social activity, which he designed into his project method of instruction. Dewey (1929) stated that "social tools" (reading, spelling, and writing) are best acquired in a social context. Piaget believed that people try to make sense of the world and actively create their own knowledge through direct experience with objects, people, and ideas (Woolfolk 1987). Vygotsky (1978, 88) argued that "human learning presupposes a specific social nature and a process by which children grow into the intellectual life of those around them."

Constructivist principles emphasize student reflection, inquiry, and higher order thinking skills. Student reflection, or metacognition, is integral to successful learning, whereas passiveness, low self-esteem, complex learning tasks, inexperience, and low comprehension can be detrimental to learning (Osman and Hannafin 1992). Brook and Brook (1993) define *constructivist teachers* as those who

- Encourage and accept student autonomy and initiative
- Use raw data and primary sources, along with manipulative, interactive, and physical materials
- Use cognitive terminology such as *classify*, *analyze*, *predict*, and *create*
- Allow student responses to drive lessons, shift instructional strategies, and alter content
- Inquire about students' understanding of concepts before sharing their own understandings of those concepts
- Encourage students to engage in conversations with the teacher and with one another
- Encourage student inquiry by asking thoughtful, open-ended questions and encouraging students to ask questions of each other
- Seek elaboration of students' initial responses

- Engage students in experiences that might create contradictions to their initial hypotheses and then encourage discussion
- Allow wait time after posing questions
- Provide time for students to construct relationships and create metaphors
- Nurture students' natural curiosity through frequent use of the learning cycle model (discovery, concept introduction, and concept application)

These teacher practices can help guide students in their own understanding and intellectual and reflective growth. The development of multimedia projects provides an ideal forum for a constructivist approach.

Applying the Theory of Constructivism to Multimedia Projects

Research has demonstrated that developing multimedia projects can help students to learn how to think, develop concepts and ideas, apply what they learn, question, and solve problems (Toomey and Ketterer 1995). Riddle (1995) reports that students are more likely to show greater descriptive detail, unique perspectives, and diverse interests and skills when using multimedia software to create and add graphics, audio, and animation to their textual communications. Turner and Dipinto (1992) suggest that developing multimedia projects can give students new insights into writing as well as organizing and synthesizing information. Furthermore, Lehrer, Erickson, and Connell (1994) report that developing multimedia projects allows students to construct and learn course content using higher level thinking skills. Developing multimedia projects requires students to find and interpret information, articulate and communicate knowledge, and use the computer as a cognitive tool. As a result of developing multimedia projects, Ayersman (1996) notes that students begin to see themselves as authors of knowledge.

According to Simons (1993), constructivist learning includes at least five components: active, cumulative, integrative, reflective, and goal-directed. Their definitions and relationship to the construction of multimedia projects are presented in table 1.3.

Herman, Aschbacher, and Winters (1992) also discuss the implications of aligning instruction and assessment with constructivist learning. Table 1.4 presents cognitive learning theories and their implications for instruction, assessment, and multimedia projects.

Multimedia projects can provide ideal learning environments for implementing a constructivist approach to learning. The creation of multimedia projects encourages divergent thinking, multiple modes of expression, goal setting, critical thinking skills, teamwork, opportunities to revise and rethink, and more. Students are active participants, constructing knowledge that is meaningful, applicable, and memorable. In addition, multimedia projects provide educators with multiple ways to assess students' progress. These strategies are discussed in chapter 7.

Constructivist Learning Component	Definition	Relationship to Creating Multimedia Projects
Active	Students process information meaningfully.	Multimedia projects allow students to be active learners by defining the content and creating the media components.
Cumulative	Learning builds on prior knowledge.	Multimedia projects allow students to connect current knowledge to new ideas through a variety of formats.
Integrative	Learners elaborate on new knowledge.	Multimedia projects offer environments in which students can create increasingly complex programs, as well as present current and new knowledge in new ways.
Reflective	Students assess what they know and need to learn.	Multimedia projects incorporate multiple levels of assessment at various phases throughout the design and development process.
Goal-directed	Learners engage in purposeful learning activities.	When assigning multimedia projects, the teacher and students work together to define specific learning outcomes.

Table 1.3 Constructivist components and their relationships to creating multimedia projects

Summary

Multimedia is the use of several media to present information. Computer-based multimedia involves the computer presentation of multiple media formats to convey information in a linear or nonlinear format. Creating multimedia projects reinforces students' technology skills and invites students to use a variety of media to express their understanding and work cooperatively. It is a process approach to learning, encouraging students to think differently about how they organize and present information. It supports a collaborative writing environment, self-reflection, authentic learning, and use of the computer as a cognitive tool. In addition, multimedia projects provide an effective alternative for assessing student learning and help to prepare students for the real world.

Research demonstrates that multimedia development tools provide students with opportunities to show greater descriptive detail, unique perspectives, and diverse interests and skills. It is possible that these tools may help students to develop what may otherwise be paralyzed or "shut-down" intelligences. Opportunities to explore concepts and express understanding through multimedia may create positive turning points in the development of a student's intelligences. Students report a desire to learn, feel more confident, and consider themselves producers of knowledge rather than consumers when creating multimedia projects. By working cooperatively and constructing knowledge, students become empowered learners.

Cognitive Learning Theory	Implications for Instruction/Assessment	Relationship to Creating Multimedia Projects
Learning is a process of creating personal meaning from new information and prior knowledge.	Encourage discussion, divergent thinking, multiple links and solutions, varied modes of expression, critical thinking skills; relate new information to personal experience; apply information to new situations.	Projects encourage knowledge construction and group efforts, stimulating discussion and divergent thinking. Media elements provide various modes of expression.
Learning is not necessarily a linear progression of discrete skills.	Engage students in problem solving and critical thinking.	The development of flowcharts and storyboards requires problem-solving and critical thinking skills to "chunk" and organize information into linear and nonlinear formats. Students see how data relate to each other.
There is a variety of learning styles, attention spans, developmental paces, and intelligences.	Provide choices in task, varied means of showing mastery and competence, time to think about and do assignments, opportunities to revise and rethink, and concrete experiences.	Design teams offer task options, allowing students to demonstrate their skills in a variety of ways. The process of developing projects requires students to revise and rethink, and provides students with hands-on, concrete learning experiences.
Students perform better when they know the goal, see models, and know how their performance compares to the standard.	Discuss goals and let students help define them (personal and class); provide and discuss examples of student work and allow them to have input into standards; give students opportunities for self-evaluation and peer review.	Rubrics, goals, and standards for projects can be decided as a whole class without sacrificing the teacher's basic objectives. Sample projects can help to clarify project expectations. The process of developing projects encourages self-evaluation and peer review.
It is important to know when to use knowledge, how to adapt it, and how to manage one's own learning.	Provide real-world opportunities (or simulations) to apply or adapt new knowledge; provide opportunities for students to think about how they learn, why they like certain work, etc.	Multimedia projects support real-world learning experiences, plus they have the potential to enhance students' communication and metacognitive skills.
Motivation, effort, and self-esteem affect learning and performance.	Motivate students with real-life tasks and connections to personal experiences; encourage students to see the relationship between effort and results.	Projects provide students with real-life tasks that they can connect to their personal interests and experiences. Projects serve as visual outcomes of students' efforts.
Learning has social components. Group work is valuable.	Provide group work; establish heterogeneous groups; enable students to take on a variety of roles; consider group products and group processes.	Multimedia projects encourage cooperative grouping techniques.

Table 1.4 Cognitive learning theories' relationships to multimedia project creation

References

Adams, D. M., and M. E. Hamm. 1990. *Cooperative learning: Critical thinking and collaboration across the curriculum*. Springfield, IL: Charles C. Thomas.

Armstrong, T. 1994. *Multiple intelligences in the classroom*. Alexandria, VA: Association for Supervision and Curriculum Development.

Association for Supervision and Curriculum Development (ASCD). 1992. Wanted: Deep understanding. "Constructivism" posits new conception of learning. *ASCD Update* 34(3): 1–5.

Ayersman, D. J. 1996. Reviewing the research on hypermedia-based learning. *Journal of Research on Computing in Education* 28(4): 500–25.

Bennett, D. T. 1996. Assessment through video. *Electronic Learning* 15(4): 16–17.

Blythe, T., and H. Gardner. 1990. A school for all intelligences. *Educational Leadership* 47(7): 33–37.

Bolanos, P. J. 1994. From theory to practice: Indianapolis' Key School applies Howard Gardner's multiple intelligences theory to the classroom. *School Administrator* 51(1): 30–31.

Brook, J. G., and M. G. Brook. 1993. *In search of understanding: The case for constructivist classrooms.* Alexandria, VA: Association for Supervision and Curriculum Development.

Chun, D. M., and J. Plass. 1995. Project Cyberbuch: A hypermedia approach to computer-assisted language learning. *Journal of Educational Multimedia and Hypermedia* 4(1): 95–116.

Dewey, J. 1929. *The sources of a science of education.* New York: Horace Liveright.

Ellison, L. 1992. Using multiple intelligences to set goals. *Educational Leadership* 50(2): 69–72.

Fowler, C. 1990. Recognizing the role of artistic intelligences. *Music Educators Journal* 77(1): 24–27.

Frey, D., and M. Simonson. 1993. Assessment of cognitive style to examine students' use of hypermedia within historic costume. *Home Economics Research Journal* 21(4): 403–21.

Gardner, H. 1983. *Frames of mind: the theory of multiple intelligences.* New York: Basic Books.

Gayeski, D. M. 1993. *Multimedia for learning.* Englewood Cliffs, NJ: Educational Technology Publications.

Gray, J. H., and J. T. Viens. 1994. The theory of multiple intelligences: Understanding cognitive diversity in school. *National Forum: Phi Kappa Phi Journal* 74(1): 22–25.

Hearne, D., and S. Stone. 1995. Multiple intelligences and underachievement: Lessons for individuals with learning disabilities. *Journal of Learning Disabilities* 28(7): 439–48.

Herman, J. L., P. R. Aschbacher, and L. Winters. 1992. *A practical guide to alternative assessment.* Alexandria, VA: Association for Supervision and Curriculum Development.

Hoerr, T. R. 1994. The multiple intelligence approach to giftedness. *Contemporary Education* 66(1): 32–35.

Hoerr, T. R. 1992. How our school applied multiple intelligences theory. *Educational Leadership* 50(2): 67–68.

Johnson, D. W., and R. T. Johnson. 1991. *Learning together and alone: Cooperative, competitive, and individualistic learning.* 3d ed. Englewood Cliffs, NJ: Prentice Hall.

Johnson, D. W., R. T. Johnson., and E. J. Holubec. 1994. *Cooperative learning in the classroom.* Alexandria, VA: Association for Supervision and Curriculum Development.

Jones, T., and C. Berger. 1995. Students' use of multimedia science instruction: Designing for the MTV generation? *Journal of Educational Multimedia and Hypermedia* 4(4): 305–20.

Kilpatrick, W. H. 1918. The project method: The use of the purposeful act in the educative process. *Teachers College Bulletin* (Columbia, SC: Columbia University).

Large, A., J. Beheshti, A. Breuleux, and A. Renaud. 1995. Multimedia and comprehension: The relationship among text, animation, and captions. *Journal of the American Society for Information Science* 46(5): 340–47.

Lehrer, R., J. Erickson, and T. Connell. 1994. Learning by designing hypermedia documents. *Computers in the Schools*, 10(1/2): 227–54.

Levin, H. M. 1994. Commentary: Multiple intelligence theory and everyday practices. *Teachers College Record* 95(4): 570–75.

Milone, M. N. 1994. Multimedia authors, one and all. *Technology and Learning* 15(2): 25–31.

Moeller, B., and L. Jeffers. 1996. Technology for inclusive teaching. *Electronic Learning* 16(3): 44.

Najjar, L. J. 1996. Multimedia information and learning. *Journal of Educational Multimedia and Hypermedia* 5(2): 129–50.

Osman, M. E., and M. J. Hannafin. 1992. Metacognition research and theory: Analysis and implications for instructional design. *Educational Technology Research and Development* 40(2): 83–99.

Riddle, E. M. 1995. *Communication through multimedia in an elementary classroom (Report no. 143).* Charlottesville, VA: Curry School of Education, University of Virginia. (ERIC ED 384 346)

Rieber, L. P. 1995. Using computer-based microworlds with children with pervasive developmental disorders: An informal case study. *Journal of Educational Multimedia and Hypermedia* 4(1): 75–94.

Rouet, J., J. J. Levon, A. Dillion, and R. J. Spiro. 1996. An introduction to hypertext and cognition. In *Hypertext and cognition*, edited by J. Rouet, J. J. Levon, A. Dillion, and R. J. Spiro. Mahwah, NJ: Lawrence Erlbaum Associates, Inc.

Samples, B. 1992. Using learning modalities to celebrate intelligence. *Educational Leadership* 50(2): 62–66.

Schroeder, E., and A. Zarinnia. 1994. Multimedia production: Long distance. *Multimedia Schools* 1(3): 47–51.

Sharan, S. 1990. Cooperative learning: A perspective on research and practice. In *Cooperative learning: Theory and research*, edited by S. Sharan. New York: Praeger.

Simons, P. R. J. 1993. Constructive learning: The role of the learner. In *Designing environments for constructive learning*, edited by T. Duffy, J. Lowyck, and D. Jonassen. Heidelberg, Germany: Springer-Verlag.

Slavin, R. E. 1990. *Cooperative learning: Theory, research, and practice.* Englewood Cliffs, NJ: Prentice Hall.

———. 1987. *Cooperative learning: Student teams.* Washington, DC: National Education Association.

Sternberg, R. J. 1994. Diversifying instruction and assessment. *Educational Forum* 59(1): 47–52.

Toffler, A. 1990. *Powershift.* New York: Bantam Books.

Toomey, R., and K. Ketterer. 1995. Using multimedia as a cognitive tool. *Journal of Research on Computing in Education* 27(4): 472–82.

Turner, S. V., and V. M. Dipinto. 1992. Students as hypermedia authors: Themes emerging from a qualitative study. *Journal of Research on Computing in Education* 25(2): 187–99.

Vygotsky, L. S. 1978. *Mind in society: The development of higher psychological processes.* Cambridge, MA: Harvard University Press.

Wilson, K., and W. Tally. 1991. *Designing for discovery: Interactive multimedia learning environments at Bank Street College (Report no. 15).* New York: Bank Street College for Technology in Education. (ERIC ED 337 147)

Woolfolk, A. E. 1987. *Educational psychology.* 3d ed. Englewood Cliffs, NJ: Prentice Hall.

CHAPTER 2

A Model for the Design and Development of Multimedia Projects

A Scenario

Mr. Fisher spent the summer increasing his computer literacy skills and becoming more familiar with multimedia software. He read several books, attended workshops, and practiced the skills required to produce media components and to author a multimedia program.

As Mr. Fisher prepared to assign his eighth-grade students their first multimedia project, he decided he needed a little more information about the overall process. He had learned about all of the benefits of integrating multimedia and was confident that his students would be very enthused; however, he also recognized some potential pitfalls in the implementation process.

At the next district meeting of middle-school science teachers, Mr. Fisher made a point to ask teachers from nearby schools about their experiences with the implementation of multimedia projects. He spoke to Mr. Impetuous and Mr. Plan from Clearview Middle School.

Mr. Impetuous and Mr. Plan were both middle-school teachers who had integrated multimedia projects into their classrooms within the last year. As he listened to them recount their projects, Mr. Fisher was amazed by the contrast in their experiences. Mr. Impetuous scoffed at the thought and said that his attempt to implement multimedia projects into the curriculum had been disastrous. He blamed the results on his students, stating that they were disruptive, unorganized, and noisy. His advice was to continue teaching in a traditional mode (lecture) to maintain maximum control at all times. Upon further investigation, Mr. Fisher learned that Mr. Impetuous had provided little or no guidance for his students. He simply introduced HyperStudio to them and set them loose for a week to produce a project. There were no agreed-upon project goals, no systematic procedure for producing the project, and no evaluation plan.

In contrast, Mr. Plan was extremely positive about his experience and was continuing to expand the integration of multimedia projects into his curriculum. Although he taught basically the same group of students as Mr. Impetuous, Mr. Plan found that his students worked well together and completed their projects on time. Mr. Plan emphasized the need for specific goals and procedures, noting that his students knew exactly what was expected of them. He commented that through the project design and development, he had been able to cover the topics in more depth and the students appeared to develop a greater understanding of the material. Yes, the classroom had been a little noisier than during a lecture, but the students stayed on task and were very enthusiastic about their projects.

Before Mr. Fisher returned to his school, he asked Mr. Plan for some advice on implementation techniques. "My advice," said Mr. Plan, "is to use a systematic design and development model. If the students realize the importance of the overall process, which includes analyzing the content, designing the structure, and developing the program, it is easier for them to create a quality project. In addition, you must clarify how the project will be evaluated and how student performance will be assessed."

Overview

Every teacher knows that good instruction involves careful planning. Whether or not a teacher creates detailed lesson plans, he or she understands the value of preparing the content, sequence, and instructional materials for each lesson. In addition, experienced teachers always have a backup plan in case the lesson does not progress as expected.

Careful planning is critical in the development of multimedia projects. Planning saves time, reduces frustration, eliminates fragmented learning experiences, and results in a better project. Hence, conveying ideas and instruction through a computer involves a wide variety of considerations, including how to best present the information, which media elements to use, and how to assess the effectiveness of the program. Following a systematic plan and development model is recommended. To assist teachers in this process, this chapter focuses on the systematic design of multimedia projects and introduces a model based on 3Ds and an E: DECIDE, DESIGN, DEVELOP, and EVALUATE. The topics of this chapter include:

- An overview of design models
- The DDD-E Model
  - — DECIDE phase: Assign groups, brainstorm, and research the content
  - — DESIGN phase: Determine the program structure and detail the content
  - — DEVELOP phase: Gather and create the media elements, author the program, review, and debug
  - — EVALUATE phase: Evaluate the program
- DDD-E benefits

Overview of Design Models

Implementing multimedia projects in a classroom environment requires a great deal of planning. A multitude of issues will surface, such as: How many students should work in each group? Which media components are appropriate? Should the project be produced in a hypermedia program (such as HyperStudio) or on the World Wide Web? How many hours should the students work on the project? What are the goals of the project? How should it be evaluated? The questions (and possible answers) are endless.

One way to address the numerous issues involved in the design and development of multimedia projects is to follow a systematic plan that outlines the analysis, design, development, and evaluation of the project. Since World War II, when an enormous number of people had to be trained within a short period of time, instructional systems design (ISD) models have helped to structure instructional projects. These models are not rigid, but they can help to sequence the major phases of the process and minimize the potential of neglecting a crucial component.

ISD models vary in complexity and structure; however, all models stress and include the generic phases of analysis, design, development, and evaluation (Alessi and Trollip 1991). The model proposed by this book consists of DECIDE, DESIGN, DEVELOP, and EVALUATE (DDD-E). This model is intended to serve as an general outline for projects, but it can be modified or expanded to meet individual needs.

The DDD-E Model

Creating a multimedia project is similar to cooking a gourmet meal. First you must DECIDE exactly which dishes you plan to serve (which may be influenced by who is coming to dinner and which foods are available). If more than one person is cooking the meal, you also must decide who is going to be responsible for preparing each dish.

Next, the DESIGN of the meal includes locating the recipes and organizing the instructions. Recipes, like flowcharts and storyboards, provide the structure for the dishes, detailing the required ingredients and the sequence of cooking events.

The meal is DEVELOPed by gathering all of the ingredients, mixing everything in the right order, and combining the ingredients into the final dishes. As each individual dish is prepared, the overall meal must be considered. For example, appetizers are usually prepared first and served before the main course.

You EVALUATE throughout the process of making the meal (e.g., licking the spoon and making sure a dish is not burning). Dinner guests provide the final assessment of the meal by providing feedback after the meal has been served.

The DDD-E model consists of three main phases (DECIDE, DESIGN, DEVELOP), surrounded by and ending with EVALUATE (see fig. 2.1). This chapter provides a general outline of the model. Subsequent chapters (3 through 7) provide in-depth treatments of each phase, with recommendations for classroom implementation.

Each of the phases in the DDD-E model involves activities for the teacher and activities for the students. The DECIDE phase focuses on determining the goals and content of the project; the DESIGN phase specifies the program structure; and the DEVELOP phase includes production of the media elements and the programming of the project. The

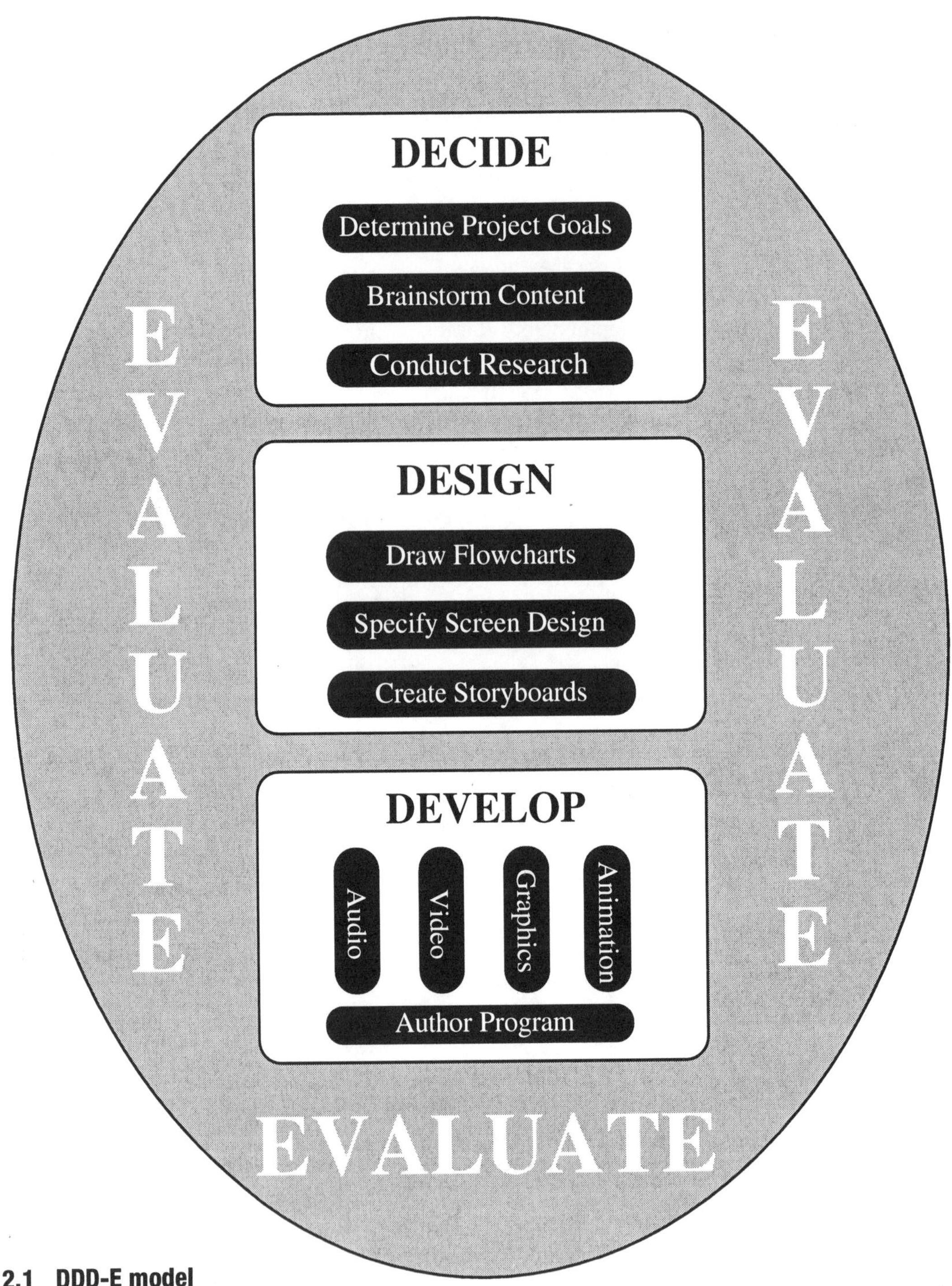

Figure 2.1 DDD-E model

EVALUATE phase occurs throughout the design and development process. At each phase of the process, the project should be reviewed, and, if necessary, revised. Table 2.1 outlines each phase in the DDD-E model.

DECIDE

The first phase in a multimedia project is DECIDE. This phase sets the stage for the entire project. The DECIDE phase is influenced by many variables, including the location and number of computers, available software, and students' experiences. These are discussed in chapter 3.

Phase	Activities: Teacher	Activities: Student
DECIDE	Set instructional goals and decide on a project Assess resources, prerequisite skills, and background knowledge Provide project guidelines Assign groups Assign roles	Brainstorm content Conduct research
DESIGN	Present design guidelines Demonstrate flowchart techniques Provide storyboard templates	Outline content Draw flowcharts Specify screen design Create storyboards
DEVELOP	Demonstrate multimedia tools Outline alternatives in multimedia production Emphasize constraints of storage/transfer rates	Produce audio Produce video Create graphics Construct animations Author program Debug program
EVALUATE	Conduct teacher evaluations	Evaluate peers Conduct self-evaluations

Table 2.1 Teacher and student activities in the DDD-E model

The DECIDE phase includes the following steps for teachers and students:

- Set instructional goals and decide on a project
- Assess resources, prerequisite skills, and background knowledge
- Provide project guidelines
- Assign groups
- Assign group roles
- Brainstorm
- Conduct research

Set Instructional Goals and Decide on a Project (Teacher)

Before assigning a multimedia project, educators need to consider whether it is the most effective way to achieve the desired learning outcomes; alternative approaches might be more effective or efficient. For example, if the instructional goal is to convince adults to vote in an upcoming election, designing a flyer or brochure may be more appropriate.

Content for multimedia projects may be assigned by the teacher or decided by the students. For example, teachers may assign students to create projects demonstrating their knowledge of photosynthesis, or students may be given the option to create a project demonstrating their knowledge of a scientific process of their choice.

When assigning a multimedia project, consider the following:

1. It should be relevant to the student. Projects are more meaningful if the students can see how they are affected by the areas of study. In other words, a project about pollution can be introduced by focusing on how pollution has affected the beaches or air quality in the local area.

2. It should be relevant to the curriculum. Technology should be used as a tool, not an end in itself. Therefore, each multimedia project should be closely related to instructional objectives.
3. There should be sufficient resources. Some topics do not lend themselves to multimedia simply because there are not enough resources. For example, it may not be fair to ask students to create a multimedia project about authors and assign Mark Twain to one group and Catherine Gregory to another. Before selecting topics, review the resources that the students will have available, such as books, clip media, the Internet, and videos.

Assess Resources, Prerequisite Skills, and Background Knowledge (Teacher)

Teachers need to assess the number of computers and other resources that will be necessary for the projects. This will help teachers to schedule computer time, arrange groups, and provide students with the necessary materials to complete their projects.

It is crucial that students have the necessary prerequisite skills for using the computer and multimedia tools. Teachers should ensure that students are familiar with basic computer skills (turning on and off the computer, formatting a diskette, saving to a diskette, copying files, navigating through folders and directories, and handling the computer hardware) and the skills necessary for creating the assigned multimedia project.

Teachers may need to expand on or provide more depth to students' background knowledge, depending on the multimedia assignment. For example, before students can brainstorm about a particular topic (such as xerophytes), they should be familiar with and have some knowledge of the topic.

Provide Project Guidelines (Teacher)

When the project begins, it is important to inform the students about the goals and the method of assessment. Sample rubrics for multimedia projects are included in chapter 7.

Assign Groups (Teacher)

In most cases, the multimedia projects will be completed by groups of two to six students. It is important to establish the size and membership of the groups early in the process because the group members will need to work together to brainstorm and research their approach.

There are many alternatives for assigning students to a group, including student learning styles, multiple intelligences, student interests, and expertise. Chapter 3 provides detailed information on alternatives in group size, group composition, and group structure.

Assign Roles (Teacher)

Within each group, the members should take on the roles of a multimedia design and development team. The primary team members are listed in table 2.2.

The team roles need not be independent of each other. In other words, one student may serve as both the program author and the graphic artist. Likewise, all students can take on all roles and work together for the final product. Chapter 3 provides more information about how to assign student roles.

Brainstorm (Students)

After placing the students into design teams, allow them time to explore the project by brainstorming with their group members. (Note: Brainstorming is effective only if the students are somewhat familiar with

Team Member	Roles in Multimedia Project
Project manager	Organize the team members Set the schedules Track the progress
Instructional designers	Determine the screen layout Create the flowcharts Specify the project design in the storyboards
Graphic artists	Create the graphics Create the animations
Production specialists	Record and edit the audio Record and edit the video
Program authors	Produce the program Debug and test the program

Table 2.2 Multimedia team members

the content.) Be sure to allow plenty of time for the students to thoroughly explore the content.

Conduct Research (Students)

Every project should include some time for the students to research the content. For this step, students should have access to as many resources as possible, including CD-ROM databases, the Internet, books, and journals. It may be necessary to provide assistance to help students get started and to provide a rubric of required components for the project. For example, if the project is focusing on a country, you may require students to include information about the imports, exports, history, geography, politics, culture, and so on.

DESIGN

The DECIDE phase outlines the goals and content of the project. In the DESIGN phase, students organize the sequence of the program with flowcharts and specify the exact text, graphics, audio, and interactions of each screen on storyboards. It is crucial to emphasize the importance of the DESIGN phase to students. If they do not dedicate sufficient time and energy to this phase, they may end up wasting valuable time during the DEVELOP (production) phase. The DESIGN phase should represent approximately 50 percent of the total time committed to the project.

In the DESIGN phase, students should:

- Outline content
- Create flowcharts
- Specify screen design
- Write storyboards

Outline Content

After the research and brainstorming steps of the DECIDE phase, the students should synthesize, organize, and outline the content for the project. This step helps to set the stage for the flowcharts.

Create Flowcharts

The flowcharting process illustrates the sequence and structure of a program. It is important that students visualize how the various parts of a lesson fit together. Students should be encouraged to experiment with different ways of presenting content. To help them determine the best options, ask questions such as "Does one idea logically follow another throughout the program?" "Is there a central point from which all of the other ideas should be linked" "Can you start with three or four choices and then subdivide the selections?" Be sure to demonstrate different projects with various structures to illustrate the alternatives. Additional information about flowcharts is provided in chapter 4.

Specify the Screen Design

The storyboards for the project detail all of the text, graphics, and interactions on each screen. Before they write the storyboards, it is important that you work with the students to determine the screen design (the layout or template for each screen). Each screen should contain specific functional areas (title, text, graphics, prompts, navigation options, and feedback) to make the program more consistent and easier to follow. Sample templates are provided in chapters 4, 8, 9, and 10.

Write Storyboards

After the screen templates and functional areas have been determined, the students can proceed with the storyboards. Storyboards should contain all of the information that will be placed on the screens, in addition to information that will assist the programmer and production specialists in development of the media components. It is at this point that the students (instructional designers) determine the best way to present the information, how much information goes on each screen, and the like. Sample storyboard templates are provided in chapter 4.

DEVELOP

After the storyboards are complete, the development process can begin. Depending on the complexity specified in the storyboards, the DEVELOP phase may involve the production of audio elements, video segments, graphics, and text. These components can be developed simultaneously by different members of the project team, or they can be developed in sequence by all of the members working together. The DEVELOP phase also includes the programming (often referred to as *authoring*) of the program. The components of the DEVELOP phase include:

- Create graphics
- Construct animations
- Produce audio
- Produce video
- Author program
- Debug program

Create Graphics

Graphics, in the form of pictures, charts, diagrams, and drawings, can play a major role in conveying the content of a multimedia program. After the requirements are specified in the storyboards, students work to create the appropriate graphics. The procedures for creating graphics with software programs, scanners, and digital cameras are outlined in chapter 5.

Construct Animations

In some cases, the project may also include animations—graphics that move in rapid sequence to create the illusion of motion. Animations can convey many complex abstractions, such as the movement of water in a pipe, or they can be used to attract attention to a particular screen or project.

Produce Audio

All of the sound elements of a program (narration, music, and sound effects) are referred to as *audio*. Students can record the audio elements of a project, or they can incorporate sounds from the Internet or other sources. The procedures and alternatives for audio production are outlined in chapter 5.

Produce Video

Students are very accustomed to viewing video in the form of videotapes, television, and (perhaps) videodiscs. Video segments can also be recorded on a computer and played through a hypermedia program such as HyperStudio. Many factors must be considered in the production, editing, and implementation of video segments, as discussed in chapter 5.

Author Program

One of the last steps in the DEVELOP phase is to incorporate all the text, graphics, and other media components into a finished program. Many tools can be used to author a multimedia project, including hypermedia programs (such as HyperStudio), presentation programs (such as PowerPoint), and Web-based programs (such as HTML). Throughout this book, all of these software environments are considered as possible development tools. Chapter 6 outlines the most popular programming options for school-based projects. Chapters 8, 9, and 10 focus on sample projects created with HyperStudio, PowerPoint, and HTML.

Debug Program

Throughout the project development, students should test and debug the program. This process includes testing the media elements on various computers, locating grammar and punctuation errors, and testing the program for inoperative links. When students complete their projects, student groups should review each others' programs for possible bugs before the projects are submitted for final evaluation.

EVALUATE

The evaluation of multimedia projects is both formative and summative. Formative assessment is done throughout project development by both the teacher and the students. For example, the teacher should assess the research and brainstorming during the DECIDE phase. She or he should also provide feedback for the students on their flowcharts and storyboards before they begin the development process.

Summative evaluation takes place at the end of the project. The steps in the EVALUATE phase include:

- Evaluate peers
- Conduct self-evaluations
- Provide student assessment

Evaluate Peers (Student)

Group dynamics are an important part of most multimedia projects. In addition to the teacher's assessment, students should be encouraged (or required) to evaluate the projects of their peers. Instruments for peer evaluation are included in chapter 7.

Conduct Self-Evaluations (Student)

It is also important for students to conduct self-evaluations and to report on their progress through journal entries or other assessment tools. For more information on self-evaluations, see chapter 7.

Provide Student Assessment (Teacher)

Multimedia projects are a great way to provide alternate assessments for students. Rather than judging their knowledge based on a multiple-choice, A–F grading system, you can assess their abilities to construct knowledge and communicate it through a variety of media. The exact method for determining the overall grade for a multimedia project will vary. The important factor is to provide a means of communicating to

Phase	Student Activities	Cognitive Skills
DECIDE	Brainstorm content Conduct research	Formulate questions Design search strategies Analyze, synthesize information
DESIGN	Outline content Draw flowcharts Specify screen design Create storyboards	Develop structure Create timeline Write scripts Chunk information Determine appropriate media elements
DEVELOP	Produce audio Produce video Create graphics Construct animations Author program Debug program	Convey information through different media Transfer storyboard information into media elements Determine appropriate media formats
EVALUATE	Evaluate peers Conduct self-evaluations	Analyze program effectiveness Practice assessment techniques

Table 2.3 Cognitive skills for students

students and their parents about the students' progress. See chapter 7 for more information on student assessment and assessment techniques.

DDD-E Benefits

There are many learning benefits for students who engage as multimedia designers (Lehrer, Erickson, and Connell 1994). Studies have also found that designing multimedia programs is motivational for students and incorporates a variety of cognitive skills (Beichner 1994; Lehrer, Erickson, and Connell 1994; Spoehr 1994). Table 2.3 outlines student activities and correlates them to some of the cognitive skills that are involved in each phase of the DDD-E process.

Summary

Careful planning is critical in the development of multimedia projects. It is important to follow a systematic process. Models such as DDD-E can help teachers and students structure the development of multimedia projects. The DDD-E model provides a framework for students to work collaboratively in the design and development of their projects, and allows opportunities for ongoing evaluation throughout each phase of the DDD-E process. Chapters 3 through 7 focus on each phase of the DDD-E model; chapters 8 through 10 provide multimedia project ideas based on the DDD-E model.

References

Alessi, S. M., and S. R. Trollip. 1991. *Computer-based instruction: Methods and development.* Englewood Cliffs, NJ: Prentice Hall.

Beichner, R. J. 1994. Multimedia editing to promote science learning. *Journal of Educational Multimedia and Hypermedia* 3(1): 55–70.

Lehrer, R., J. Erickson, and T. Connell. 1994. Learning by designing hypermedia documents. *Computers in the Schools* 10(1/2): 227–54.

Spoehr, K. T. 1994. Enhancing the acquisition of conceptual structures through hypermedia. In *Classroom lessons: Integrating cognitive theory and classroom practice*, edited by K. McGilly, 75–101. Cambridge, MA: MIT Press.

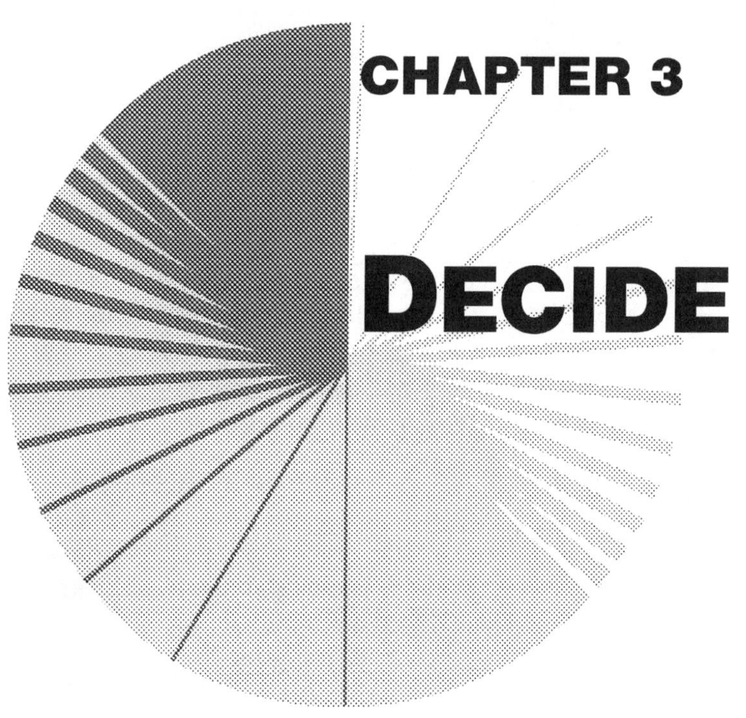

CHAPTER 3

DECIDE

A Scenario

With the recent reduction in class sizes, Mr. Snyder hesitated to dismantle the school's computer lab and place the computers in teachers' classrooms. He had no other choice, however. The room was needed for the new first-grade classes. Mr. Snyder took the necessary precautions to secure the computers in their new homes.

Within the next year, Mr. Snyder was amazed at how teachers began integrating the use of technology into the curriculum. In the past, teachers would sign up for weekly, 40-minute time slots in the computer lab. Students would use the computers to word process their class stories, practice their math skills, and have adventures along the Oregon Trail. He always saw the computer lab as a good reinforcement of what the students were learning in class, but he never observed an integral connection between lab time and class time. He never imagined that teachers would be using the computer as an integral part of their classroom instruction.

It was true, however, in several of the classrooms that Mr. Snyder visited. Students were using the computer as an integral tool in the development of multimedia projects. It was fascinating to observe. For example, in Mrs. Garcia's fourth-grade classroom, students were collaborating with each other and working on a number of different projects. Some students sat together at the computer, while others worked on a script for a newscast, created brochures, added to a classroom mural, or worked on a story. Mrs. Garcia worked with individual groups and monitored the students' progress. Mrs. Garcia explained that the students were working on a unit about pollution, developing multimedia projects, brochures, a video show, a classroom mural of the trash collected from the playground, and storybooks for their second-grade buddies about why it is important not to pollute.

Mrs. Garcia elaborated on the students' multimedia projects and explained how having the computers in the classroom allowed her more control over integrating technology into her instruction. She also commented on the importance of classroom management. With a limited number of computers, it was important to plan concurrent activities, organize procedures, and provide the students with a schedule of events. Mrs. Garcia enjoyed having her students work together and express their learning in a variety of ways. She also believed very strongly in the computer's potential as a tool for thought and knowledge construction. She wanted learning to dictate the use and time commitment of the computers, not vice versa.

Mrs. Garcia showed Mr. Snyder the unit's organization, assessment sheets, an activity schedule, and other strategies that she had developed to help make the students' learning experiences worthwhile. Just then, an assembly bell rang. Mrs. Garcia's students stopped what they were doing and lined up at the door. Mrs. Garcia commented that her class would continue where they left off after the assembly. This was not always possible when classes were assigned a computer lab schedule. Mr. Snyder understood. Imagine having access to other teaching tools (such as chalkboards, overhead projectors, and pencils) for only 40 minutes a week!

Overview

The location and number of computers significantly influence the DECIDE phase. Other issues include available computer time, grouping options, the time needed to complete a project, and the students' experience with computers. The DECIDE stage sets the foundation for the remaining stages of the DDD-E process; hence, the planning and organization of the DECIDE phase contribute to the overall success of the students' multimedia projects. The DECIDE stage includes determining the goals of the project (planning and organizing), brainstorming, and conducting research. Much of the teacher's time will be spent on planning and organizing the projects. Topics in this chapter include:

- Planning multimedia projects
  - Setting instructional goals
  - Deciding on a project
  - Developing prerequisite skills
  - Assessing resources
- Organizing multimedia projects
  - Examining grouping alternatives
  - Creating cooperative groups
  - Scheduling computer time
- Managing brainstorming and research activities

Planning Multimedia Projects

DECIDE is the first phase of the DDD-E process, and it involves a significant amount of planning and organization. Planning includes setting instructional goals, deciding on a project, developing prerequisite skills, and assessing computer availability and other necessary resources.

Setting Instructional Goals

Before choosing to assign a multimedia project, educators need to consider whether such a project is the most effective way to achieve the desired learning outcomes. Textbooks, worksheets, independent research, field trips, or other hands-on activities may address an instructional goal more effectively. For example, students may more effectively learn how to square dance by actually square dancing, rather than researching and presenting a multimedia project about it. This is not to say that a multimedia presentation could not assist with square dance instruction, but the students' time may be better spent in dancing than in creating a multimedia project.

When setting instructional goals for multimedia projects, it is critical that students learn something beyond computer skills, and that the appearance of the end presentation does not overshadow the content of the project. It is easy to get caught up in multimedia special effects (such as sound, animation, video, transitions, and so on) and to forget about the purpose of the project. This is like rating a car based on its exterior instead of its engine, or judging a cake's taste by its looks.

In addition to identifying specific content learning, instructional goals may be designed to:

- Accommodate multiple learning styles and interests
- Encourage cooperative learning and social skills
- Foster active learning by promoting interdisciplinary investigations
- Develop critical thinking, reasoning, problem-solving, and metacognitive processes
- Enhance presentation and speaking skills

Instructional goals will vary depending on the ability level of the learner, available resources, and the learner's experience.

Deciding on a Project

After defining the instructional goals, the teacher can select and design a project to meet the desired goals. Assuming it is a multimedia project, the teacher will need to decide if the instructional goals can best be achieved through a hypermedia, World Wide Web, or presentation project. More experienced students may make this decision on their own (see ch. 4). Ideas for projects are endless. Table 3.1 presents a variety of projects by subject area.

In addition to instructional goals, time must also be considered when deciding on a multimedia project. Students need to be given projects that can be completed within a prescribed period of time. For example, if the multimedia project is part of a three-week unit on the California Gold Rush, teachers should limit the size and complexity of the project to what their students are capable of completing in a two- to three-week period.

Developing Prerequisite Skills

Once the instructional goals and project have been defined, teachers must ensure that their students have the skills needed to successfully complete the project. These include basic computer operations and use of the assigned multimedia tool. Additional or more advanced skills can be taught as needed as the students design and prepare their projects.

Subject	Project Ideas
Language arts	• book reports • interactive and multiple-ending stories • poetry collections • news reports • phonemic awareness activities for younger students • famous authors • parodies • mythology • reports on stories from multiple cultures or time periods • word origins • grammar, spelling, or vocabulary activities • rhyming games • story starters • prompted writing • creative writing
Mathematics	• problem-solving adventures • famous mathematicians • number recognition activities for younger students • number systems • geometry concepts • math puzzles and solutions • addition, subtraction, multiplication, or division concepts • history of mathematics • units of measure • currency exchange • stock market • inflation • finance • retailing • advertising • proofs
Science and health	• space exploration • pollution • animals • plant growth • weather • insects • nutrition • inventions and inventors • body systems • dissection • simple machines • chemical properties • ocean life • diseases • light and colors • science magic tricks • drugs, alcohol, or smoking • home remedies • exercise • senses
Social studies	• state or country reports • famous people in history • world wars • Industrial Revolution • Civil War • Holocaust • Gold Rush • geography • Westward Movement • community events and history • family tree • explorers • hobbies and interests • government • careers • cultural holidays, foods, or celebrations
Fine arts	• famous artists • film history • cinematography • history of music • musical instruments • film or music genre • history of dance • music or movie reviews • opera • music notation • song writing • animation • special effects • music and culture

Table 3.1 Sample project ideas

Complexity and sophistication of skills should be based on the students' ability level.

Assessing Resources

After ensuring that students are familiar with basic computer skills (turning the computer on and off, formatting a diskette, saving to a diskette, copying files, navigating through folders and directories, and handling the computer hardware) and the skills necessary for creating the assigned multimedia project, educators can begin assessing the number of computers and other resources (such as software, scanners, digital cameras, and so on) needed for the projects. This will help teachers schedule computer time, arrange groups, and ensure that the necessary resources are available. For example, if a school has an Internet connection in the media center, teachers may have to ask permission or sign up to use the connection. Teachers may also plan to borrow additional computers from other classrooms, request diskettes for their students, or ensure that the necessary software is installed on all of the computers. Once a teacher has gathered all the necessary components, she or he is ready to introduce the project to the class.

Organizing Multimedia Projects

In addition to planning, the DECIDE phase of the DDD-E process involves organizing the student's learning environment. This includes examining grouping alternatives, creating cooperative groups, and designing computer schedules.

Examining Grouping Alternatives

Depending on the project, teachers may group students before or after introducing the multimedia project topic. Students may work collaboratively or cooperatively. Students in collaborative groups work toward the same goal, but they are not necessarily accountable for each other's learning. Success may not depend on the efforts of all group members, allowing some students to loaf while others do all the work. Students in cooperative groups work toward a common goal and are accountable for each other's learning, providing both academic and personal support. Group members are taught social skills to help them coordinate their efforts, and teamwork is emphasized.

As mentioned in chapter 1, there are many types of cooperative group methods: Student Teams Achievement Divisions (STAD), Teams Games Tournament (TGT), Team Assisted Individualization (TAI), Jigsaw, Group Investigation, and Learning Together. Groups may be heterogeneous or homogeneous. Most research supports the use of heterogeneous groups (Johnson and Johnson 1991; Watson 1992). Heterogeneous groups are usually formed with a mixture of ability, gender, or race; homogeneous groups consist of students with similar abilities or interests. Johnson, Johnson, and Holubec (1994, 26) state that "[h]eterogeneous groups tend to promote more elaborate thinking, more frequent giving and receiving of explanations, and greater perspective-taking during discussions about material, all of which increase students' understanding, reasoning, and long-term retention." There may be, however, some instances when homogeneous groups are preferred, such as specific class topics or the creation of interest groups (Beane and Lemke 1971; Hooper and Hannafin 1991; Jonassen 1996; Okebukola and Ogunniyi 1984).

Grouping Variables

Both grouping styles (heterogeneous and homogeneous) have advantages and disadvantages, depending on the grouping variable. Grouping variables include (but are not limited to) ability, learning style, intelligence, cognitive preference, gender, and background. Ability grouping is based on high, middle, and low achievement. Learning styles may include textual, visual, tactile, and auditory. Intelligences include linguistic, logical-mathematical, spatial, bodily-kinesthetic, musical, interpersonal, and intrapersonal. Cognitive preference defines learners according to how they place themselves on a continuum between "global processing" and "analytical processing." Global individuals tend to be more sensitive to others, better communicators, and more socially oriented. Analytical individuals tend to be more introverted, but are better at organizing and analyzing content. The next variable, gender, is self-explanatory. Background may include race, experiences, age, and likes and dislikes. Table 3.2 presents the advantages and disadvantages of these grouping variables.

In addition to heterogeneous and homogeneous grouping, groups may be established by interest or random assignment. For example, students whose favorite pet is a cat may work together to produce a multimedia project about cats, or students may be assigned to groups by picking topics out of a hat. These grouping methods also have advantages and disadvantages. Interest groups may enhance communication among members and identify common interests and similarities among students. The disadvantage of interest groups is that they are self-selected, which may generate more off-task behavior, result in undesired homogeneous grouping (ability, race, gender, etc.), and eliminate possibilities for students to expand their circles (Johnson, Johnson, and Holubec 1994). Random assignment can provide variety in the

Grouping Variable	Type	Advantages	Disadvantages
Ability	Heterogeneous	Best opportunity for peer support and tutoring	Free-rider effect
Ability	Homogeneous	Students tend to bond and communicate more effectively	Low-ability students are often left at a significant learning disadvantage
Learning style, intelligence, or cognitive preference	Heterogeneous	Students are exposed to multiple perspectives and problem-solving methods, stimulating students' learning and cognitive development	May be hard to group if students display a preference for one dominant learning style, intelligence, or cognitive preference; communication skills may be more difficult to develop because of different interests
Learning style, intelligence, or cognitive preference	Homogeneous	Students tend to bond and communicate more effectively	Students' focus and exposure to different perspectives are limited
Gender or background	Heterogeneous	Reduces stereotypes, promotes equality among perceived ability and leadership roles	Teachers may need to ensure that social skills are in place to eliminate preconceived biases
Gender or background	Homogeneous	May benefit specific interest groups or class topics	May cause unnecessary tension between groups; not representative of the real world

Table 3.2 Advantages and disadvantages of various grouping variables

groups and is perceived as fairer (Jonassen 1996). However, general random assignment may pair incompatible students. Stratified random assignment may be used to ensure that certain students do not get placed together or that each group has students with one or two characteristics (e.g., reading level, math ability, computer skills, etc.). Stratified random assignment can be used to create groups of students with preferred intelligence. For example, by using stratified random assignment, the teacher can ensure that each group has one member with high linguistic intelligence, another member with high logical-mathematical intelligence, another member with high spatial intelligence, and another member with high interpersonal intelligence.

Groups can be teacher-selected or self-selected. Teacher-selected groups allow teachers to decide who works with whom, ensuring balance and the potential for positive relationships. At-risk students can be assigned to a group with one of the most skillful, popular, and supportive students in the class. Teachers can also ensure that students with nonachievement-oriented and disruptive behavior are not grouped together. Self-selected groups are the least recommended (Johnson, Johnson, and Holubec 1994). Typically, self-selected groups are homogeneous, spawning isolated groups of high achievers, males, minorities, socialites, females, and nonachievers. This leads to more off-task behavior and limited social experiences.

Group Numbers

In addition to grouping variables, the number of students placed in each group can make a difference in group success. Group numbers may depend on the students' abilities, number of computers in the classroom, time constraints, project requirements, cooperative group method, and other variables. Most studies on cooperative learning report group sizes ranging from two to six students. Johnson, Johnson, and Holubec (1994) provide the following points about group size:

1. As the size of the group increases, the range of abilities and viewpoints increases. Additional resources (members) may help the group succeed, and varying viewpoints will challenge the students to more critically evaluate their own viewpoints and opinions.
2. The larger the group, the more skillful the members must be at ensuring that everyone remains on task, has a chance to speak, reaches a consensus, understands the material being learned, and maintains good working relationships. Interactions increase as the group size increases, requiring additional interpersonal skills.
3. As group size increases, there is less face-to-face interaction among members and a reduced sense of intimacy. Lower individual responsibility may result, as well as a less cohesive group.
4. If a short period of time is available, smaller groups should be used. Smaller groups can take less time to get organized, and they may operate more quickly.
5. The smaller the group, the more difficult it is for students to not contribute their share of the work. Small groups make students more accountable by increasing the visibility of their work.
6. The smaller the group, the easier it is to identify group difficulties, including leadership struggles, unresolved conflicts, and learning difficulties. Problems are more visible and more easily addressed in small groups.

Advantages and disadvantages of various group sizes for multimedia design teams are listed in table 3.3.

Design teams generally consist of several people, depending on the size of the project and the number of available computers. With large groups, individuals or pairs of students can be assigned specific tasks. For example, following the group's research efforts, one person may be responsible for the graphics, one person may be responsible for the music and narration in the project, two more people may be responsible for completing the storyboards (based on a group-approved template), and two students may be responsible for entering information into the computer. Group members will have additional responsibilities as well; hence, it may not be possible for one member to complete his or her main responsibility until other members of the group complete their parts of the project. Students will need to ensure that everyone stays on task and assists other members.

Creating Cooperative Groups

The success of cooperative groups depends on positive interdependence, a group goal, and individual and group accountability. Teamwork skills must be taught just as purposefully and precisely as academic skills. For most classroom multimedia projects, teamwork is essential.

Group Size	Advantages	Disadvantages
One	• Work at own pace • Not dependent on others	• Requires more computer access time (every individual will need time on the computer) • Does not reflect real-world learning • Does not promote learning from different perspectives • Does not encourage cooperative problem solving • Takes longer to complete a project • Individual may not be capable of handling all of the project's requirements
Two or three	• Learn from each other • Share project responsibilities • Supports real-world learning, learning from different perspectives, and cooperative problem solving • Computer access time is cut in half, as students can work together at the computer	• Need to ensure that everyone contributes and has a chance to speak
Four	• Learn from each other • Tasks can be broken into smaller pieces • Supports real-world learning, learning from different perspectives, and cooperative problem solving • Increases computer access time • More talent and resources are available to create the project • Project can be completed in less time	• Need to ensure that everyone contributes and has a chance to speak • Difficult to share computer • Requires greater interpersonal skills
Five or six	• Same as four	• Same as four • Easier for a member not to contribute • More chance of group disputes, leadership difficulties, and off-task behavior, which may delay the project • Less face-to-face interaction • Group dynamics may be more appropriate for older, more mature students

Table 3.3 Advantages and disadvantages of various group sizes in multimedia design teams

Introducing Social Skills

Before placing students into cooperative groups, it is important to determine the goal of the multimedia project and what types of student interactions are desired. In most cases, students will need to be taught or reminded how to work cooperatively. To foster group cooperation, Willing and Girard (1990, 15) recommend the following guidelines:

- Model and teach appropriate communication habits, such as listening, politeness, speaking up, and not dominating the conversation.
- Structure a supportive environment in which each student has a chance to observe, demonstrate, and evaluate behavior models.
- Provide meaningful materials that will create interest because they are probing or controversial.

Teachers may want to create social skill objectives. These may be defined by monitoring student groups and diagnosing the specific problems students are having working together, or by asking students which social skill would improve their teamwork. Based on the teacher's observation and students' input, a social skill can be taught to help solve the problem.

Placing Students into Cooperative Groups

After social skills have been introduced, decide on the cooperative group method (STAD, TGT, TAI, Jigsaw, Group Investigation, or Learning Together) that will be most beneficial for the students and their assigned multimedia project (see ch. 1). Depending on the project, desired interactions, and cooperative group method, assess students' strengths and weaknesses, their interests, who they like to work with, and so on. Consider group dynamics and create heterogeneous conditions. Along with the survey found at the end of this chapter (see the Self Survey blackline master), a teacher's own observation and background with his or her students can help facilitate student placement.

Students may be placed in design teams before or after the introduction of a multimedia project. Teachers may poll student interests before introducing the project, or may wait to assess student interest until after the project has been introduced. For example, an informal survey might be created to assess students' interest in certain animals. Based on the survey results, the teacher can heterogeneously group students according to their interests before introducing a multimedia project about animals. Alternatively, the teacher could introduce a multimedia project about animals and let students group themselves according to their interests. Precautions must be taken, however, because of the disadvantages associated with self-selected groups. Hence, some students may choose groups based on the animal's popularity (not their true interest) and friends' choices. In addition, some animals may not draw enough students or attract too many students, creating bad feelings and a sense of unfairness if students are assigned to a different animal. Polling students' interests and assigning teams before introducing a project is recommended.

Assigning Roles

Another important aspect of cooperative group learning is role assignment. Assigning roles helps to ensure that all students participate and that no one person dominates a group. Roles may be based on group behaviors, computer tasks, or project assignments. For example, in a group of four students, one person may ensure that everyone gets a chance to speak (turn-taking monitor), one person may record the group's activities (record keeper), one person may ensure that the group's noise level is kept to a minimum (noise monitor), and one person may be responsible for keeping the group on task (task master). These group behavior roles may be rotated on a daily basis. Computer tasks may include keyboarder (enters information into the computer), editor (oversees computer input), and record keeper (keeps track of group's progress). Project assignment roles may include a graphic artist, instructional designer, production specialist, and program author.

Assignment roles may also become the basis for forming the groups. For example, a survey can be used to form the groups according to Gardner's Theory of Multiple Intelligences (see the Self Survey blackline master). Students are placed into teams based on their interests and observed strengths. Each design team might contain one student who ranked high in linguistics (I like to read books, write, and tell stories), one student who ranked high in logic-mathematics (I like math, strategy games, and working with puzzles), and two students who ranked high in spatial skills (I like to draw and I understand things better by looking at a picture). Student "linguistic experts" may take on the responsibilities of the subject matter experts, "spatial experts" may be considered the teams' graphic artists and storyboard designers, and "logical-mathematical experts" may be responsible for the project's flowchart and programming needs. Additional project roles may be assigned according to the students' self-rankings in the remaining areas of the survey: bodily-kinesthetic (I have a hard time sitting still), musical (I am a good singer and I know when music is off key), interpersonal (I get along well with others and I am a good listener), and intrapersonal (I am dependable and self-confident).

Scheduling Computer Time

Perhaps the most challenging aspect of designing and developing multimedia projects is computer access. Various situations are possible. Computer labs are typically available for one 30- or 40-minute time slot a week. A computer assistant may or may not be available, and stations may range from 10 to 30 or more computers. Classrooms may have one or more computers, with or without a projection system. Some schools have mobile computers available for checkout, increasing the number of computers possible in a classroom. Mobile computers may not always be available if other teachers request them, however. There are several advantages and disadvantages for each situation when creating multimedia projects (see table 3.4.)

Dublin, Pressman, Barnett, Corcoran, and Woldman (1994) contend that a minimum of three computers in the classroom is needed to ensure that every student gets some time at the computer during a single classroom period. This requires that students work in groups of three or four. While students are waiting for their group's turn at the computer, they work on a related, noncomputer task. For example, students may be engaged in a silent reading activity, follow-up materials about the computer lesson, or another related activity. Teachers should resist teaching a directed lesson when students are actively engaged on classroom computers for several reasons:

1. Students on the computers are missing the lesson.
2. Students near the computers will more likely be watching their computer classmates rather than the teacher.
3. Some computer programs require sound (interrupting the teacher's directed lesson), and headphones are not always available.
4. The teacher cannot immediately assist students on the computers if he or she is involved in a directed lesson.
5. Students not on the computers may be more concerned about the clock and their turn at the computer than what the teacher has to say.
6. Scheduling may require students to take their computer turn during the middle of the directed lesson, as well as returning students to the directed lesson without having participated in the beginning of the lesson.

Computer Setting	Advantages	Disadvantages
Lab (10 to 20 computers)	• Working in groups, all students have access to the computers at the same time; teacher can facilitate whole-class instruction • Computer coordinator may be available to assist students • Students can take turns working individually on computers with computer coordinator while other students work on noncomputer assignments with teacher • Less cost to secure and network computers; printer not required for every classroom	• Usually limited to 30 or 40 minutes a week • Fire drills, assemblies, holidays, etc., may cause lab time to be missed • Computer use is more likely to be an isolated activity than an integral part of the curriculum • Whole school uses the same computers and printers, causing more wear and tear on the systems, more variable problems, and additional software costs to meet everyone's needs • Instructional time is lost going to and from computer lab
Lab (25 to 35 computers)	• Same as other lab situation • Individual students have access to the computers at the same time; teacher can facilitate whole-class instruction • Additional computers may be available for multimedia purposes (e.g., digitizing and editing QuickTime movies)	• Same as other lab situation
1 or 2 computers in the classroom	• Computer available every day for "teachable moments" • If projection device or large monitor is available, can be used to facilitate whole-class/small group instruction • Some software is specifically designed for whole-class/small group instruction (e.g., Tom Snyder Productions, Inc.) • Software funds can be used to purchase a variety of software that meets students' and teachers' individual needs vs. lab sets that may not be used by all teachers or students	• Individual computer time is difficult to manage • Some group computer projects may take an undesirable length of time to complete due to limited access • More cost involved with purchasing computers and printers for every classroom, networking, and securing every room (alarm system)
3 or more computers in the classroom	• Same as other classroom situation • Student groups can have daily computer access • Computers are more likely to be used as an integral part of instruction and tools for learning	• Requires more classroom space than one or two computers • More cost involved with purchasing computers and printers for every classroom, networking, and securing every room (alarm system)
Mobile computers for checkout	• Can provide additional computer access for group projects • Can be removed from classroom, freeing up space, when not in use	• Not always available • Time needed to move systems in and out of the classroom • Computers may be damaged in transit

Table 3.4 Advantages and disadvantages of computer situations

For many teachers, the thought of three or more computers in the classroom may seem unrealistic. Nevertheless, the California Education Technology Task Force is recommending that every classroom be equipped with at least six computers (California Department of Education 1997). The trend is there, but how soon teachers will see the technology in their classrooms is questionable. In the meantime, teachers can place more computers in their classroom to facilitate multimedia projects by borrowing other classrooms' computers or arranging to borrow an additional computer from a computer lab. Parents and businesses may lend support, also.

Time	Computer Time	Project Assignments	Computer Classroom Daily Computer Use (Version 1)
9:00 a.m. – 9:30 a.m.	A B C D	E F G H	• 3 or 4 students per group • 24 to 32 students • 30-minute rotation schedule • When students are not at computers, they work on related, noncomputer project assignments. For example, Groups A, B, C, and D have computer time between 9:00 a.m. and 9:30 a.m. Groups E, F, G, and H work on related assignments.
9:30 a.m. – 10:00 a.m.	E F G H	A B C D	

Figure 3.1 Computer schedule for a four-computer classroom (version 1)

Time	Computer Time	Project Assignments 1	Project Assignments 2	Computer Classroom Daily Computer Use (Version 2)
9:00 a.m. – 9:20 a.m.	A B C D	I J K L	E F G H	• 2 to 3 students per group • 24 to 36 students • 20-mintues rotation schedule • When students are not at computers, they work on related project assignments. For example, Groups A, B C, and D have computer time between 9:00 a.m. and 9:20 a.m. Groups E, F, G, and H and groups I, J, K, and L work on related, noncomputer assignments (projects 1 and 2).
9:20 a.m. – 9:40 a.m.	E F G H	A B C D	I J K L	
9:40 a.m. – 10:00 a.m.	I J K L	E F G H	A B C D	

Figure 3.2 Computer schedule for a four-computer classroom (version 2)

Time	Computer Time	Project Assignments 1	Project Assignments 2	Computer Classroom Daily Computer Use
9:00 a.m. – 9:20 a.m.	A B C	G H I	D E F	•3 or 4 students per group •27 to 36 students •20-minute rotation schedule •When students are not at computers, they work on related project assignments. For example, Groups A, B, and C have computer time between 9:00 a.m. and 9:20 a.m. Groups D, E, F, G, H, and I work on related, noncomputer assignments (projects 1 and 2).
9:20 a.m. – 9:40 a.m.	D E F	A B C	G H I	
9:40 a.m. – 10:00 a.m.	G H I	D E F	A B C	

Figure 3.3 Computer schedule for a three-computer classroom

To help deal with the various computer situations possible, computer schedules have been developed to assist teachers in managing multimedia projects in their classroom (see figs. 3.1, 3.2, 3.3, 3.4, and 3.5).

Note that four computers in the classroom can provide students with 30 minutes of *daily* access to computers versus the 30 minutes of *weekly* access provided by computer labs. Two or three computers in the

Time	Computer Time	Project Assignments 1	Project Assignments 2	Project Assignments 3	Computer Classroom Daily Computer Use
9:00 a.m. – 9:15 a.m.	A B	C D	E F	G H	• 3 or 4 students per group • 24 to 32 students • 15-minute rotation schedule • When students are not at computers, they work on related project assignments. For example, Groups A and B have computer time between 9:00 a.m. and 9:15 a.m. Groups C, D, E, F, G, and H work on related, noncomputer assignments (projects 1, 2, and 3).
9:15 a.m. – 9:30 a.m.	C D	E F	G H	A B	
9:30 a.m. – 9:45 a.m.	E F	G H	A B	C D	
9:45 a.m. – 10:00 a.m.	G H	A B	C D	E F	

Figure 3.4 Computer schedule for a two-computer classroom

Time	Computer Time MW	Computer Time TTH	Project Assignments MW 1	Project Assignments TTH 2	Project Assignments MW 3	Project Assignments TTH 4	Computer Classroom MW/TTH Computer Use
9:00 a.m. – 9:15 a.m.	A	E	B F G H	B F G H	C D E	A C D	• 3 or 4 students per group • 24 to 32 students • 15-minute rotation schedule • Groups have computer time twice a week • When students are not at computers, they work on related project assignments. For example, Group A has computer time from 9:00 a.m. and 9:15 a.m. on Monday and Wednesday. Groups B, F, G, and H and groups C, D, and E work on related, noncomputer (projects 1 and 3). • On Friday, students are provided with additional time to complete their related, noncomputer assignments. Groups may send one person to work with other groups to find clip art or research via the computer. For example, one person from each of groups A, B, C, and D may work together on the computer from 9:00 a.m. to 9:30 a.m., and one person from each of groups E, F, G, and H may work together on the computer from 9:30 a.m. to 10:00 a.m.
9:15 a.m. – 9:30 a.m.	B	F	F G H	B G H	A C D E	A C D E	
9:30 a.m. – 9:45 a.m.	C	G	A D E	A C D E	B F G H	B F H	
9:45 a.m. – 10:00 a.m.	D	H	A C E	A C D E	B F G H	B F G	

Figure 3.5 Computer schedule for a one-computer classroom

classroom can provide student groups with 75 to 110 minutes of computer time a week, respectively. One-computer classrooms provide limited group access, but they can be used to facilitate whole-class projects. For example, the class may decide to create a project about African-American inventors to present to the community during Black History Month. Students may be placed in groups of three to research a specific inventor and to design a one-card or one-page presentation about their inventor. A template can be designed to assist students with their presentation. Student groups can take turns at the classroom computer (see fig. 3.5) inputting their data while others are finishing their research or working on a related small-group activity.

Managing Brainstorming and Research Activities

After the preliminary management issues of the DECIDE phase have been addressed, the teacher can provide the students with time to brainstorm and research the topic of their project. This step should be prefaced with the purpose of the students' multimedia projects, and each group should be provided with guidelines and rubrics for their project (see ch. 7). To solidify the groups, let teams develop their own name or "company" logo.

Brainstorming Activities

After student groups have established their project roles (e.g., graphic artist, instructional designer, production specialist, and program author), behavior roles (e.g., turn-taking monitor, noise monitor, record keeper, task master), and team name, provide students with time to brainstorm (see the BrainStorm and KWL Knowledge Chart blackline masters). Depending on the ability level and experience of the students, brainstorming may be conducted as a whole class or by individual groups. For high-ability and experienced groups, provide a rubric of questions or guidelines that covers the assigned instructional content. For example, if students are creating multimedia projects on Egypt, provide them with specific content questions and related pictures to research and include in their presentations. If students are creating a multimedia project about family history, provide students with guidelines as to the type of information that should be included. These guidelines can help focus the students' thoughts as they brainstorm ideas.

For younger and lower ability students, make sure students have previous background knowledge in the assigned topics. Guide them through a KWL Knowledge Chart—What we know, What we want to find out, and What we learned (see the KWL Knowledge Chart blackline master). Each student can participate in the chart activity at his or her desk as the teacher directs the whole class using a transparency of the chart on an overhead projector. Student groups can exchange their thoughts and share their ideas with the class. Following the introduction of the KWL Knowledge Chart, student groups can be assigned a particular outcome on the chart. For example, if the chart is about the solar system, student groups might be assigned to find out what the class wants to know about a particular planet. Group One might answer class questions about Pluto, Group Two might answer class questions about Mercury, and so on. Completion of the chart would occur after the students presented their final multimedia projects.

Additional brainstorming techniques include recording students' sensory experiences. For example, many teachers pop popcorn in class to facilitate the student's creative writing skills. Students experience and discuss the sound, smell, taste, texture, and sight of popcorn before they write about it. A similar approach may be taken toward a particular multimedia project. For example, if the goal of the project is to develop and present a persuasive advertisement, such as why a group's hamburger is the best, educators may bring in different hamburgers for the students to sample, as well as let the students view videos of hamburger commercials, examine newspaper and magazine advertisements for hamburgers, inspect the hamburgers' packaging, and so on. As a class, the students can brainstorm and discuss how the hamburgers and their advertisements are the same or different, and what issues (price, taste, nutrition, popularity, convenience, etc.) may affect consumer choice. Following this whole-class experience, students can return to their groups and brainstorm strategies for their projects based on their new background knowledge. Final projects might include a persuasive presentation and samples of the group's hamburger creations.

Background knowledge is a prerequisite for most brainstorming activities. Sometimes educators may want to extend or deepen their students' background knowledge before having them engage in brainstorming activities. For example, if the content of a project is on the homeless, a field trip may be arranged to visit a facility that provides shelter for the homeless. Once there, students may have the opportunity to interview, photograph, and videotape various people who live on the streets. Given this real-world learning experience, the teacher has provided the students with background knowledge that will likely produce a more meaningful brainstorming session on the homeless than a session limited to what the students may have read or seen on television.

Research Activities

After students have brainstormed about their topic, the teacher reviews the group's brainstorming chart and asks clarifying questions to ensure that the group is on track. After the group's work is approved, the students can begin researching the different areas of their topic. Students may want to assign each group member a specific task.

Research activities may take place on or off the computer. Computer schedules can be designed that allow students access to CD-ROMs and the Internet to further their research (see figs. 3.1, 3.2, 3.3, 3.4, and 3.5). Students not assigned to computers can conduct research at the school library or in the classroom, using newspapers, textbooks, literature books, magazines, and other resources. High-ability students will need time to organize and synthesize gathered information and assign further research responsibilities. Younger and lower ability students will need to work together to find the answers to their assigned questions from the KWL Knowledge Chart. Field trips, guest speakers, experiments, and other opportunities may be arranged to assist students with their research. Students can use a bibliography information sheet (see the Bibliography Information blackline master) to record and track their sources throughout the DDD-E process.

Students may also have the opportunity to conduct research at home. Groups may assign members to conduct research via the Internet, locate or create graphics, or develop narration or audio clips on their home computers. Students can also create portions of their group's multimedia project at home, provided they have the appropriate software. Many Web tools are free, and HyperStudio has a "Home Use Policy" that permits students to work on their projects at home. Groups may work together at one member's house, too. Never assume, though, that students have access to home computers or other research materials. It is inappropriate to assign homework if the students do not have the skills or resources to complete it.

Each group's record keeper should keep a journal (see the Journal Entry # blackline master) of his or her group's progress, including the time the group spent brainstorming. Journal entries can help students reflect on their work, social experiences, and how they are achieving their goals. Teachers may choose to review journal entries on a daily or every-other-day basis to help keep students focused and to address problems before they get out of hand. Groups can keep their journal entries in a binder and submit the binder with their final project. Groups may spend two to five class periods conducting the initial research for their projects.

Summary

There are many variables to consider when assigning multimedia projects: computer access, student experience, grouping variables, group size, student roles, time needed to complete the project, etc. The DECIDE phase of the DDD-E process requires teachers to address these variables before assigning multimedia projects; hence, the planning and organization of a project help teachers to determine the project goals.

After determining the project goals, appropriate background knowledge, guidelines, and rubrics are provided to assist student groups with the brainstorming and research activities. These activities provide the foundation for the next step of the DDD-E process: DESIGN. Journal entries continue throughout the DDD-E process, helping students to reflect on their progress and project goals.

There are multiple stages to the creation of multimedia projects, but the DECIDE phase is the most critical to the success of the projects. The stages that follow (discussed in chapters 4, 5, 6, and 7) depend on the planning, organization, and research activities conducted in the DECIDE phase; hence, each stage depends on its predecessor. The time needed to complete each stage will depend on the size and complexity of the project, as well as the level and number of students in each group. Well-managed classrooms and organized projects will add to the success of students' multimedia endeavors and learning.

Blackline Masters

Several blackline masters are presented in this chapter to assist teachers with the DECIDE phase. These include:

- Self Survey—one method of organizing students into groups based on Howard Gardner's Theory of Multiple Intelligences.
- Computer Schedule—a template for organizing classroom computer time.
- BrainStorm—a webbing activity designed to help students link their ideas.
- KWL Knowledge Chart—a chart to help students organize what they know and what they want to find out about a topic.
- Bibliography Information—one way to record and identify sources used throughout the DDD-E process.
- Journal Entry #—a method of recording and tracking a group's progress.

Blackline masters may be copied for educational purposes. They may also be used to assist educators in creating their own DECIDE activity and organization sheets, such as a modified survey, computer schedule, or bibliography information sheet.

References

Beane, W. E., and E. A. Lemke. 1971. Group variables influencing the transfer of conceptual behavior. *Journal of Educational Psychology* 62(3): 215–18.

California Technology Task Force, California Department of Education. 1997 (March). Connect, compute, and compete: The report of the California technology task force. [online]. Available: http://goldmine.cde.ca.gov/ftpbranch/retdiv/ccc_task/ccc.htm

Dublin, P., H. Pressman, E. Barnett, A. D. Corcoran, and E. J. Woldman. 1994. *Integrating computers in your classroom: Elementary education.* New York: HarperCollins College Publishers.

Hooper, S., and M. J. Hannafin. 1991. The effects of group composition on achievement, interaction, and learning efficiency during computer-based cooperative instruction. *Educational Technology Research & Development* 39(3): 27–40.

Johnson, D. W., and R. T. Johnson. 1991. *Learning together and alone: Cooperative, competitive, and individualistic learning.* 3d ed. Englewood Cliffs, NJ: Prentice Hall.

Johnson, D. W., and R. T. Johnson, and E. J. Holubec. 1994. *Cooperative learning in the classroom.* Alexandria, VA: Association for Supervision and Curriculum Development.

Jonassen, D. H. 1996. *Computers in the classroom: Mindtools for critical thinking.* Englewood Cliffs, NJ: Prentice Hall.

Okebukola, P. A., and M. B. Ogunniyi. 1984. Cooperative, competitive, and individualistic science laboratory interaction patterns—Effects on students' achievement and acquisition of practical skills. *Journal of Research in Science Teaching* 21(9): 875–84.

Watson, S. B. 1992. The essential elements of cooperative learning. *American Biology Teacher* 54(2): 84–86.

Willing, K. R., and S. Girard. 1990. *Learning together: Computer-integrated classrooms.* Markham, Ontario: Pembroke Publishers Limited.

Self Survey

Rank the following statements according to how well they describe you. Give the statement that describes you the best a "1," the second best a "2," and so on.

☐ **I like to read books, write, and tell stories.**
(linguistics)

☐ **I like math, strategy games, and working with puzzles.**
(logic-mathematics)

☐ **I like to draw and I understand things better by looking at a picture.**
(spatial)

☐ **I have a hard time sitting still.**
(bodily-kinesthetic)

☐ **I am a good singer and I know when music is off key.**
(musical)

☐ **I get along well with others and I am a good listener.**
(interpersonal)

☐ **I am dependable and self-confident.**
(intrapersonal)

Name ______________________________

Computer Schedule

		Mon.	Tues.	Wed.	Thur.	Fri.	Sat.
Team Name:	Comp.						
______	Time						
Team Members: ______	Role						
______	Role						
______	Role						
______	Role						
		Mon.	Tues.	Wed.	Thur.	Fri.	Sat.
Team Name:	Comp.						
______	Time						
Team Members: ______	Role						
______	Role						
______	Role						
______	Role						
		Mon.	Tues.	Wed.	Thur.	Fri.	Sat.
Team Name:	Comp.						
______	Time						
Team Members: ______	Role						
______	Role						
______	Role						
______	Role						

BrainStorm

Create a web or "brainstorm" of your related ideas. Add additional thoughts as necessary.

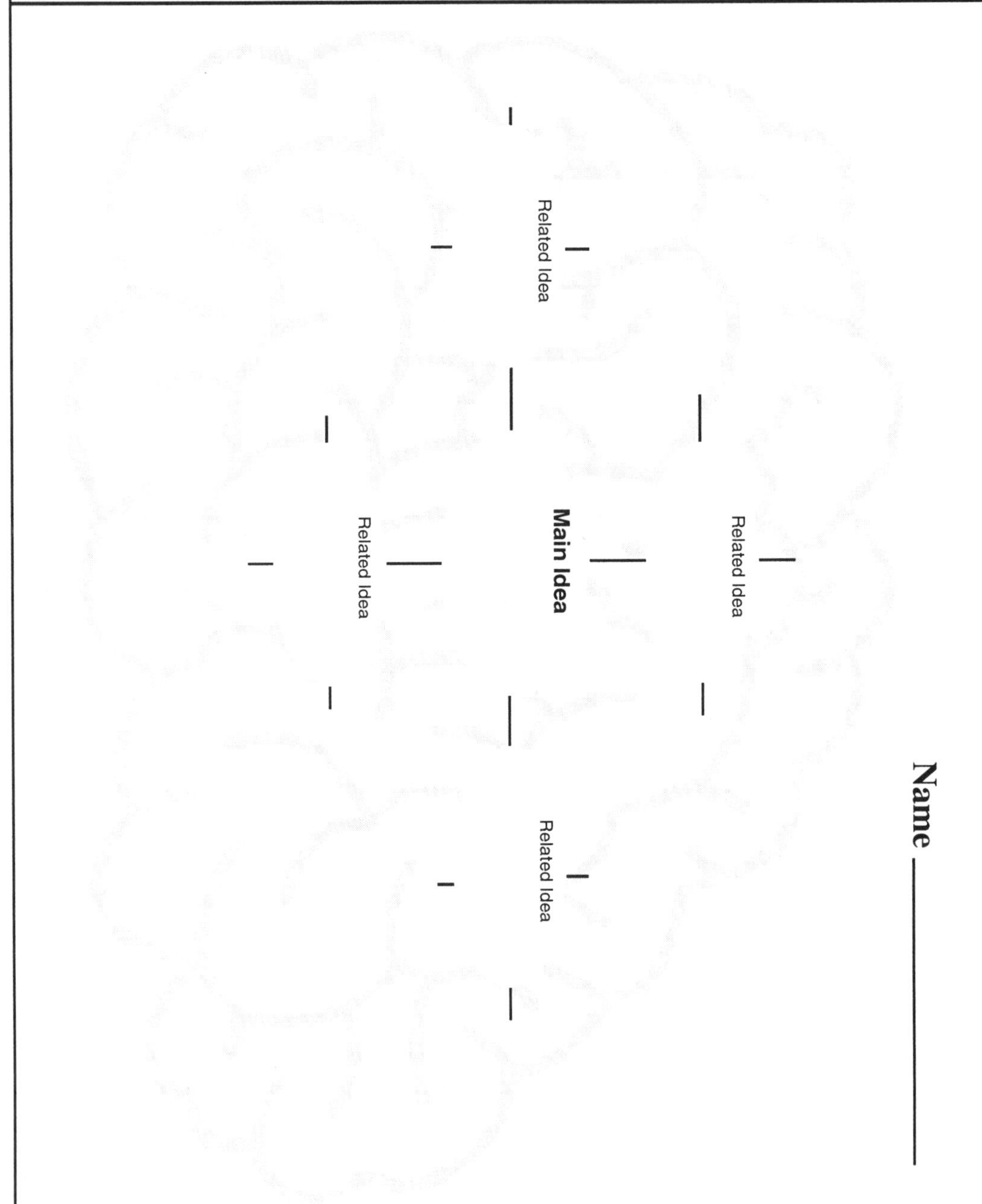

KWL Knowledge Chart

What we know	What we want to find out	What we learned

Bibliography Information

Team Name ______________________

Description	Media Type	Story-board#	Source

Journal Entry

Date ______________________ Team Name ______________________

Today's accomplishments: ______________________

____

____

____

____

Today's problems: ______________________

____

____

____

Goals for tomorrow: ______________________

____

____

____

Group dynamics:

1	2	3
poor	okay	great

Recorder's initials:

Comments: ______________________

____

____

CHAPTER 4

DESIGN

A Scenario

Sally's group was frantically trying to finish a multimedia project for class. The assignment was to create a multimedia project about the imports and exports of a country in South America. At first, the assignment seemed easy. Sally's group had finished its research over a week ago, and they were already quite proficient with HyperStudio. They were sure they would be able to throw together the final project very quickly.

The other groups in the class had worked a couple of days writing out storyboards and design ideas, but Sally's group had jumped ahead and immediately started recording sounds, drawing pictures, and making movies. After all, those elements were a lot more fun than writing storyboards. Now, however, they had a problem: The project was still a jumble of incomplete cards with no structure, and it was due tomorrow!

Sally called Charlene over to ask her advice. Charlene's project was complete, so maybe she knew some secrets for saving time. After a quick review of the unfinished project, Charlene asked if she could see Sally's storyboards and flowchart. Sally replied that her group had felt it was a waste of time to write out a detailed plan. Instead, their approach had been to develop the program on the fly. By skipping the DESIGN phase, they had rationalized, they would save valuable time and be able start development much sooner than their classmates.

Charlene agreed that it was tempting to jump right into the development of a multimedia project, but said that the secret to saving time was to *take* the time to develop flowcharts and storyboards. Charlene had learned this the previous semester when she, too, was tempted by the fun of digital media—and ended up spending more time fixing her program than her classmates spent on flowcharts and storyboards! Charlene had vowed that she would never put herself through that frustration again, so she could empathize with Sally. Charlene pointed out several problems with Sally's project:

- There was no structure to the project; a user would wander aimlessly.
- Some of the cards that Sally had created were lost because none of the other cards linked to them.
- Some of the icons and links were endless loops that trapped the user between cards, with no apparent exit.
- Some of the cards had titles, some did not; some of the cards had icons, some did not.
- The sounds and video were of good quality, but they distracted from the content and seemed irrelevant.

Charlene shared her group's flowcharts and storyboards with Sally, explaining how the problems in Sally's project could have been avoided. Charlene helped Sally's group straighten out its project as much as possible. As the hours passed, Sally's group realized that their time could have been better spent during the DESIGN phase, developing flowcharts and storyboards.

Overview

The DESIGN phase is extremely important because it produces the blueprint for the entire project, in the form of screen templates, flowcharts, and storyboards. Before they begin production of the media elements and programming, students must "chunk" and organize the information to convey meaning; specify the necessary graphics, sounds, animations, and video; and sequence the project elements in a flowchart.

At the beginning of the DESIGN phase, teachers may want to recommend or assign a minimum and maximum number of pages or cards for the project, as well as provide student teams with a list of other requirements or expectations, depending on the ability level of the students, available resources, and the type of multimedia project. (See the Project Checklist blackline master at the end of this chapter.) It is also a good idea to show examples of well-designed projects and poorly designed projects.

To assist teachers with the DESIGN phase of students' projects, this chapter provides design guidelines and recommendations for the structure and format of multimedia projects. The chapter concludes with several blackline masters to assist students and teachers during the DESIGN phase. Topics include:

- Outlining the content
  - The target audience
  - Development time
  - Project requirements
- Creating flowcharts
  - Linear structures
  - Tree structures
  - Cluster structures

- Star structures
- Flowchart symbols

- Specifying screen design
  - Hypermedia programs
  - Presentation programs
  - Web-based programs
- Writing storyboards
  - General planning sheet
  - Detailed storyboards
  - Design guidelines

Outlining the Content

In the DECIDE phase, the broad goals are stated and a brainstorming session helps to determine the possible topics. In addition, research is conducted to further delineate the topics that will actually be included in the project. As the students enter the DESIGN phase, the content must be solidified in the form of a content outline. Many factors will influence the content outline, including the target audience, development time, and project requirements.

The Target Audience

The students should determine who will be the primary users of the project and how users might influence the design and the content. For example, if the project is a presentation that will be displayed in class by the student group, the students will not have to include extensive navigation options, because they will be presenting the project. Students may also choose to present part of the content orally. If the project is designed to be used individually, however, there must be sufficient prompts to move users through the project, and all the content must be included.

The background, age, and experience of the target audience may affect the design of the project. For example, if a project is designed for third-graders, the content, presentation, and elements will be noticeably different from the content, presentation, and elements of a project designed for adults.

Development Time

The amount of time devoted to the development of a project will also affect the content outline. If a project must be designed and developed in a few hours, it will include substantially less content than a project that is produced over a semester period. In a similar manner, computer access time and the number of students in a project group can impact the content scope.

Project Requirements

When a project is assigned, it is often wise for the teacher to specify the project requirements in terms of content and components. For content, teachers may assign a topic, such as a famous author, and require that the project provide background information on the childhood of the author, a synopsis of his or her publications, and the author's impact on society. Teachers can require that students complete an outline of intent, specifying the project title, the goals and outcomes of the project, its target audience, and an outline of the content (see the Intention Outline blackline master at the end of this chapter). When the intention outlines are complete, the teacher should review them to ensure that the students' goals are clearly stated and aligned with the assignment's instructional objectives, that the content outline contains the depth required for the project, and that the topics are organized logically.

As to project components, the requirements may specify the number of screens (pages) or the number of graphics or media files that must be included in the project (see the Project Checklist blackline master at the end of this chapter). Requirements may be based on the students' ability level, available resources, time constraints, and appropriateness.

Creating Flowcharts

A *flowchart* is a visual depiction of the sequence and structure of a program. There are several common structures for flowcharts, including linear, tree, star, and cluster. A linear design consists of program elements that follow one after another; tree structures generally begin with a Main Menu and then branch into submenus; clusters are similar to tree structures, except that they do not branch into submenus; star designs are generated from a single point or idea. The specific structure is determined primarily by the project's goals and content.

Students should be encouraged to experiment with different ways of presenting content. In addition, teachers should demonstrate various projects that use different structures and point out the advantages and disadvantages of each. Teachers can use the Project Structures blackline master at the end of this chapter to help their students differentiate the various project structures and choose the appropriate structure for their project.

Linear Structures

Linear structures are appropriate when there is a specific sequence or a step-by-step procedure (see fig. 4.1). Presentations (such as those created with PowerPoint) are usually linear in design. For example, a student may create a linear project that details the steps required to dissect a frog.

Movement options in a linear structure generally consist of branching forward or backward. Most linear structures also include the option to start over at the beginning.

Tree Structures

A tree structure is appropriate when the main idea branches into a few other topics, which in turn are subdivided further (see fig. 4.2). Tree structures are common in both Web and hypermedia projects. A tree-shaped project might involve a Main Menu where the user can select any of three different states. When he or she clicks on any of the states, a submenu appears with other options, such as state politics, state history, or state industries. These selections may branch into further subdivisions.

Movement options in a tree structure usually allow users to branch forward and backward, return to the previous menu, and return to the Main Menu. Links among different branches of the tree are also possible, but they may confuse the students.

Cluster Structures

The cluster approach is a combination of the tree and linear structures (see fig. 4.3). In this case, the Main Menu (first card or page) may contain several options, but thereafter the program proceeds in a linear manner. A cluster structure would be appropriate if several procedures were available in one program.

Movement options in a cluster structure allow users to branch forward and backward within the linear segments and to return to the

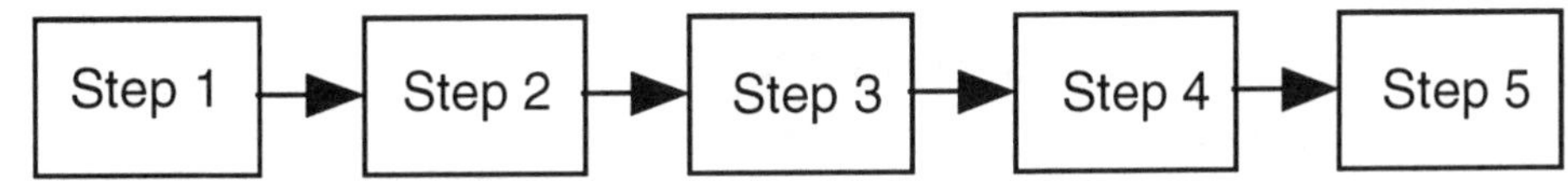

Figure 4.1 Linear structure

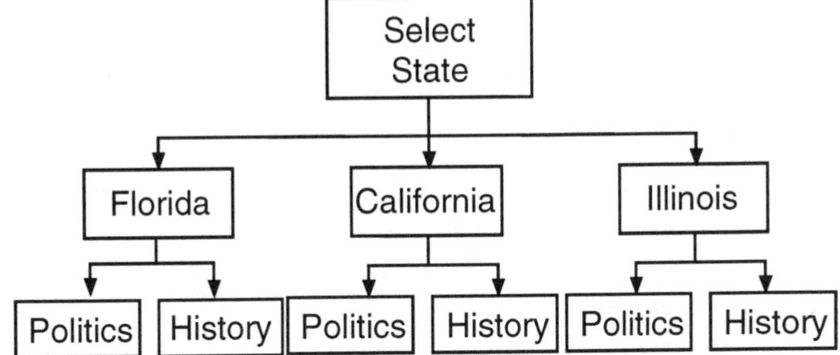

Figure 4.2 Tree structure

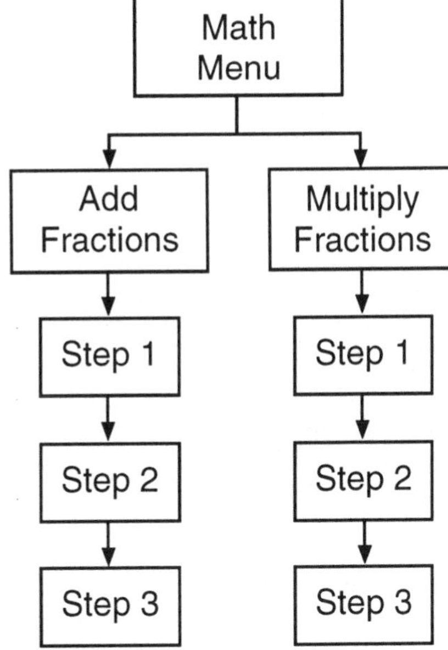

Figure 4.3 Cluster structure

Main Menu. In most cases, the linear segments should not contain more than five or six screens.

Star Structures

Star structures are used when one idea branches to several other, single ideas (see fig. 4.4). Many Web pages and hypermedia programs are designed with a star format. For example, a Web page may provide information about a school. From the main page, hyperlinks allow access to other pages with the sports schedule, school address, student activities, and so on. Each of the linked pages branches directly back to the introduction page.

The navigation of a star structure allows the user to branch out in any direction from the Main Menu. In most cases, the only option thereafter is to branch back to the Main Menu to make another selection.

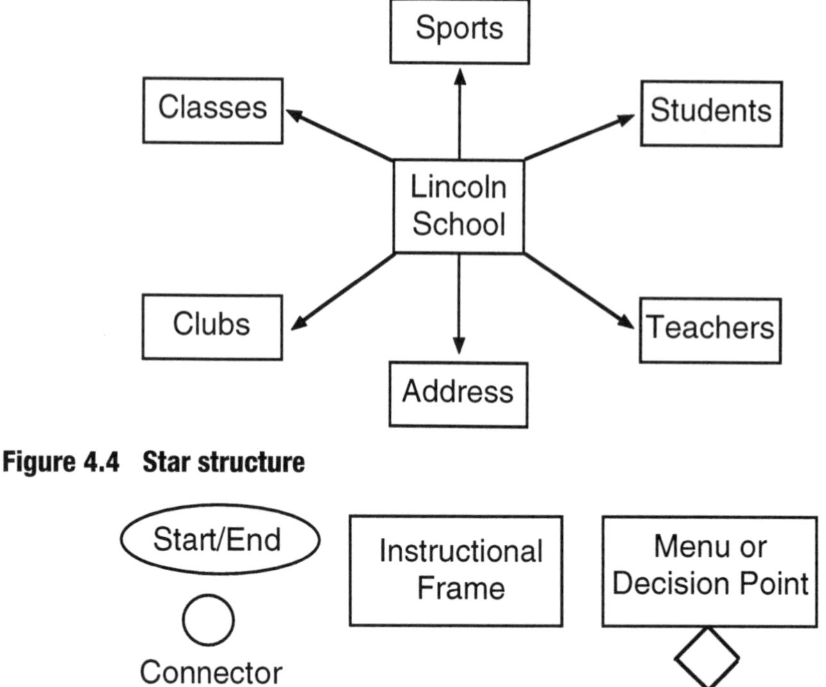

Figure 4.4 Star structure

Figure 4.5 Common flowchart symbols

Flowchart Symbols

Several standard symbols are commonly used in flowcharts (see fig. 4.5). These symbols can be created by hand, with rulers, with drawing templates, or in computer graphics programs.

When creating flowcharts, insist that the students label each element of the flowchart. With proper labeling, they will be able to easily correlate the flowchart components with the details of the program. Figure 4.6 is a flowchart of a program (in the tree structure) about Florida. Each symbol has a short description, and connectors are used to return to the menu.

Students should be encouraged to flowchart their lessons after the content outline is complete. Several flowchart activities are included at the end of this chapter (see The Bunny Hop, Medusa's Market, and Flowchart blackline masters) to assist students in structuring and designing their own flowcharts.

Specifying Screen Design

After the general flow of the lesson is diagrammed, the students should determine the screen templates that will be used in the project. For consistency, each screen should contain defined functional areas. The functional areas will vary based on the purpose of each screen (menu versus presentation) and on the programming tool used (PowerPoint versus HyperStudio). The primary functional areas include:

- *Title.* The title of each screen is usually located at the top or on the left side.
- *Informational/instructional text.* The text should be consistently located in the central part of the screen.
- *Graphics.* The graphics are usually placed on the side of the text, above it, or below it (see fig. 4.7).

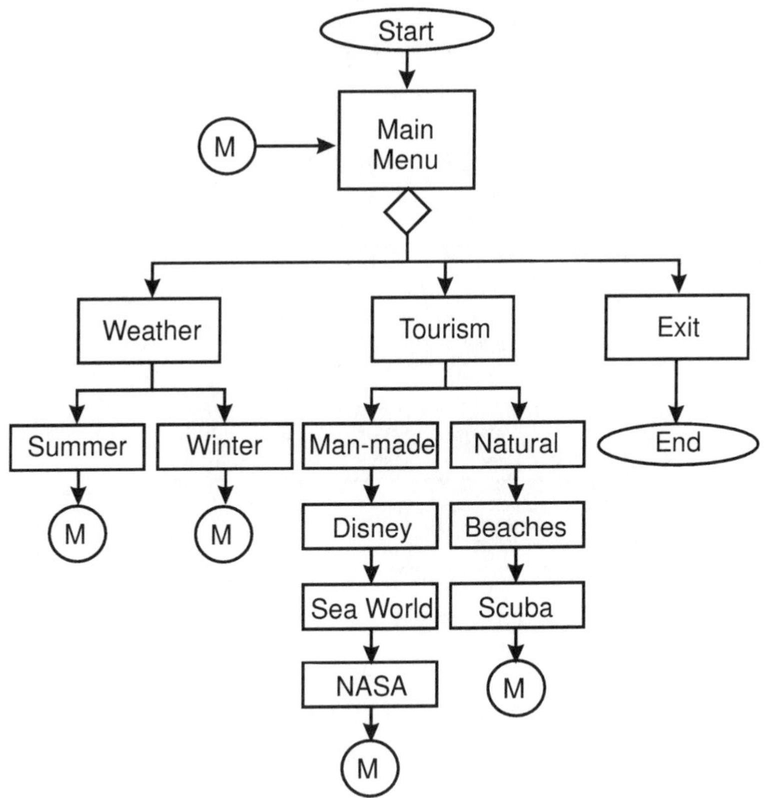

Figure 4.6 Flowchart for lesson about Florida

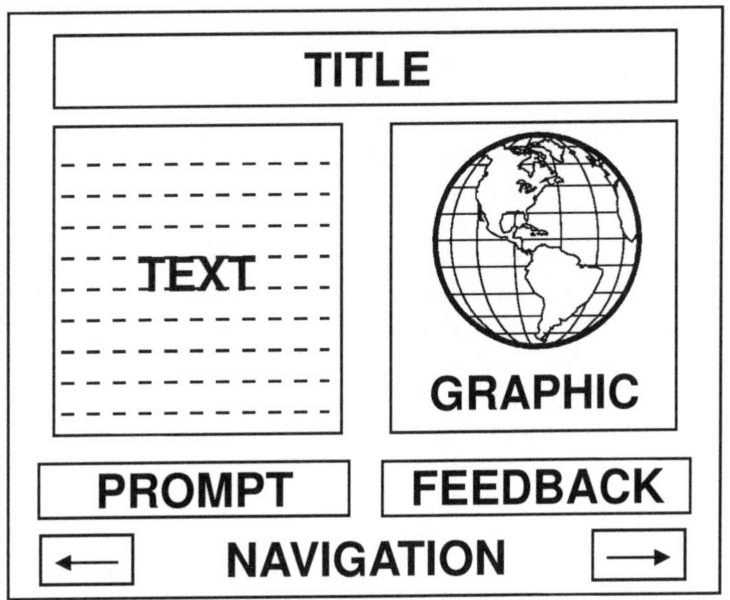

Figure 4.7 Instructional screen template for hypermedia program

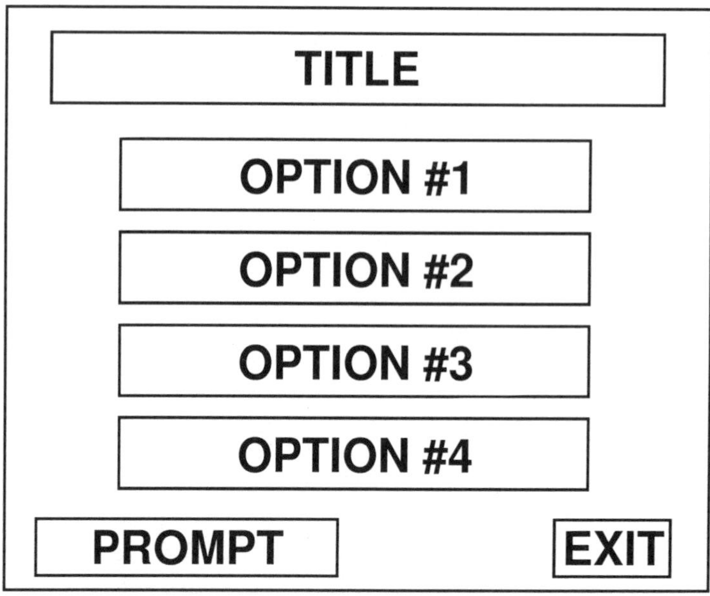

Figure 4.8 Menu screen template for hypermedia

- *Directions or student prompt.* If the directions are located in a consistent place, it will be easier for users to navigate through the program.
- *Feedback.* Feedback may appear in a pop-up dialog box or in a consistent location on the screen.
- *Icons or navigation options.* The navigational options (icons or buttons) are usually located at the bottom or one of the other edges of the screen.

Hypermedia Programs

Hypermedia programs, such as HyperStudio, usually contain at least three screen types: instructional screens, menu screens, and question screens. Figure 4.7 provides a template for an instructional screen. Note that in this case the text is on the left, the graphic is on the right, and the navigation options are on the bottom. This is only one example of the numerous possibilities for screen templates. For example, the text could be on the top with the graphic under it; there may be only a graphic on the screen; or it may be a text-only screen. See chapter 8 for additional examples of hypermedia card designs.

Another common template for hypermedia programs is a menu screen. In this case, the navigation is usually based on the menu options. There may or may not be additional buttons, such as an Exit. The menu template in figure 4.8 is based on four text options. In many cases, the menu selections will be graphics, and they may be arranged horizontally on the screen rather than vertically. When designing a menu screen, it is best to provide three to six menu options.

Because of the branching ability, question screens are often used in hypermedia programs. These screens look and operate very much like menu screens (see fig. 4.9). The directions should always be clearly stated, and there should always be an option to Exit.

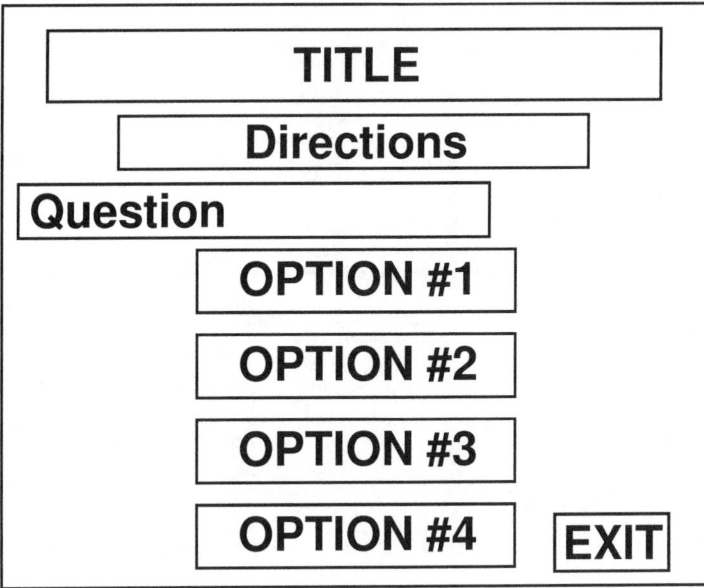

Figure 4.9 Question screen template for hypermedia

The exact design of the screen template will depend on the type of information, the authoring program being used, the experience level of the students, and several other factors. There may be more than one template for each project. For example, there may be one template for informational screens, another for question screens, and a third for menu screens.

Presentation Programs

Presentation programs, such as PowerPoint, are not designed to provide as much interactivity as hypermedia programs (although the latest version of PowerPoint does allow the creation of buttons). Presentation programs generally supply templates that have been professionally developed for communicating with a large audience. Figure 4.10 illustrates some of the layouts that are provided with PowerPoint, and figure 4.11 shows a sample presentation template. Note that these layouts and templates are designed to be projected for a large audience. In most cases, the font is large and the text is presented in bulleted lists.

Web-Based Programs

A wide variety of screen templates are appropriate for Web pages. Because large graphics take too long to transfer over the Internet, it is usually advisable to use primarily text, with small graphic banners or bullets. Navigational links on a Web page should be well defined so that users will know where the links will lead. Although feedback in the form of pop-up windows is possible on Web pages, the programming is quite complex. In most cases, school-based Web pages will consist of text and hyperlinks to other pages or media files. Templates and examples of Web-based pages are provided in chapter 9.

Writing Storyboards

After the screen templates and functional areas have been determined, the students can proceed to write the storyboards. Storyboards contain all the information that will be placed on the screens (in the screen templates), in addition to information that will assist the programmer and production specialists in development of the media components.

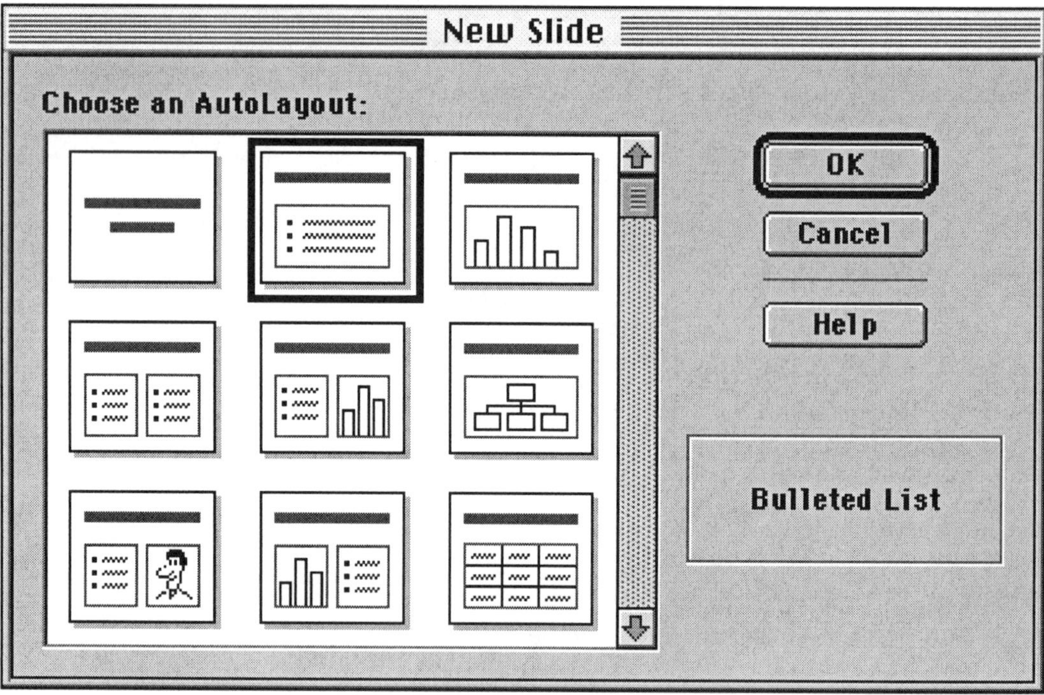

Figure 4.10 PowerPoint layouts

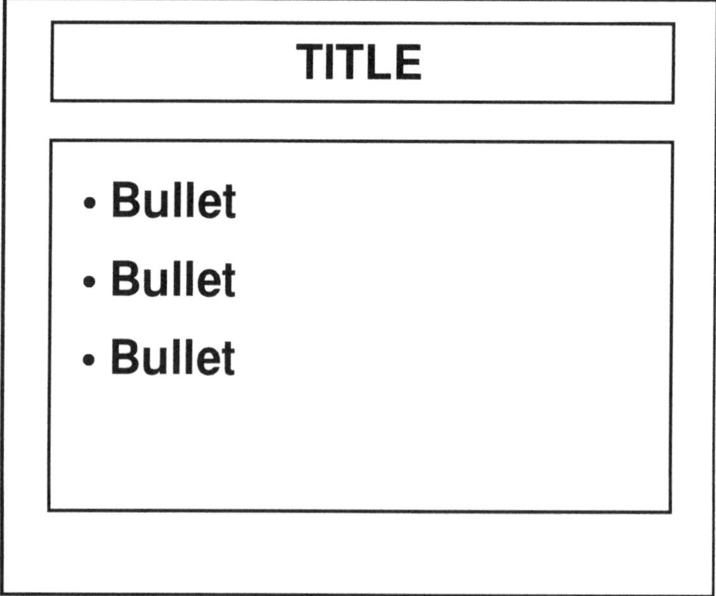

Figure 4.11 PowerPoint template

General Planning Sheet

Before writing the storyboards, it may be helpful to have the students fill out a general planning sheet. This sheet provides an opportunity for the students to allocate, or chunk, the information into separate screens without specifying all the details. Figure 4.12 illustrates the manner in which a title screen and instructional screen can be completed. (A Planning Sheet blackline master is provided at the end of this chapter as a tool for students.)

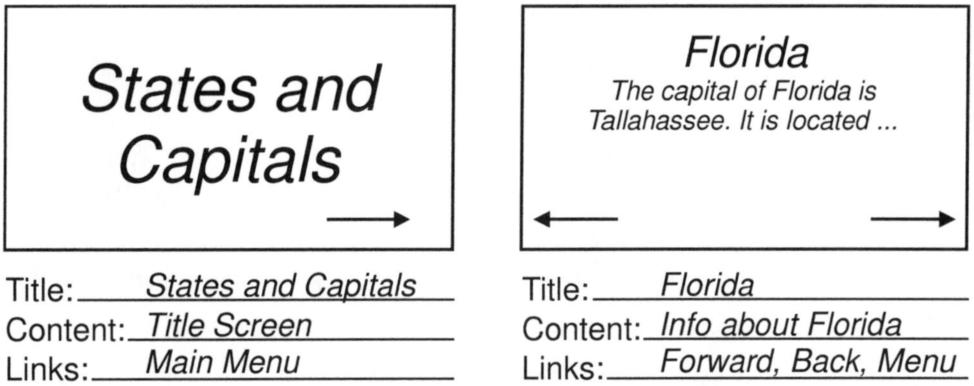

States and Capitals →	Florida The capital of Florida is Tallahassee. It is located ... ← →
Title: *States and Capitals* Content: *Title Screen* Links: *Main Menu*	Title: *Florida* Content: *Info about Florida* Links: *Forward, Back, Menu*

Figure 4.12 General planning sheet

An alternative to using the planning sheet is to have the students outline their screens on 3×5 or 5×8 index cards. Each card can be used to represent one computer screen or page. The students can divide each card into functional areas and place the content (text and graphics) on the screen in the appropriate places. The backs of the cards can be used to provide information for navigation and media elements. An advantage of using this method is that the students can arrange the cards on a desk in the sequence that they will be accessed in the program.

Detailed Storyboards

After the general plan is created, the students should be encouraged to write detailed storyboards for each screen. These storyboards serve as the blueprint for the program. Storyboards contain all the descriptive information required to produce the text, graphics, animations, audio, and video for the project. In addition, the links for each button or interaction are specified. Several storyboard templates are provided at the end of this chapter. The Hypermedia Storyboard is primarily targeted for hypermedia programs; the Presentation Storyboard for presentation programs; and the Web Storyboard for Web-based programs. These storyboards can be copied and distributed to the students. Advanced students may want to create their own storyboards in a database program, draw program, or word processor.

The storyboards should provide all of the information that will appear on the final screens. It is at this point that the students (instructional designers) determine the best way to present the information, how much information goes on each screen, and which media elements are appropriate. Each storyboard should contain a display area, branching information for the programmer, details about the font size and color, and a list of media elements.

Design Guidelines

There are several design rules that can help students as they work to specify the details of their programs. These guidelines cover each of the elements that may be included in a project.

Guidelines for Text

Left-justify the text (not centered).

Use mixed case (not all caps).

Avoid long lines of text.

Double-space text if possible.

Keep sentences short and sweet.
Use active tense.
Chunk information into short paragraphs.
Do not blink text unnecessarily.
Use at least 12 point font size for hypermedia and Web pages.
Use at least 24 point font size for presentation projects.
Use generic fonts that are available on all computers.
Do not place text on a background that has a pattern or graphic.

Guidelines for Menus

Provide between three and six options on a menu.
Include an exit option on all menus.
Clearly state the directions for selecting menu options.
Include titles on all menus.
Place menu options in logical sequence.

Guidelines for Icons and Navigational Buttons

Place icons in consistent locations throughout the program.
Use common icons (such as arrows) for navigation.
If an icon is inactive, remove it or make it dim.
Make icons big enough for users to easily click on them.
Provide instructions to help users navigate.
Make permanent buttons small and unobtrusive.
Place permanent buttons along the edge of the screen.
Include options for users to back up and exit.

Guidelines for Color

Use fewer than seven colors per screen.
Use consistent background colors.
Use consistent text colors.
On dark backgrounds, use light text.
On light backgrounds, use dark text.
Highlight key words in a contrasting color.
Do not use red backgrounds.

Guidelines for Graphics

Use graphics to enhance the program.
Do not include graphics that distract from the program.
Use simple graphics.
Add arrows or highlight boxes to help focus attention.
Be consistent in the placement of graphics.
Add text labels to graphs and charts.

Guidelines for Audio

Use audio only where it is appropriate.
Keep audio segments very short (about 10 seconds).
Use conversational style for narration.
Do not include audio that conflicts with the text.
Use sound effects as cues and transitions.

Guidelines for Video

Use video only when necessary.

Keep video segments short.

Include a replay button for video.

Additional information and guidelines about media elements (graphics, animations, audio, and video) are provided in chapter 5. Additional information about authoring programs and their options are included in chapter 6.

After the storyboards are complete, they should be reviewed by the teacher (see the Storyboard Review blackline master). Students should not begin the DEVELOP phase until their storyboards are approved. A final storyboard evaluation sheet is provided in chapter 7.

Summary

The DESIGN phase is a crucial element in the development of a multimedia project. The content outline, flowchart, planning sheets, and storyboards serve as the blueprints for the program and help to ensure that the goals of the project will be met. In the DESIGN phase, students participate in organizing information for optimal presentation; determining the most appropriate sequence; and outlining the details of the text, graphics, audio, video, and interactivity.

Blackline Masters

A variety of blackline masters are presented in this chapter to assist teachers and students with designing a multimedia project. Practice activities are included to help students with flowcharting. The following blackline masters conclude this chapter:

- Project Checklist—a general checklist of expectations for multimedia projects
- Intention Outline—an outline of intent that specifies the goals and content of a project
- Project Structures—illustrations of different flowcharts
- The Bunny Hop—a flowchart sequencing activity
- Medusa's Market—a flowchart sequencing activity
- Flowchart—a grid for designing flowcharts
- Planning Sheet—a tool to assist students in planning their storyboards
- Hypermedia Storyboard—a sample hypermedia storyboard template
- Presentation Storyboard—a sample presentation storyboard template
- Web Storyboard—a sample storyboard template for Web projects
- Storyboard Review—a preliminary evaluation sheet to guide students in the production and revision of storyboards

Project Checklist

Team Name ____________________

Before developing your project at the computer, complete the following:

- ☐ Intention Outline
- ☐ Flowchart
- ☐ Planning Sheet
- ☐ Storyboards

Make sure your project has:

- ☐ a minimum of _____ pages (or cards).
- ☐ a maximum of _____ pages (or cards).
- ☐ a Title page (or card).
- ☐ credits (designers and bibliography information).
- ☐ a Main Menu.
- ☐ appropriate navigation options.
- ☐ text that is easy to read and is accurate.
- ☐ complete sentences with correct punctuation, grammar, and spelling.
- ☐ the assigned media requirements.

_____ Clip Art _____ Animation _____ Video

_____ Scanned Image _____ Digitized Camera Photo

_____ Original Audio _____ Clip Sound (digitized)

_____ MIDI File _____ Original Graphic

- ☐ Other: ____________________

____

Intention Outline

Project Title: ______________________________

General Goal: ______________________________

Specific Outcomes: ______________________________

____

Audience

Who will use this project (students, teachers, parents, etc.)?

Content Outline

I. ______________________________

A. ______________________________

B. ______________________________

C. ______________________________

II. ______________________________

A. ______________________________

B. ______________________________

C. ______________________________

III. ______________________________

A. ______________________________

B. ______________________________

C. ______________________________

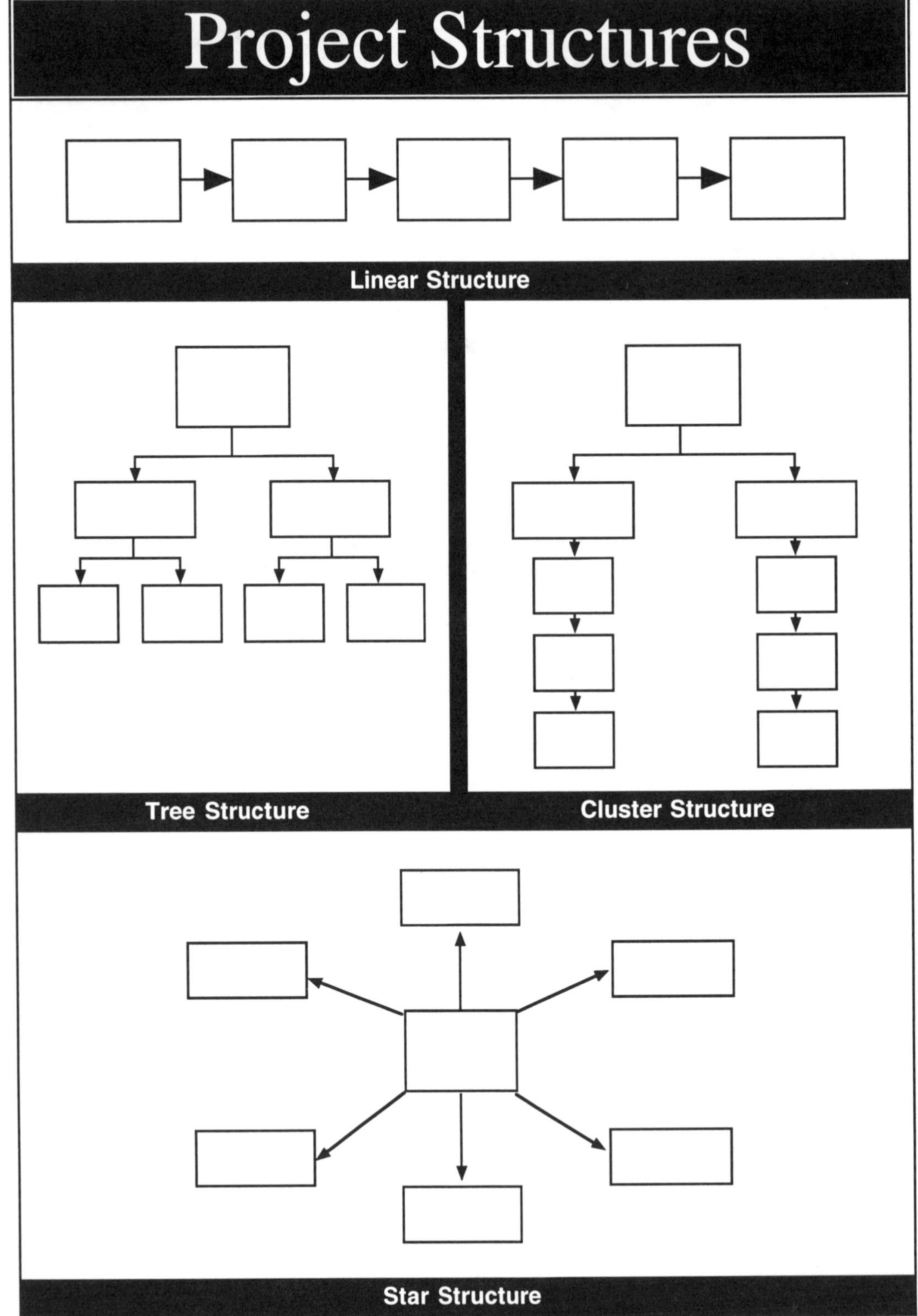
Project Structures
Linear Structure
Tree Structure
Cluster Structure
Star Structure

The Bunny Hop

Benjamin Bunny is helping his friend hide eggs. Help Benjamin figure out what to do by placing a letter in the correct section of the flowchart. Remember that diamond shapes are for asking questions and box shapes are for decisions. Two are already done for you.

_____ A. Wait ten minutes.

_____ B. Hide egg.

_____ C. Is anyone peeking?

_____ D. Continue to hop down the bunny trail.

_____ E. Place colored eggs into basket.

_____ F. Are there eggs in the basket?

_____ G. Hop down the bunny trail.

_____ H. Look for a place to hide egg.

_____ I. Go home.

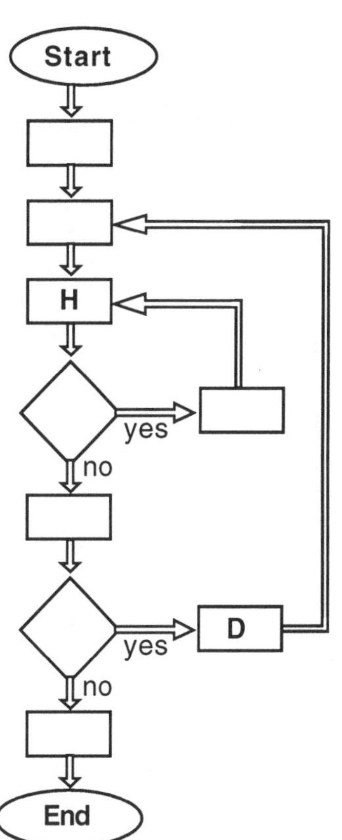

Extension ideas: Create a flowchart for getting ready for school in the morning, cooking your favorite meal, packing for a vacation, etc.

Answer: E, G, H, C (yes is A), B, F (yes is D), I

Medusa's Market

Medusa needs to go to the grocery store. Help her get into her car and drive to the grocery store's parking lot by placing a letter in the correct section of the flowchart. Remember that diamond shapes are for asking questions and box shapes are for decisions. Three are already done for you.

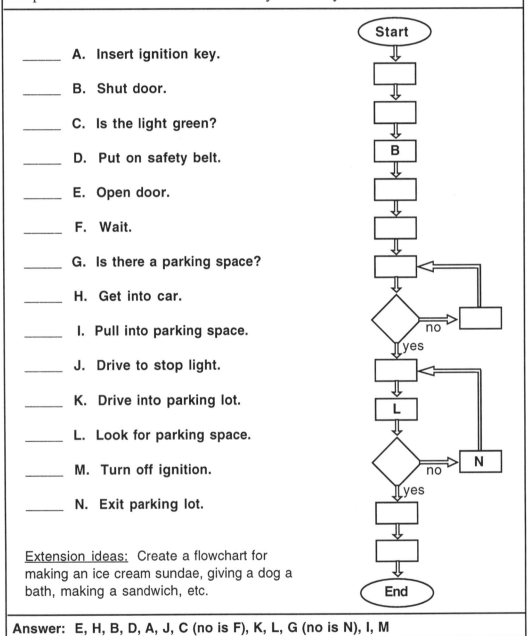

_____ A. Insert ignition key.

_____ B. Shut door.

_____ C. Is the light green?

_____ D. Put on safety belt.

_____ E. Open door.

_____ F. Wait.

_____ G. Is there a parking space?

_____ H. Get into car.

_____ I. Pull into parking space.

_____ J. Drive to stop light.

_____ K. Drive into parking lot.

_____ L. Look for parking space.

_____ M. Turn off ignition.

_____ N. Exit parking lot.

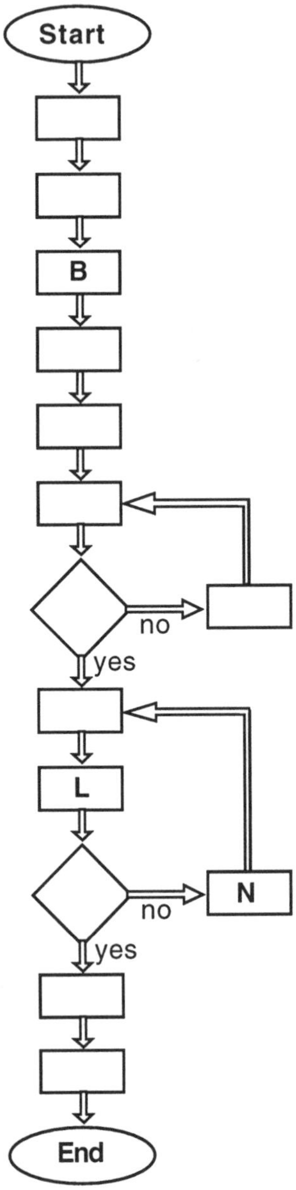

Extension ideas: Create a flowchart for making an ice cream sundae, giving a dog a bath, making a sandwich, etc.

Answer: E, H, B, D, A, J, C (no is F), K, L, G (no is N), I, M

Flowchart

Use these symbols to create a flowchart of your project:

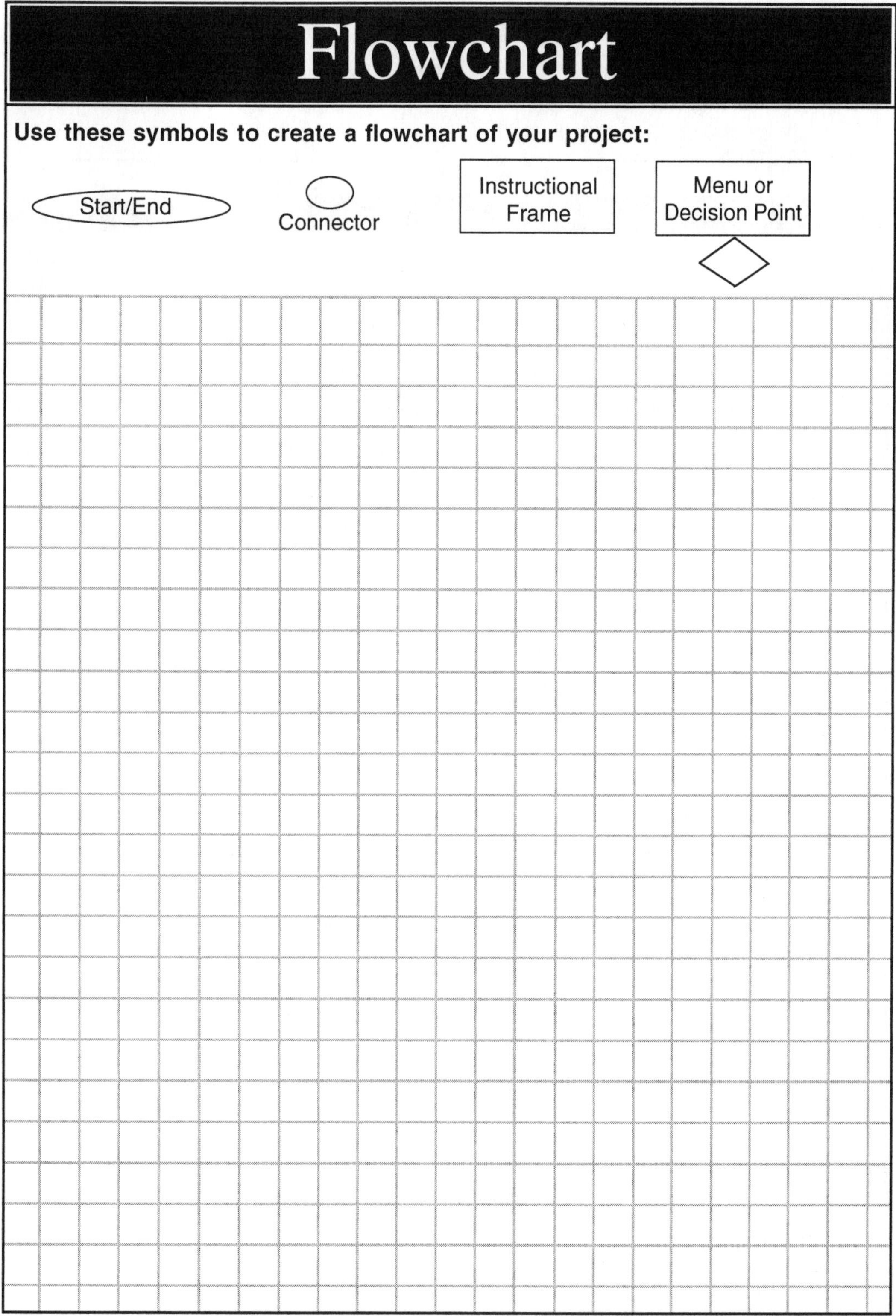

Planning Sheet

Name of group: ______________________

Use this sheet to plan the general content of your pages.

Title: ______________
Content: ______________
Links: ______________

Title: ______________
Content: ______________
Links: ______________

Title: ______________
Content: ______________
Links: ______________

Title: ______________
Content: ______________
Links: ______________

Title: ______________
Content: ______________
Links: ______________

Title: ______________
Content: ______________
Links: ______________

Hypermedia Storyboard

Name of group: ______________________ Storyboard Number: ______________

Use this sheet to specify the details of the project.

Navigation

Button: _______________ Link to: _____________ Action: ______________
Button: _______________ Link to: _____________ Action: ______________
Button: _______________ Link to: _____________ Action: ______________

Text

Color: _______________ Size: _____________ Font: ____________________

Audio

Source: __________________________
File: ____________________________
Description: ______________________
____
____

Video

Source: __________________________
File: ____________________________
Description: ______________________
____
____

Presentation Storyboard

Name of group: ____________________ Storyboard Number: ______________

Use this sheet to specify the details of the project.

Template

Name: __________________ Color: ____________ Layout: _______________

Text

Color: _________________ Size: ____________ Font: ____________________

Transition: _______________________ Build: ___________________________

Audio

Source: ________________________
File: __________________________
Description: ____________________
____
____

Video

Source: ________________________
File: __________________________
Description: ____________________
____
____

Web Storyboard

Name of group: ____________________ Storyboard Number: ____________

Use this sheet to specify the details of the project.

Navigation

Hyperlink: ________________ Link to: ______________________________

Hyperlink: ________________ Link to: ______________________________

Hyperlink: ________________ Link to: ______________________________

Text and Background

Text Color: ________________ Size: ____________ Font: ____________

Background Color: ____________ Background Graphic: ________________

Audio	Graphic
Source: ______________________	Source: ______________________
File: ______________________	File: ______________________
Description: ________________	Description: ________________
______________________________	______________________________

Storyboard Review

Students included:	Yes	No	N/A
a title screen	___	___	___
a credit screen	___	___	___
directions/information for the user	___	___	___
a main menu	___	___	___
forward and back links	___	___	___
factual and interesting information	___	___	___
consistent and clear layout designs	___	___	___
required media elements	___	___	___
font information for text boxes	___	___	___
font information for titles	___	___	___
background information	___	___	___
___________________________	___	___	___
___________________________	___	___	___
___________________________	___	___	___

Comments:

____

____

____

____

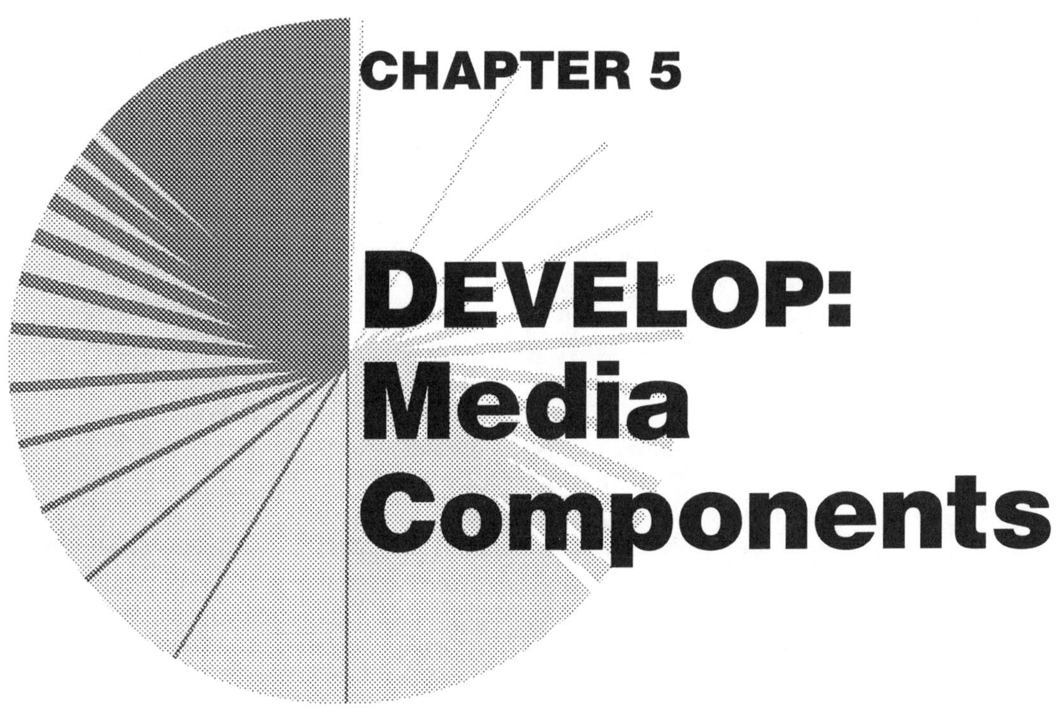

CHAPTER 5

DEVELOP: Media Components

A Scenario

John's group was creating a project about Spain. Through their research, they discovered that art and music are very important parts of Spanish culture. Rather than making a project with just text, they decided to add some other elements, such as graphics and sound.

After they completed their flowcharts and storyboards, their next step was to create the graphics. The students were using HyperStudio to develop the project, and they were pleased to learn that HyperStudio includes a toolbox with some paint tools. The HyperStudio paint program was easy to use, and they were able to create a few simplistic graphics of Spanish art and architecture. Then they looked at the clip art provided with HyperStudio and found maps and other images that fit the theme of their program.

Next, they wanted to include spoken translations for Spanish words. Luckily, José was bilingual and could serve as the narrator. They attached a microphone to a Macintosh computer and recorded Spanish words into the audio recorder of HyperStudio. They were having so much fun that they even considered reading all of the text in both languages. After the first few attempts, however, they discovered that the program size had grown too large to fit on a diskette! "We'd better record just a few short words," John decided.

The group also wanted to find some Spanish music for the program. Mr. Thomas suggested that they search on the Internet. The students were very surprised when they immediately located a site with hundreds of MIDI songs. Most of them were very small files, too. After their experience with the narrated words, they thought that the songs would be very short because the files were small. Instead, they were pleased to find that some of the songs played almost three minutes. "How can this be?" they asked Mr. Thomas. "It's a MIDI file," he explained. "Music stored in a MIDI format has a much smaller file size than the digital audio files that you narrate and record."

The groups was almost finished when Clara (who was still searching the Internet) shouted, "Wow! Look what I found! It's a movie of a bullfight!" Sure enough, she had located a short digital movie. Mr. Thomas showed them how to download it and include it in their program. Even though it was short, it was almost a megabyte in size (which meant they had to keep it on a separate diskette or on the hard drive). Their project was a success, and they were already talking about how they would make their own movie for the next assignment!

Overview

After the flowcharts and storyboards have been approved, students begin developing their multimedia projects on the computer. The third phase of the DDD-E model is DEVELOP. The DEVELOP phase includes the production of the media components, such as text, graphics, animations, audio, and video. It also covers the programming (or authoring) of the program. This chapter focuses on the design and production of the media; chapter 6 outlines the authoring process.

Media elements (graphics, animation, audio, and video) are key components of multimedia projects. They can help bring a presentation to life by providing realism, color, motion, and sound. Used effectively, media elements add many instructional benefits, enhance visual literacy, and address several of the students' different intelligences and learning styles. This chapter outlines the procedures for creating and editing graphics, animations, audio, and video elements. It concludes with classroom management strategies for gathering and creating media elements and an appendix of media resources. Topics include:

- Graphics
  - Creating a graphic file
  - Importing an existing graphic file
  - Scanning graphics
  - Digitizing graphics with a camera
  - Graphics guidelines
- Animations
  - Path animations
  - Frame animations
  - Animations guidelines
- Audio
  - Digital audio
  - Recording audio with computers
  - Compact disc-audio
  - Synthesized speech
  - MIDI
  - Digital audio file formats
  - Obtaining the rights to audio files
  - Obtaining sound files from the Web

   - Obtaining sound files from CD-ROM discs
   - Audio guidelines
- Digital video
   - Procedure for digitizing video
   - Constraining the file size of digital video
   - Digital video file formats
   - Obtaining the rights to video files
   - Video resources on the Web
   - Video resources on CD-ROM
   - Video guidelines
- Managing the gathering and creation of media

Graphics

The term *graphics* can be used to refer to images or any information in the computer that is presented via pictures, drawings, or paintings. As computer display systems evolved to include more and more colors, images became increasingly prevalent. Now, it is very rare to find a computer program or multimedia project that does not contain at least a few images.

There are many ways to obtain graphics for a computer project: they can be created from scratch with a computer program; they can be imported from an existing file; they can be scanned from a hard copy; or they can be digitized with a camera. Each method has advantages and disadvantages.

Creating a Graphic

Many graphics creation programs are available, including ClarisDraw, CorelDraw, Adobe Photoshop, SuperPaint, ColorIt, and Adobe Illustrator. These programs vary in price, sophistication, and many other attributes, but they can all be used to create computer graphics and save them in various file formats. Computer graphics (and graphics creation programs) can be roughly divided into two different types: paint (bitmapped) or draw (vector).

Paint (Bitmapped) Graphics

Paint or bitmapped images are made up of individual pixels (picture elements), which are small dots on the screen. The individual pixels are usually represented as horizontal and vertical lines in a matrix. The small pixels can be arranged to form a graphic—similar to a Lite-Brite toy. It is important to note that in this type of program, the pixels retain their independence. In other words, even if the pixels are positioned to form the appearance of a square, when you zoom in, you can see that the square is made up of tiny, individual pixels (see fig. 5.1).

There are numerous software programs that can be used to create bitmapped graphics. These programs are often referred to as *paint programs*. Popular examples include Adobe Photoshop, SuperPaint, and ColorIt. These programs are appropriate when you want to use a brush effect or apply a mixture of colors. With these programs, you can add effects such as distortions, textures, or gradients.

Many hypermedia programs, such as HyperStudio, include a simplistic paint program. For example, in HyperStudio's toolbox, the bottom four rows are paint tools that allow students to create squares, circles, and so forth (see fig. 5.2). All of the images created with these tools will

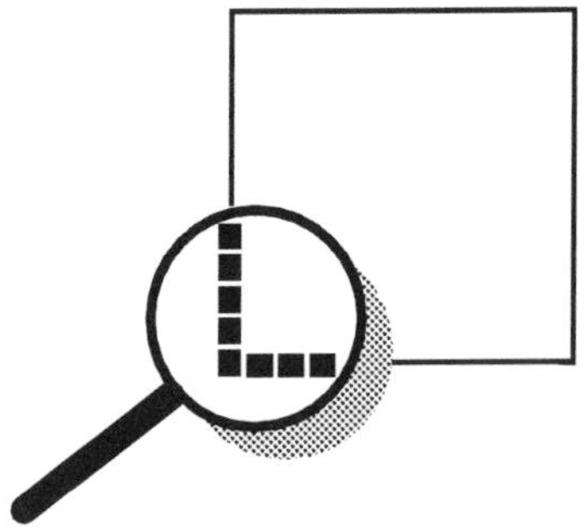

Figure 5.1 A bitmapped graphic is made up of individual pixels

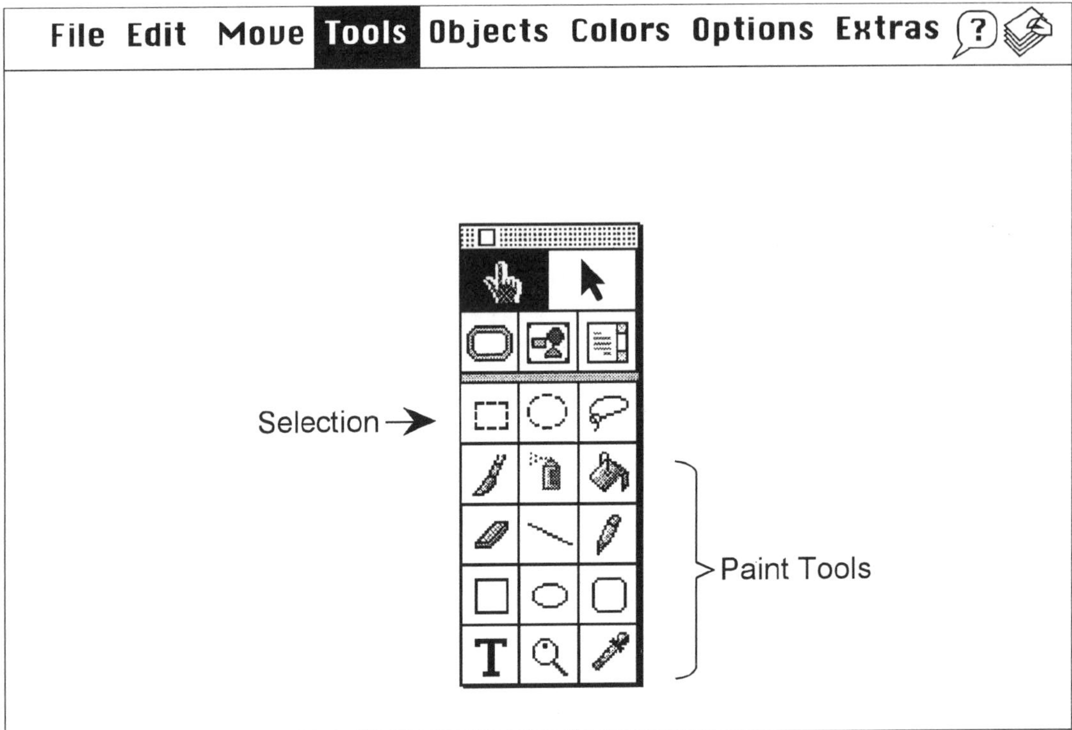

Figure 5.2 HyperStudio toolbox

be bitmapped and thus will consist of individual pixels. If students want to move a graphic (such as a square) after it has been created, they must use a selection tool (such as the lasso) to select all of the pixels that are to be moved.

Draw (Vector) Graphics

A vector graphic might look similar to a bitmapped image when it appears on the computer screen, but it is stored in a very different manner. In a vector image, every component of a graphic, such as a circle, square, or line (sometimes called an *object*), is defined by a precise mathematical formula. The image is stored as a collection of the formulae. If you were to zoom into the graphic, you would not see individual pixels (see fig. 5.3).

Vector images are ideal for geometric drawings such as blueprints, charts, or line drawings. Vector software programs (such as ClarisDraw or Adobe Illustrator) are popular because simple modifications to the

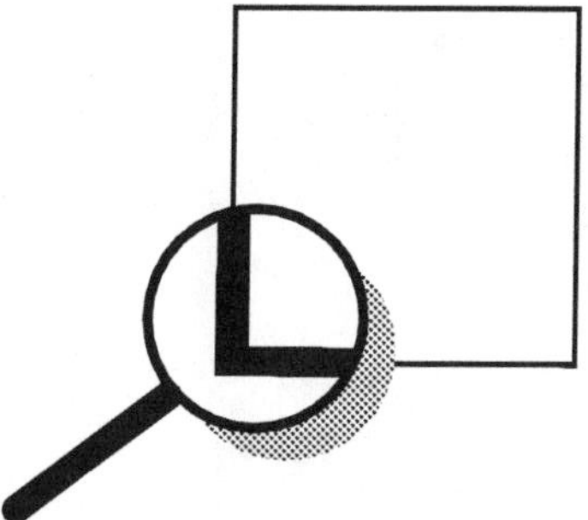

Figure 5.3 Vector graphics do not contain individual pixels

Extension	Description	Platform	Application
BMP	Windows bitmapped	Windows	Windows applications
PICT	Picture Format	Macintosh	Macintosh applications
TIFF	Tagged Image File Format	Windows and Mac	Common format for exchanging files between platforms
EPS	Encapsulated PostScript	Windows and Mac	Common in desktop publishing
GIF	Graphics Interchange Format	Windows, Mac, UNIX	Common on the Web
JPEG	Joint Photographic Experts Group	Windows, Mac, UNIX	Common on the Web

Table 5.1 Common graphics formats

formulae make it possible to rescale images, layer the objects, or select and move one object without affecting the rest of the objects.

Importing an Existing Graphic File

In many cases, the students may not have the time or software programs required to create their own graphics, and they may find it more expedient to use existing files. Some programs, such as PowerPoint and HyperStudio, provide a collection of clip art that can be easily imported into the programs. For example, HyperStudio contains a command: *Add Clip Art...*; PowerPoint has a similar option called *Insert...Clip Art....* These commands insert the clip art into the program where it can be repositioned and resized.

Both PowerPoint and HyperStudio also allow users to import picture files that are not provided as clip art. The key to importing existing graphics files into a program is to make sure that the files are stored in the correct format. For example, PowerPoint will open and display graphics files that have the extension BMP, PICT, TIF, and others. Some versions of PowerPoint may not open GIF or JPEG files. In contrast, graphics files on the Web are almost always stored in GIF or JPEG format. See table 5.1 for a list of common graphics formats.

If you have a graphic that is not in the appropriate format, you can use a graphic converter program to change the format. For example, if you had a PICT graphic and you wanted to place it on a Web page, you could open it in Adobe Photoshop and save it as a GIF file. Adobe Photoshop will open and save a variety of graphic file formats. There are also shareware programs, such as Graphic Converter (available at http://www.goldinc. com/Lemke/gc.html) and GIFConverter (available

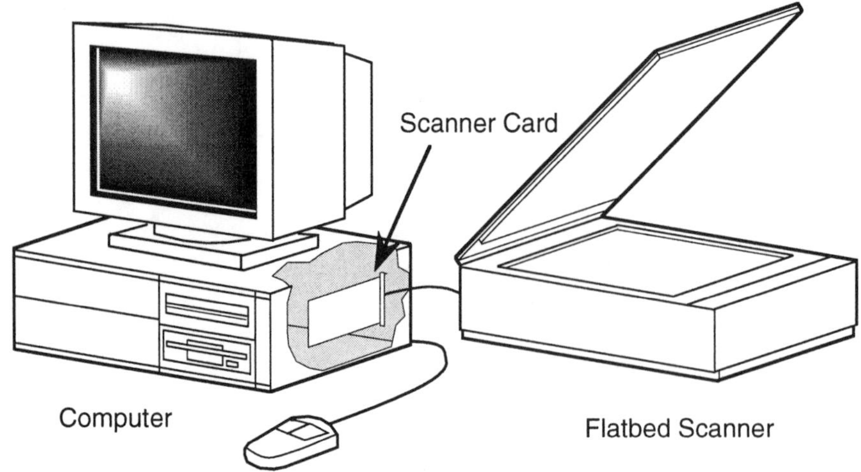

Figure 5.4 Configuration for scanning

at http://www.kamit. com/gifconverter.html), that can be used to convert image formats. Many shareware and freeware programs are available on the Web to assist students and teachers with multimedia projects. An appendix of resources appears at the end of this chapter.

Scanning Graphics

There are many times when you may want to use an image in a multimedia program that currently exists only as a hard copy, such as a photograph or a picture in a book. *Scanners* are computer peripherals used to convert print materials (hard copies) into images on a computer. Capturing images with a scanner makes it possible to incorporate complex images into multimedia projects.

The typical scanning process is very similar to copying a piece of paper on a photocopy machine. The paper copy is placed on a scanner, a light passes under it, and a bitmapped image is created. The difference is that instead of producing a copy on paper, the image is transferred to the computer screen. If a Windows computer is used for scanning, an additional scanner card must be installed (see fig. 5.4).

Scanners come with software that offers a variety of settings. These settings can help to constrain the file size of a scanned image by specifying:

- the amount of the image that is scanned,
- the number of colors displayed in the final image, and
- the resolution (number of dots per inch) of the image.

When students scan graphics, caution them to scan only the portion they need, to keep the file sizes as small as possible. Also, they should select a resolution of about 72 dots per inch (dpi). Scanning at a higher resolution for display on a computer screen is probably a waste of disk storage space.

After an image is scanned into a computer, it can be modified or enhanced with a computer graphics program. Scanners can produce graphics in black and white, shades of gray, or a wide range of colors. The recommended color setting for scanning graphics for multimedia projects is 256 colors or less. Using more colors (such as thousands or

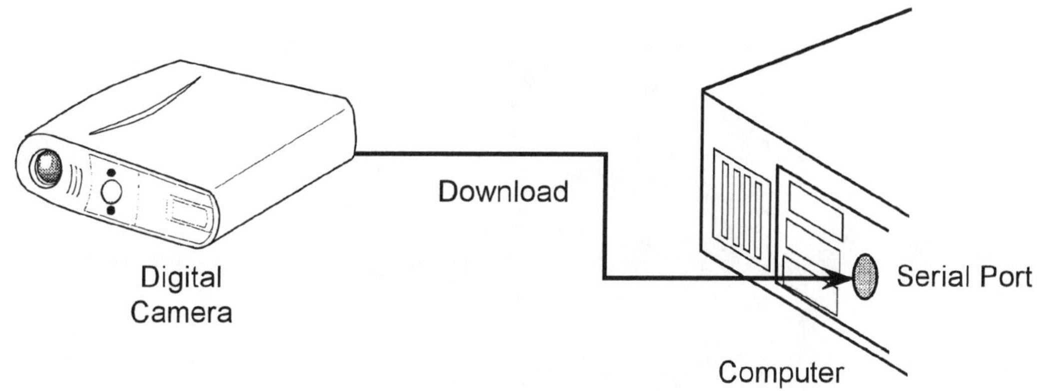

Figure 5.5 Downloading digital pictures from a camera

millions) may make the size of the image file too big, without resulting in a significantly better display on the computer.

Digitizing Graphics with a Camera

A photograph of a person is very difficult to draw from scratch on a computer. If your students have a photograph and a scanner, they can scan the image. However, if they do not already have a photo that has been developed on film, they may want to use a digital camera to capture the image.

Digital cameras, such as Apple's QuickTake, simplify the capturing process by enabling students to capture still images without film. The procedure for using a digital camera is very simple: simply point and click the camera to take pictures. To transfer the pictures to a computer, connect the camera to the computer, open the special software that is supplied with the camera, and click to download the images onto the computer drive (see fig. 5.5). After the images are downloaded into a computer, they can be enhanced, resized, or repositioned and integrated into a multimedia project.

Digital cameras have decreased tremendously in price. The average cost is now around $500. They are great for taking pictures during field trips and other school events.

Graphics Guidelines

The following guidelines can help you and your students determine the appropriate use of graphics in multimedia projects.

- Use graphics to enhance the program and illustrate important concepts.
- Do not include graphics that distract from the program.
- If possible, use several simple graphics rather than one complex graphic.
- If complex graphics are required, add arrows or highlight boxes to help focus attention on the relevant areas.
- If graphic icons are used for buttons, or other similar elements, be consistent—always use the same icon for the same function.

Figure 5.6 Picture for animation

- Be consistent in the placement of graphics—designate one part of the screen for graphics and another part for text, title, and so on.
- Use 256 colors or fewer to help keep file sizes as small as possible.
- Graphics should be created or scanned at 72 dpi.
- Check copyright restrictions on all graphics that will be used outside of the classroom.

Animations

Animations are graphic files that include movement. Animations can add excitement to multimedia projects; however, they can also be time-consuming to develop. This section outlines two different types of animations (path and frame), and discusses some animation procedures used in HyperStudio and on the Web.

Path Animations

A *path animation* involves moving an object on a screen that has a constant background. For example, an airplane may fly across the page or a ball may bounce through a scene. Some programs include features that can easily create path animations. For example, in HyperStudio there is a New Button Action, called Animator, that allows you to select a graphic or a portion of the screen and define an animation sequence.

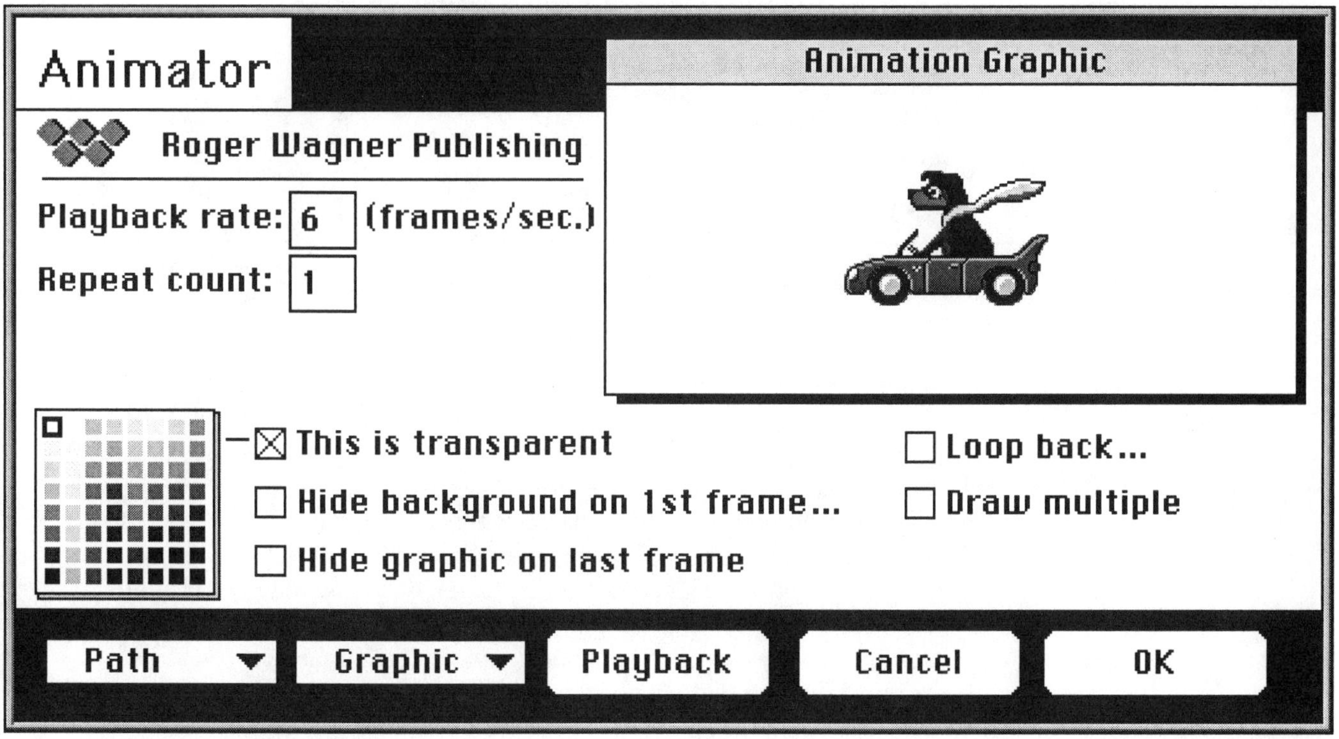

Animator

Roger Wagner Publishing

Playback rate: 6 (frames/sec.)

Repeat count: 1

Animation Graphic

☒ This is transparent

☐ Hide background on 1st frame...

☐ Hide graphic on last frame

☐ Loop back...

☐ Draw multiple

Path ▼ Graphic ▼ Playback Cancel OK

Figure 5.7 Path animation window

For example, if you wanted to animate the car in figure 5.6 and move it across the screen, you would follow these steps:

1. Create a button on the screen. For the Button Action, select "New Button Actions: Animator."
2. Select the car (or whatever portion of the screen you want to animate).
3. Click the mouse and hold it down as you move the car to define the path.
4. Release the mouse when you reach the end of the path.
5. When you release the mouse, the Animator dialog box in figure 5.7 will appear and allow you to select additional mouse options for your animation.

When a student clicks on the button, the car will animate across the predefined path and the background will stay the same.

Frame Animations

Path animation is a great way to move a single object; however, more sophisticated sequences may involve frame animations. With frame animation, several objects can move at the same time, the background can change, or the object itself can change (*morph*) into another object. With frame animation, there is a different screen for each step (*frame*) in the animation.

Movie animators create their effects by drawing many images with very slight differences between the images. When the images are played in rapid sequence (usually about 15 frames per second), they blend together and we see the illusion of motion. Likewise, to create frame

Figure 5.8 Graphics for a frame animation

animations on a computer, you must draw several frames and play them in rapid sequence (see fig. 5.8). HyperStudio includes a button action called "Play Frame Animation" that allows students to play the animation frames.

GIF animations are common frame-based formats that are used on Web pages. To create a GIF animation, you can use almost any graphics program to produce a series of still images that have slight alterations from one image to the next. Then, using software tools such as GifBuilder (available at http://www.pascal.com/mirrors/gifbuilder), you can set the play time so that each image will display a split second before the next one appears.

Animation Guidelines

The following guidelines can help you and your students determine the appropriate use of animations.

- Use animations to illustrate an abstract concept, such as erosion on a river.
- Keep the animation sequences short, or allow the user an option to interrupt and proceed with the program.
- Test the animations on various computers to ensure that the speed is appropriate.
- Use path animations to move one or two objects on a screen.
- Use frame animation for more complex sequences involving multiple changes.
- Do not include animations that distract from the content.
- To keep animation files small, limit the number of colors and the number of frames per second.

Audio

Audio refers to sound elements in a program. These elements can include recorded narration, music, and sound effects (such as a bird singing or telephone dial tone). Audio can assist students' learning, as well as add realism, excitement, and motivation to the program.

There are many ways that your students can add audio components to their projects. They can record the audio with a microphone (digital audio); they can control a CD with audio; they can use synthesized speech; they can create music with a MIDI input device; or they can use clip audio (elements that are available for free or for sale).

Sampling Rate	Storage for 1 Second of Sound	Seconds of Sound per 1 MB Storage
44 kHz	44 kilobytes	22 seconds
22 kHz	22 kilobytes	45 seconds
11 kHz	11 kilobytes	90 seconds

Table 5.2 Comparison of file sizes and sampling rates

Digital Audio

Audio can be recorded with a computer and stored in a digital format on computer disks or CD-ROMs. The audio files can be accessed and played by a computer program. A major advantage of this technology is that teachers and students can record their own voices or sounds and store them on a computer disk.

Bringing sound into the digital domain of computer bits and bytes requires a sampling process. At small but discrete time intervals, the computer takes a "snapshot" of the level of the sound. This process is called *sampling*, and the number of samples taken each second is referred to as the *sampling rate*. The more samples, the better the sound quality. For example, audio sampled 44,000 times per second (44 kilohertz or kHz) will provide better quality than audio sampled 22,000 times per second (22 kHz).

The selection of a sampling rate is based primarily on two factors: the quality of sound needed and the disk storage space available. The two factors are interrelated: the higher the quality, the more disk space required, and vice versa. For most educational applications, a sampling rate of 11 kHz is sufficient. If storage space is at a premium, even 5 to 8 kHz rate will provide intelligible narration. For music programs, higher quality and therefore higher sampling rates are recommended. Table 5.2 compares the file sizes generated when a one-second audio clip is recorded at various sampling rates.

Recording Audio with Computers

The recording process for digital audio is not difficult. Macintosh computers have the necessary hardware components built in for recording audio. If you have a PC, it will need a digital audio board (such as SoundBlaster) installed to record and play audio files. To digitize audio, follow this procedure:

- Plug a microphone into the audio input of the computer or audio board.
- Open an audio recording program. (SoundBlaster provides a sound recording/editing program and HyperStudio has a built-in sound recording program.)
- Select a sampling rate and other parameters if they are available.
- Choose "Record" on the menu of the software program.
- Speak into the microphone.
- Select "Stop" when you have recorded the segment you want.
- Test the recording with the "Play" command. If it is acceptable, name the file and save it to the disk.

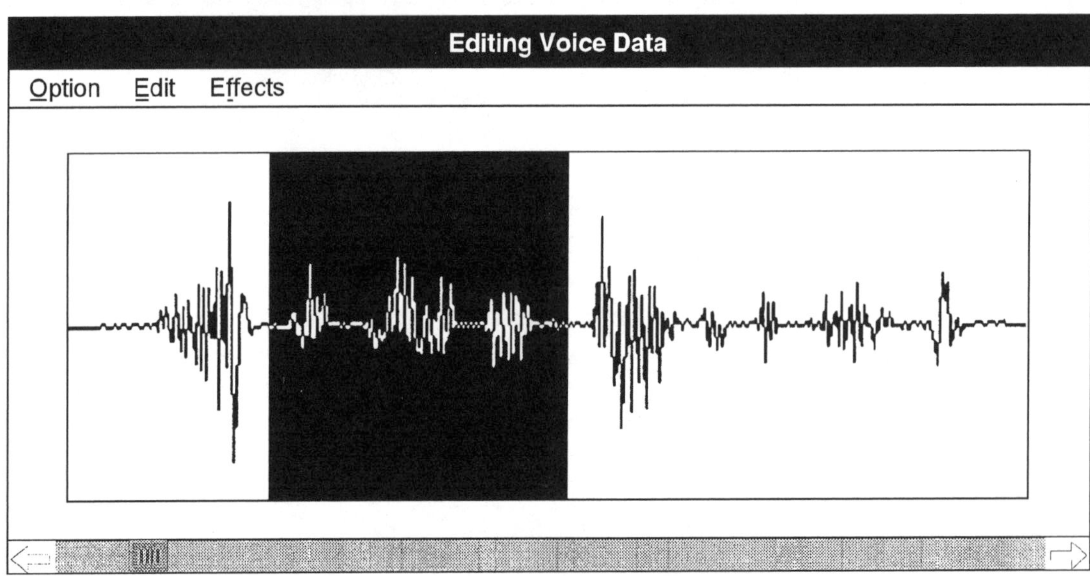

Figure 5.9 Editing an audio wave

Figure 5.10 Controlling a compact disc audio with HyperStudio

Digitized sounds can be viewed and edited like text (see fig. 5.9). With the appropriate software program, sounds can be selected, cut, copied, pasted, and mixed with other sounds. Audio editing is a powerful tool that allows you to rearrange sounds or cut out parts you do not need.

Compact Disc-Audio

Compact disc-audio (CD-Audio or CD-A) is a popular consumer format that can store up to 74 minutes of high-quality music on a compact disc. The standard sampling rate for CD-Audio is 44.1 kHz, which provides very high-quality sound.

In most cases, students will not have the equipment necessary to record a CD-A; however, they can use commercial CDs to enhance their multimedia projects. Commercial CD-Audio discs can be controlled through software programs by specifying the timecode in a hypermedia or authoring program. For example, if students want to create a multimedia program that plays a particular section of Beethoven's Fifth Symphony, HyperStudio will allow students to set the start and end times (in minutes, seconds, and frames). The control panel in figure 5.10 is used to select the track (song), time, and other parameters for a CD-Audio clip. It is important to note that the audio is not recorded; HyperStudio merely controls the CD-Audio disc.

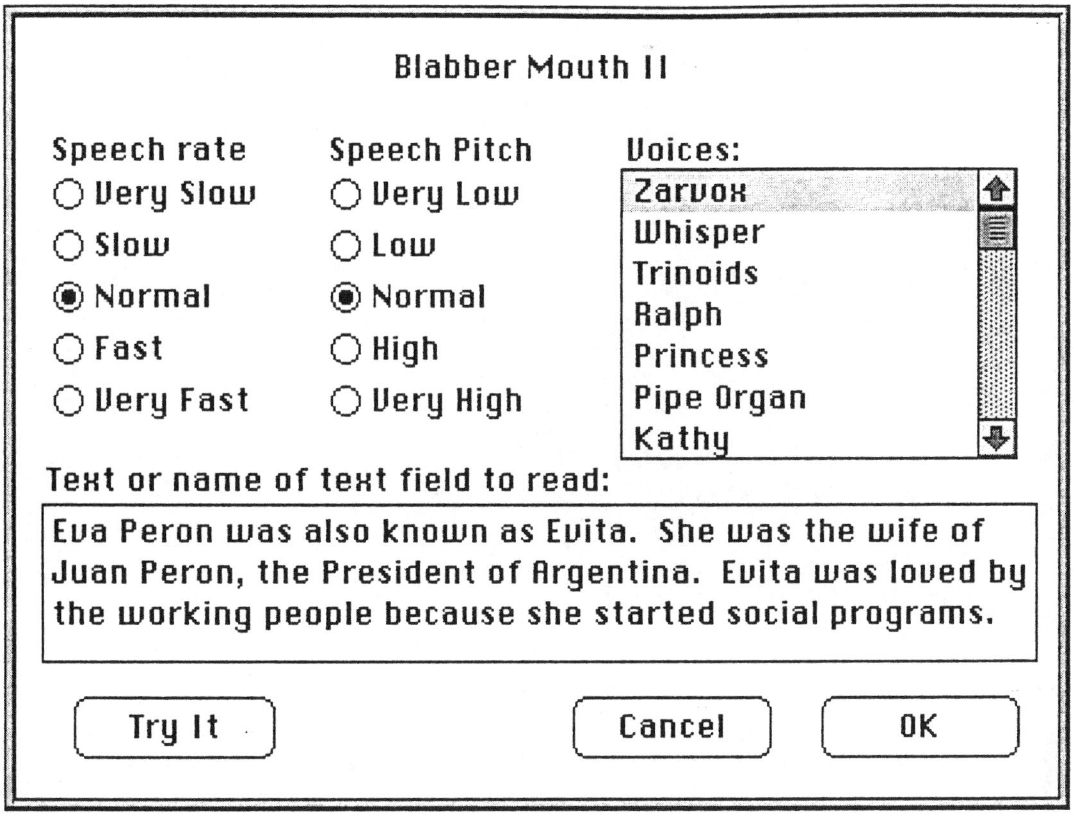

Figure 5.11 Blabber Mouth dialog box in HyperStudio

Synthesized Speech

Synthesized speech uses a computer program to translate text into spoken output without any recording process. It simply applies its phonetic rules to pronounce all of the words. The disadvantage of the text-to-speech synthesis method is the unnatural and mechanical sound. For instance, problems arise with words such as *live* that do not follow consistent rules of pronunciation. Most computer synthesizers cannot accurately differentiate between the use of *live* in these two sentences: "I live in Florida" and "We are using live bait."

Another problem with synthesized speech is that synthesizers do not have the natural inflections of a human voice; they do not "drop off" to indicate the end of a sentence as we do in natural speech. The robotic sounds can be a problem in educational settings, where realistic speech is important for teaching pronunciation and language.

An example of synthesized speech is the Blabber Mouth II feature of HyperStudio. With this feature, students can type in text and select one of many "voices"; the computer then does its best to read the text (see fig. 5.11). Because the only component that the computer has to store is the text, the file size is very small for this type of audio.

MIDI

A *synthesizer* is a musical instrument or device that generates sound electronically. Synthesizers have existed in various forms for many years, but many of them were incompatible with each other. In the early 1980s, several manufacturers agreed on a hardware standard for the instruments and the MIDI (Musical Instrument Digital Interface) specification was developed.

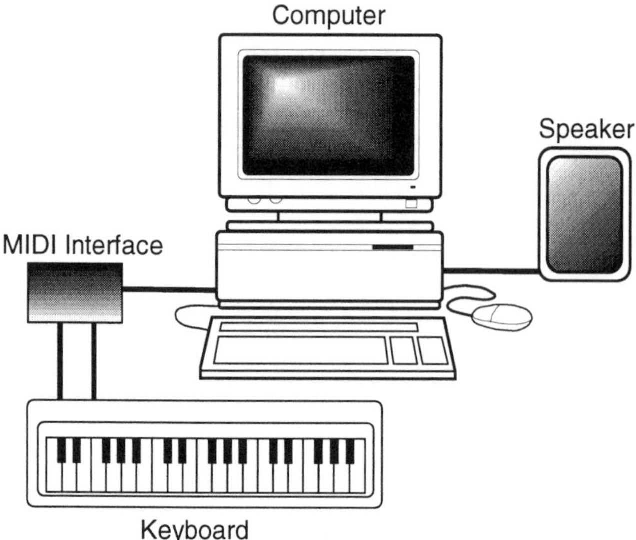

Figure 5.12 Configuration for MIDI

It is important to note that MIDI music is *not* sampled and digitized like digital audio files. Instead, MIDI contains information *about* the sound (such as the note value, the duration, and the pitch), not the sounds themselves. MIDI files provide the instructions on how to reproduce the music. The computer then interprets the MIDI instructions and produces the music using the sounds that are embedded in the sound card, MIDI instrument, or sound module.

An advantage of MIDI technology is that it can produce very complex music with very small files. It can play the sounds for stringed instruments, woodwinds, brass, and percussion simultaneously. To produce a MIDI composition, one uses a MIDI input device (such as a keyboard) and software that captures everything as it is played (see fig. 5.12). After the musical information is loaded into the computer, it can be edited or revised in relation to its rhythm, meter, tone, and many other parameters. With MIDI sequencing software, you can experiment with harmonies, record different parts, and play them back as a complete arrangement.

MIDI files are often used in multimedia projects because the file sizes are very small. For example, a file that is less than 10K may play a song that is two or three minutes long. If your school does not have the equipment to record MIDI files, you may be able to locate copyright-free files on the Internet. A list of MIDI sites on the Internet is available in the appendix at the end of this chapter.

Digital Audio File Formats

Many different audio file formats are used for digital audio. Some of the formats work only on Macintosh computers; others work only on Windows computers. Also, some file formats may be recognized by one program and not another. For example, .SND and .AIFF formats are common on Macintosh computers and .WAV is the most common format for Windows computers. A common format on the Web is .AU, which works on both Macintosh and Windows computers.

If you have an audio file that is not in the correct format, there are programs that will convert files from one format to another. For example, SoundApp (available at http://wwwhost.ots.utexas.edu/mac/pub-mac-sound.html) will convert an .AIFF file to an .AU file and GoldWave (available at http://www.goldwave.com) will convert from .WAV to .AU.

Obtaining the Rights to Audio Files

The fair use portion of the copyright law is generally interpreted as allowing students to use copyrighted music in a classroom situation to fulfill an instructional objective (such as an assignment to create a multimedia project). If the students want to use music on their Web site, however, they must be very careful that they have the rights to record and/or play the music files. Recording a song from the radio and adding a link to it from a Web site would definitely violate copyright laws.

To be on the safe side, it is best to purchase the rights to any song your students may use. There are several options for obtaining musical rights, including locating shareware sound files on the Web or on a CD-ROM.

Obtaining Sound Files from the Web

Numerous shareware sound files are available on the Web, including archives of Macintosh audio files (.AIFF or .SND format), audio files for Windows computers (.WAV format), and files designed to play on both Macintosh and Windows (.AU and .MID format). Prior to incorporating these files into a Web page or an application that will be distributed beyond the classroom, you should carefully read the permission statements. If there is no permission statement associated with the file or Web site, send an e-mail message to the site administrator to request permission.

Obtaining Sound Files from CD-ROM Discs

If you are seeking music or sound effects for a multimedia project, you can locate "clipmusic" discs. Clipmusic discs are designed to distribute musical files that can be legally copied and used by the person who purchased the disc. Some of these clipmusic discs contain sounds (such as trains, planes, cars, etc.); others have short music files that are in the public domain (generally those that are over 75 years old). Public domain music can be used freely in any environment.

In most cases, when you buy clipmusic discs, you also purchase the rights to duplicate and use the files. However, always read the fine print (or place a call) to make sure you can use the files on a Web site or in a multimedia project that will be distributed beyond the classroom.

Audio Guidelines

There are many situations when audio is appropriate in a multimedia program. For example, if the program is designed for nonreaders, or if it contains music, then audio is definitely required. In addition, audio is a great way to teach someone a different language or to include sound effects (such as heartbeats). However, audio files can be quite large, and students should be cautioned to use them only when necessary. The following guidelines should be considered for audio.

- Use audio only when it is appropriate to the content of the program.
- Record audio at the lowest acceptable sampling rate to save file space.
- Use synthesized speech for programs that require a lot of spoken words.

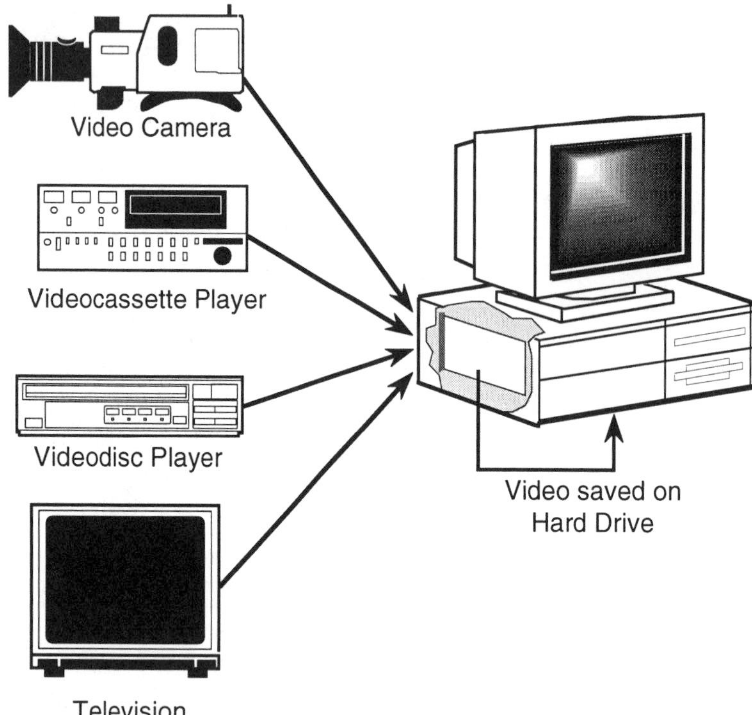

Figure 5.13 Configuration for digitizing video

- If possible, use MIDI for music—the files are much smaller than digital audio.
- Do not add audio that will distract from the screen display.
- Check copyright restrictions if the audio will be played outside the classroom environment.
- If the audio file format is not recognized by your software program, locate an audio converter program to change the file format.

Digital Video

Digitized video refers to motion sequences that have been recorded with a computer and saved as a computer file. Digital video has the potential to add realism to multimedia projects, but beware: The files sizes can be extremely large.

Procedure for Digitizing Video

When video is digitized, it must be processed through a special card in the computer. Video-digitizing cards (or peripherals) convert the electronic signals of regular video into digital bits of information for each pixel of the computer screen. The conversion process makes it possible to use a camera, videotape, videodisc, or broadcast television as a computer input device and to display the video on a standard computer monitor (see fig. 5.13).

To digitize video with a digitizing card, follow this procedure:

- Open the software program that controls the digital video card.

Screen Size and Rate	16 Colors	256 Colors	16.7 Million Colors
¼ screen; 15 fps	.55 MB	1.1 MB	3.4 MB
¼ screen; 30 fps	1.15 MB	2.3 MB	6.8 MB
Full screen; 15 fps	2.25 MB	4.5 MB	13.5 MB
Full screen; 30 fps	4.5 MB	9.0 MB	17.0 MB

Table 5.3 File sizes of one second of motion digital video

- Connect a video source (camera, videotape, or videodisc) to the video input on the card. If you are also recording audio, connect an audio source (microphone, tape recorder, videodisc, etc.) to the audio input on the computer.
- Choose "Record" on the menu of the digitizing software program.
- Select "Stop" when you have recorded the segment you want.
- Test the recording with the "Play" command. If it is acceptable, save the file to the computer disk.

Constraining the File Size of Digital Video

If you are capturing video segments, you will discover very quickly that the files generated by digitizing motion video can be huge. A one-minute sequence can easily take up many megabytes of storage space. To constrain the size of digital video files, you can adjust several factors: the number of colors, the size of the video window, and the frame rate.

Number of Colors

When you capture video, you can choose to digitize in black and white or with various numbers of colors (usually 16, 256, 65,000, or 16.7 million). The more colors you use, the larger the file size will be. In most cases, 256 colors is more than sufficient for multimedia projects.

Size of Video Window

Three basic display sizes are used for digital video, although other sizes are possible. A full screen on a computer display that is set for digitized video is usually 640 pixels by 480 pixels; one-quarter of a screen is 320 × 240; and one-sixteenth of a screen is 160 × 120. The file sizes are proportional—an image saved in full screen will result in a file that is four times bigger than one for a quarter screen. Generally, the video window should be set to 1⁄16 or ¼ screen.

Frame Rate

The standard display rate for video on a videotape or videodisc is 30 frames per second (fps). In many cases, however, digital video will be captured at a slower rate, because the computer is too slow to process 30 frames per second or because the file size would be too large. Frame rates of 10 to 15 frames per second are common with digital video.

Table 5.3 illustrates how these factors (colors, size, and frame rate) affect the size of the video file. Note that the file sizes listed in the chart represent only one second of digital video!

After the video segments or single images are captured, editing software (such as Adobe Premier) can be used to edit the sequences, add special transitions, and construct a movie. Development of digital movies requires at least 16 megabytes of RAM and a very large hard drive.

Digital Video File Formats

Three common file formats are used for digital video: QuickTime, AVI, and MPEG. Of the three, QuickTime is by far the most common because it can be used on both Macintosh and Windows computers without a special digital video board. The AVI format can also be used without a digital video board, and it is very common on Windows computers. The MPEG format can provide higher quality movies, but it requires special hardware (a digital video board) to play back the movies at top quality.

If you have a video file that is not in the best format for a particular program or application, there are programs that will convert one format to another. These are listed in the appendix at the end of this chapter.

Obtaining the Rights to Digital Video Files

If you do not have the inclination, equipment, or time to produce your own digital video movies, you may be able to obtain appropriate files through the Web or archives on a CD-ROM. Again, be sure you check the copyright restrictions, especially for applications that will be used or accessed outside the classroom.

Video Resources on the Web

Several video sites on the Web provide a collection of clips in various formats. These files can be downloaded to your computer. However, before downloading the movies, always check the permission statements, send an e-mail, or call the owner to find out if you have the rights to use these movies in your projects.

Video Resources on CD-ROM

As with clip art, there are clipmovie archives that are distributed on CD-ROM. In most cases, when you purchase the disc, you are also purchasing distribution rights. You must, however, read the fine print to find out exactly how and where you can use the movies. In addition, check the format of the movies to make sure they will run in your program.

Video Guidelines

Digital video files are generally very large; therefore, you must assess very carefully whether you want to use video in a multimedia project—especially one for the Web. The following guidelines should be considered for video:

- Use digital video only when absolutely necessary.
- Keep the window size as small as possible (about ¼ screen) to help improve performance.
- Check the size of the video files after they are recorded, especially if you want to transfer them with a floppy diskette.
- Make sure there is adequate lighting when recording digital movies.
- Check copyright restrictions on video segments, especially for material that will be used outside the classroom.

Managing the Gathering and Creation of Media

Graphic artists and production specialists need to work closely with instructional designers to ensure that the appropriate media elements are gathered or created. Each graphic artist and production specialist may want to keep a list of the necessary media, as well as each element's bibliographical information, for inclusion in the group's program or final report (see the Bibliography Information blackline master

Figure 5.14 Designated graphic artists within student groups

in chapter 3). Teachers need to schedule computer use to facilitate each group's needs (see ch. 3).

One way of assigning computer use is by using a Jigsaw cooperative learning approach. For example, each team's graphic artists can work with the graphic artists from other teams to select and review each other's media needs on the class computers. For example, if there are eight groups of students, one person from each group would be designated as the group's graphic artist (designated as "A" in fig. 5.14). These students would form their own group (eight students) to help create and research each other's graphics on the classroom computers. In a four-computer classroom, this allows two graphic artists to share a computer (see fig. 5.15).

Other team members can assist the graphic artists by taking digitized pictures, researching additional graphics, and working with production specialists to record video and audio clips. In addition, team members can meet and discuss project strategies with their counterparts in other groups, as well as working on other project-related materials, until the media elements are complete. A Jigsaw approach can be used for creating audio, too. Each group should continue to reflect on their progress through daily journal entries (see ch. 3).

If limited peripherals (such as a scanner, modem, and so on) and graphic software are available, the teacher may rotate student computer groups so that they are assigned a different computer each day. For example, a scanner might be attached to Computer One; Adobe Photoshop might be installed on Computer Two; a 3-D modelling program might be installed on Computer Three; and Computer Four may have a modem connection to the Internet. Rotating computer assignments allows student groups to plan their time using a scanner, a single copy of Adobe Photoshop, or other limited resources. Students may also use a sign-up sheet to use a particular computer, a digital camera, a camcorder, or other equipment.

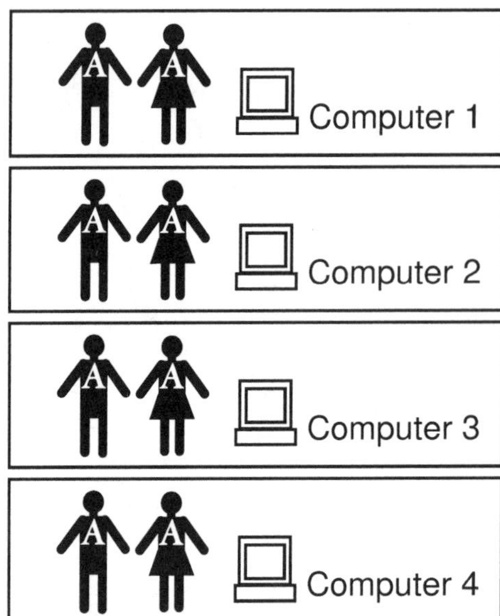

Figure 5.15 Jigsaw example of graphic artists using computers

Summary

Graphics, animations, audio, and video files can add life and interest to multimedia projects. They can also be used to illustrate and convey abstract concepts, and they can enhance students' visual literacy and their ability to think, learn, and communicate through visuals and other media. The design and development of media files allow students to be creative and to investigate the presentation of information from several perspectives. Most students are very enthusiastic about working with sound, graphics, and video!

Creating media files, however, also presents some challenges for educators and students. The media files can be stored in many different formats, and problems may arise when students have media files ready to incorporate into a project, but the program will not "see" or open the files. In addition, recording and editing generally require additional software and hardware, which may be in limited supply in classrooms.

This chapter presented a wide array of options for incorporating graphics, animations, audio, and video files. Although each software program will incorporate the media elements in a slightly different manner, almost all software programs (including basic word processors) now have the ability to add graphics, sound, and video. The potential is limited only by the imagination (and hardware) available to the students.

Appendix

Graphics Archives and Information on the Web

Barry's Clip Art Server: http://www.barrysclipart.com/

GIFConverter: http://www.kamit.com/gifconverter.html

Graphic Design Links: http://fcit.coedu.usf.edu/workshops/graphics.htm

Graphic Converter: http://www.goldinc.com/Lemke/gc.html

LView Pro: http://www.lview.com

Media Links Free Graphics Page: http://www.erinet.com/cunning1/tiles.html

Animation Archives and Information on the Web

GIF Animations on the WWW: http://member.aol.com/royalef/gifanim.htm

GifBuilder: http://www.pascal.com/mirrors/gifbuilder

Killersites: http://www.killersites.com/core.html

Sound Archives and Information on the Web

Audio: http://www.comlab.ox.ac.uk/archive/audio.html

Classical MIDI Archives: http://www.prs.net/midi.html

GoldWave: http://www.goldwave.com

Harmony Central: http://www.harmony-central.com/MIDI/

MIDI Farm: http://www.midifarm.com/

MIDI Home Page: http://www.eeb.ele.tue.nl/midi/index.html

Multimedia Music SND Stuff:
http://www.wavenet.com/~axgrindr/Snd.html

Sites with Audio Clips: http://www.eecs.nwu.edu/~jmyers/other-sounds.html

SoundApp: http://wwwhost.ots.utexas.edu/mac/pub-mac-sound.html

Worldwide Internet Music Resources:
http://www.music.indiana.edu/music_resources/

Movie Archives and Information on the Web

Audio and Video Clips: http://jhunix.hcf.jhu.edu/%7Erau_c/

CNN Video Vault: http://www.cnn.com/video_vault/index.html

The Movie Sound Page: http://www.moviesounds.com/

Paul Bauer's Multimedia City Movie Sites:
http://www.geocities.com/Broadway/2876/movies.html

Video Utilities and Players on the Web

FastPlayer: ftp://ftp.ncsa.uiuc.edu/Mosaic/Mac/Helpers/

Sparkle: http://hyperarchive.lcs.mit.edu/HyperArchive/Archive/gst/mov/

AVI-Quick: http://hyperarchive.lcs.mit.edu/HyperArchive/Archive/gst/mov/

Additional Resources

Adobe Illustrator
Adobe Systems
P.O. Box 1034
Buffalo, NY 14240
800-492-3623

Adobe Photoshop
Adobe Systems
P.O. Box 1034
Buffalo, NY 14240
800-492-3623

Adobe Premiere
Adobe Systems
P.O. Box 1034
Buffalo, NY 14240
800-492-3623

Adobe SuperPaint
Adobe Systems
P.O. Box 1034
Buffalo, NY 14240
800-492-3623

AutoDesk Animator Pro
AutoDesk, Inc.
111 McInnis Parkway
San Rafael, CA 94903
800-879-4233

ClarisDraw
Claris Corporation
5201 Patrick Henry Drive
Santa Clara, CA 95052
800-3CLARIS

ColorIt
MicroFrontier, Inc.
P.O. Box 71190
Des Moines, IA 50325
800-388-8109

CorelDraw
Corel Corporation
1600 Carling Avenue
Ottawa, ON K1Z 8R7
Canada
800-772-6735

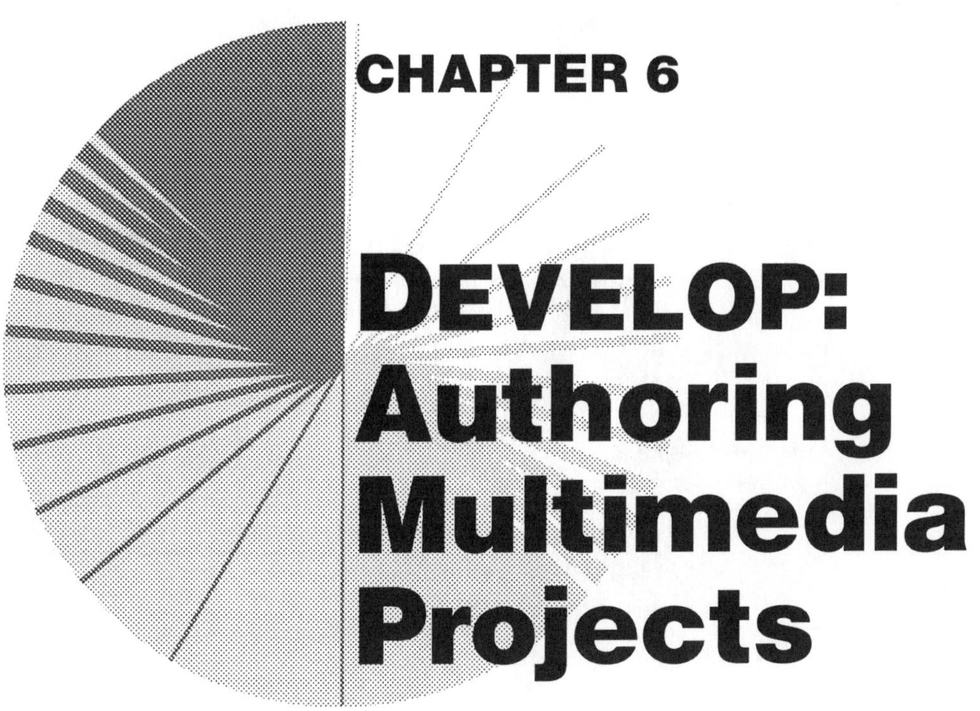

CHAPTER 6

DEVELOP: Authoring Multimedia Projects

A Scenario

Ronda, Paul, Carlos, and Kerry were just starting to design their project. Ms. Martinez, their sixth-grade teacher, had already outlined the parameters and told the students that they could create their project in either PowerPoint, HyperStudio, or HTML. Each of these formats was familiar to the students because they had used each tool for development of a project in the past.

They knew that PowerPoint was a presentation program that they could use to produce a linear slide-show type report; that HyperStudio was more interactive and could include buttons to branch from one card to another; and that HTML was used to author Web pages that could contain graphics, text, and limited media elements. The hard part was deciding which tool would be the best for their project about the War for Independence.

Ronda suggested that they use PowerPoint because it was the easiest tool and because she liked the colorful templates that were provided for backgrounds. Carlos argued that HyperStudio would be best because the design could include a menu with selections about different aspects of the war. Paul and Kerry both liked the idea of making Web pages for the project and uploading them to the Web server at the district office. They realized that they would not be able to include as many audio and video clips, but they wanted to solicit feedback from students in other countries, especially the United Kingdom.

As the students worked through the DECIDE phase of the project, conducting their brainstorming and research activities, it became clear that the Web was the best authoring environment. They were amazed at how many excellent sites existed that focused on the independence of the United States. By developing their project for the Web, they would be able to include links to these sites as a part of the project, as well as to share their project with the world.

Overview

After the media elements are created, they are brought together into a final project with a software program called an *authoring tool*. There are many affordable software programs that can be used to author a multimedia project. This chapter provides an overview of two programs that are common in school environments: PowerPoint and HyperStudio. It also presents information on authoring multimedia Web pages with HTML. All of these options are cross-platform (they work on both Macintosh and Windows computers), inexpensive, relatively easy to use, and can include text, graphics, audio, and video. This chapter includes:

- Authoring options for multimedia projects
  - — Presentation programs
  - — Hypermedia programs
- Overview of PowerPoint
  - — Developing a PowerPoint presentation
- Overview of HyperStudio
  - — Developing a HyperStudio program
- Overview of HTML
  - — Developing an HTML program
- Selecting an authoring tool
- Guidelines for managing the authoring process

Authoring Options for Multimedia Projects

In the past, computer programming involved stark lines of text that had to be created and compiled by a computer science major. Now there are several easy-to-use computer programs designed specifically for developing multimedia projects. Many of these programs are inexpensive and available in school environments. With these tools, students and teachers can combine video, audio, text, and graphics to enhance their classroom presentations and to develop their projects.

The authoring tools for multimedia fall into three primary categories: presentation programs, hypermedia programs, and Web-based development tools. These tools vary in structure, the methods used to access media elements, and complexity.

Presentation Programs

Presentation programs, such as PowerPoint, are generally used to create linear projects, where one screen follows another when the user clicks the mouse or presses a key. Class lectures and multimedia reports are easy for teachers and students to develop with presentation software. As the term *presentation* implies, presentation programs are often used for projects that will be presented to a large group, rather than projects designed for individual use.

There are many popular presentation programs, including PowerPoint by Microsoft Corporation, Action by Macromedia, and Harvard Graphics by Software Publishing Corporation. All of these programs are inexpensive, easy to learn, and easy to use, and all can incorporate multimedia elements such as graphics, digital video, and digital audio. They all include a variety of predesigned templates with colorful backgrounds and preformatted fonts to make the presentations look professional.

Hypermedia Programs

With hypermedia programs, information stored as text, graphics, audio, video, or animations can be accessed in associative, nonlinear ways. For example, the opening screen of a hypermedia application might contain a menu with four options. Buttons (areas) on the menu can be activated, allowing students to select one of the options and branch to the corresponding screen, audio file, video file, or animation. Hypermedia applications are often used for stand-alone projects because they enable users to make their own choices and follow their own paths.

Although the concept of hypermedia has existed for many years, technical advances in computers and software have only recently made it a reality for educators. Currently several inexpensive hypermedia programs are in common use in schools. These include HyperCard by Apple Computer, HyperStudio by Roger Wagner, Digital Chisel by Pierian Spring Software, and ToolBook II by Asymetrix. See the appendix at the end of this chapter for additional information and resources.

Web-Creation Programs

The World Wide Web offers great potential for the delivery of multimedia projects on a worldwide basis. If your school has an Internet service provider and the necessary hardware, it is possible to create projects with hyperlinks, text, graphics, audio, and video that will be accessible to schools throughout the world at minimal cost.

There are many alternatives for creating Web pages, ranging from a simple text editor (such as SimpleText or NotePad) to sophisticated Web page creation programs, such as Adobe PageMill, Claris HomePage, Netscape Gold, and Microsoft FrontPage. In addition, many of the latest word processors and other programs include the option to save documents in HTML (the format required for Web pages).

Overview of Microsoft® PowerPoint®

PowerPoint® is a presentation program that is primarily designed for creating electronic slide shows. In other words, its strengths lie in being able to quickly produce a presentation that is designed to be used in a linear fashion, moving from one slide to the next. However, you can also add interactivity and multimedia elements to PowerPoint by embedding audio, video, and hyperlinks.

One of the best features of PowerPoint is that it is almost 100 percent cross-platform. That means that you can create a presentation on a Macintosh, save it on a disk that is formatted for DOS, and then run the presentation on a Windows computer. Although there may be minor differences in the fonts used on the two systems, the vast majority of the colors, graphics, and text will look and act exactly the same as it did on the Macintosh. The program is equally flexible in the other direction, too: You can create a presentation on a Windows computer and then run or edit the presentation on a Macintosh.

Another benefit of PowerPoint is that the program provides numerous predefined templates with professionally designed backgrounds, text, and colors. These templates are very useful for novices who are developing their first multimedia projects. PowerPoint also includes a wide array of clip art and media elements to incorporate into projects.

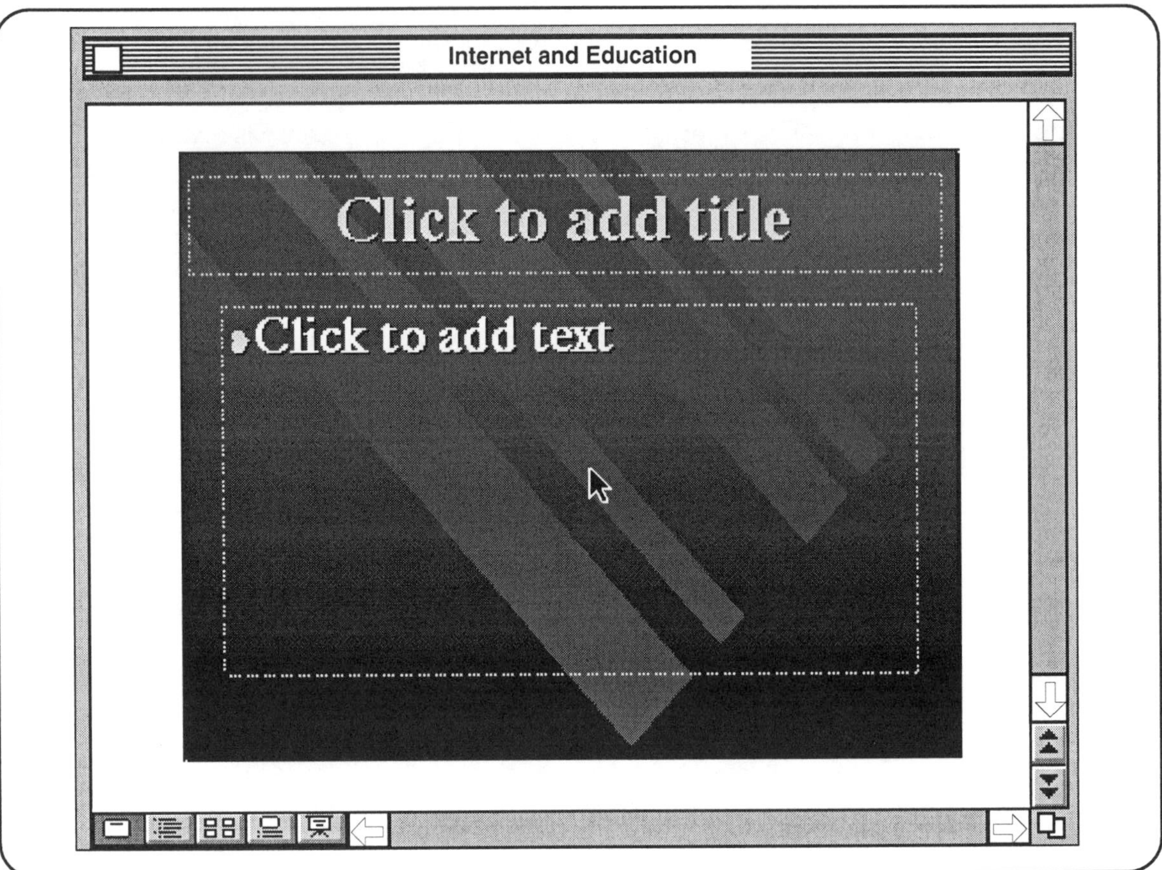

Figure 6.1 PowerPoint slide view

Developing a PowerPoint Presentation

This section outlines the major steps required to create a project with PowerPoint. There may be minor differences between different versions of the program and different platforms (Macintosh and Windows).

Step 1. Select a Background Template

Most presentation programs have a number of predefined background templates available for use. When you create a new PowerPoint file, you will have the choice of several templates that are specifically designed for use as black-and-white overheads, color overheads, on-screen presentations, or 35mm slides. By using one of the templates, you can save time and produce a presentation with professional style.

The templates determine the text colors, fonts, and sizes; background colors and patterns; and arrangement of information on the screen. Some of the templates have a particular theme (such as a beach or party); others are more generic. Advise the students to select a template that offers high contrast between background and text so that the words will be easy to read.

Step 2. Create Screens with Text and Graphics

PowerPoint offers two different interfaces to create screens for a project: Slide View and Outline View. Slide View works best if you have a lot of graphics and different layouts. Outline View works best if you have a title at the top of each screen and four or five bullets on each slide.

To create a slide in Slide View, simply click in the title box to enter a title, and click in the body area to type in the bullets (see fig. 6.1). When you are ready for a new slide, select "Insert...New Slide," and a

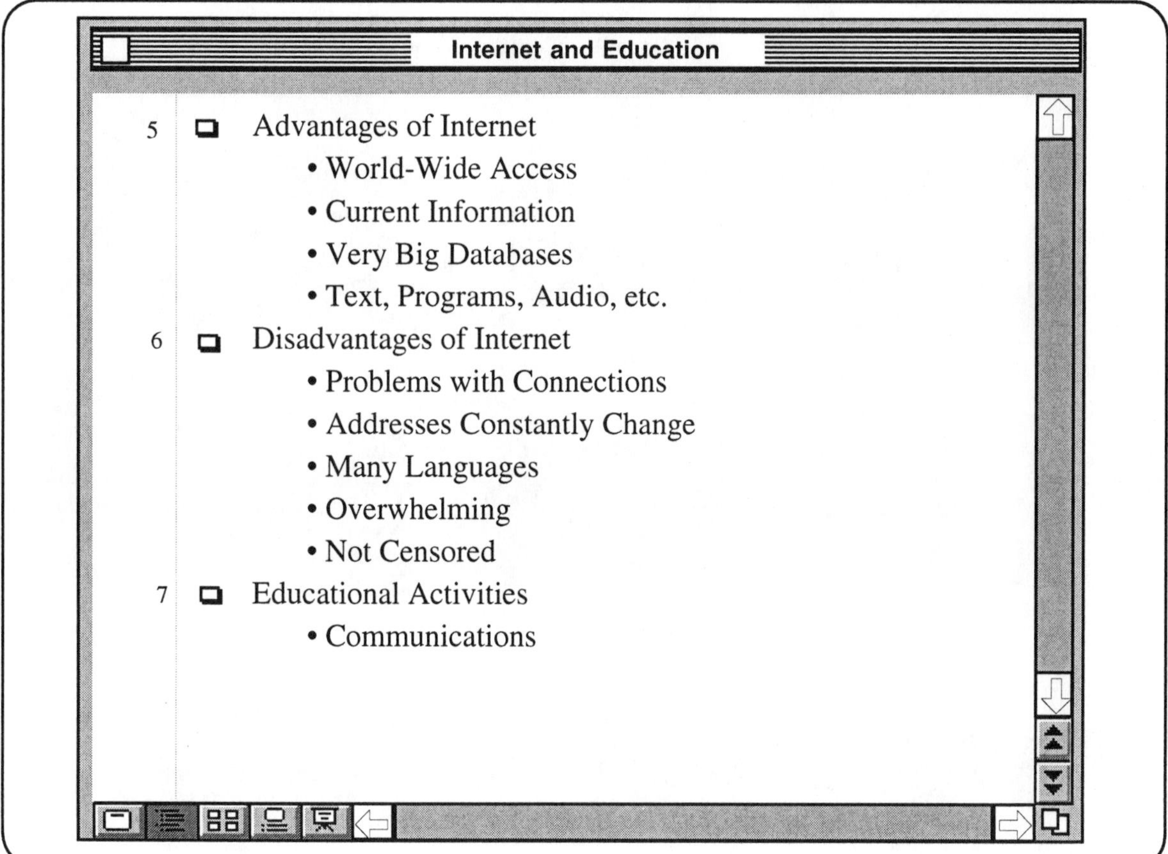

Figure 6.2 PowerPoint outline view

new slide will appear with the same background template as the first screen. Graphics can be added with the "Insert" options. "Insert...Clip-art" accesses the PowerPoint gallery. "Insert...Picture" allows you to insert graphics that were scanned or saved in other formats (such as .PIC or .BMP).

Outline View is a good way to create screens for a project that is primarily text. In Outline View, you simply type in your titles and bullets, and the screens are automatically created with the template that you specified (see fig. 6.2).

Step 3. Sequence the Presentation

PowerPoint has another view, called Slide Sorter, that allows you to change the order of the screens. In this view, you can see a miniature view of each screen and alter the sequence by using a mouse to click and drag slides into their new positions (see fig. 6.3).

The Outline View also allows you to add transitions and builds. *Transitions* are special effects that occur between slides, such as dissolves or wipes. *Builds* are techniques for using progressive disclosure of the bullets on a slide; the bullets can fly in from the left, from the right, from the top, and so on.

Step 4. Add Media Elements

It is very easy to add media elements to PowerPoint projects. By using the "Insert" options, you can quickly integrate digital audio, MIDI music, digital video, or animations into your presentation. Each of these elements can be embedded into a screen with instructions to play as

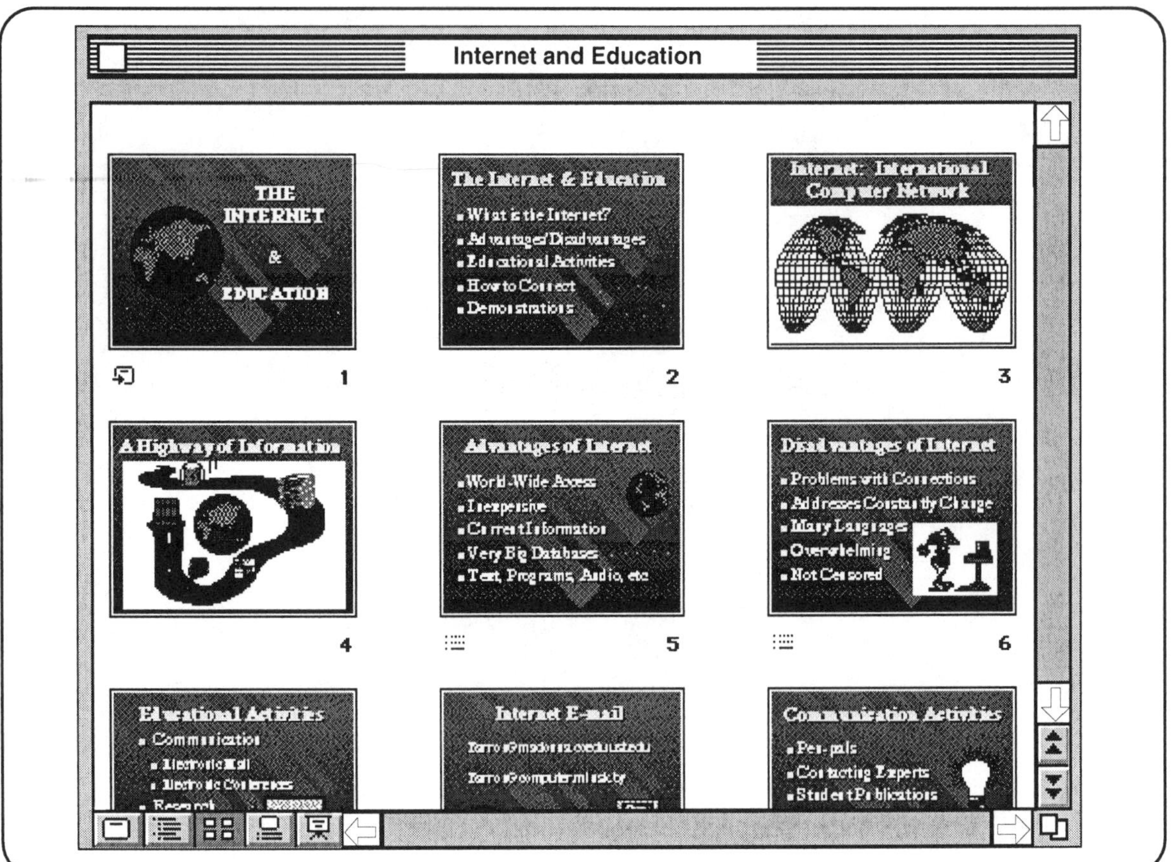

Figure 6.3 PowerPoint slide sorter

soon as the screen is displayed, to play after a specified number of seconds, or to play when an object is clicked.

In most cases, the media elements will be created in a different program prior to developing the PowerPoint presentation (see ch. 5 for more information about creating media elements). However, it is possible to record audio within PowerPoint by calling up the Windows Media Player. The latest versions of PowerPoint can also include objects that branch to another screen or that link to a World Wide Web site.

Step 5. Pilot Test the Presentation

PowerPoint, like most other presentation software, provides a separate runtime program (viewer) for delivery of the show. The viewer allows you to show the presentation on a computer that does not have the PowerPoint program. For example, if you have a limited license for PowerPoint, the students can copy their presentations and the viewer to a disk and test their presentations on computers at home or at school—whether or not PowerPoint is loaded on those computers. In addition, you and your students can freely distribute their presentations and the viewer to others.

Step 6. Print the Screens

In some cases, the students may want to print their PowerPoint projects. There are many options for printing with PowerPoint:

- *Slides.* This option will print full-size slides. This is a great way to produce overhead transparencies for backups.

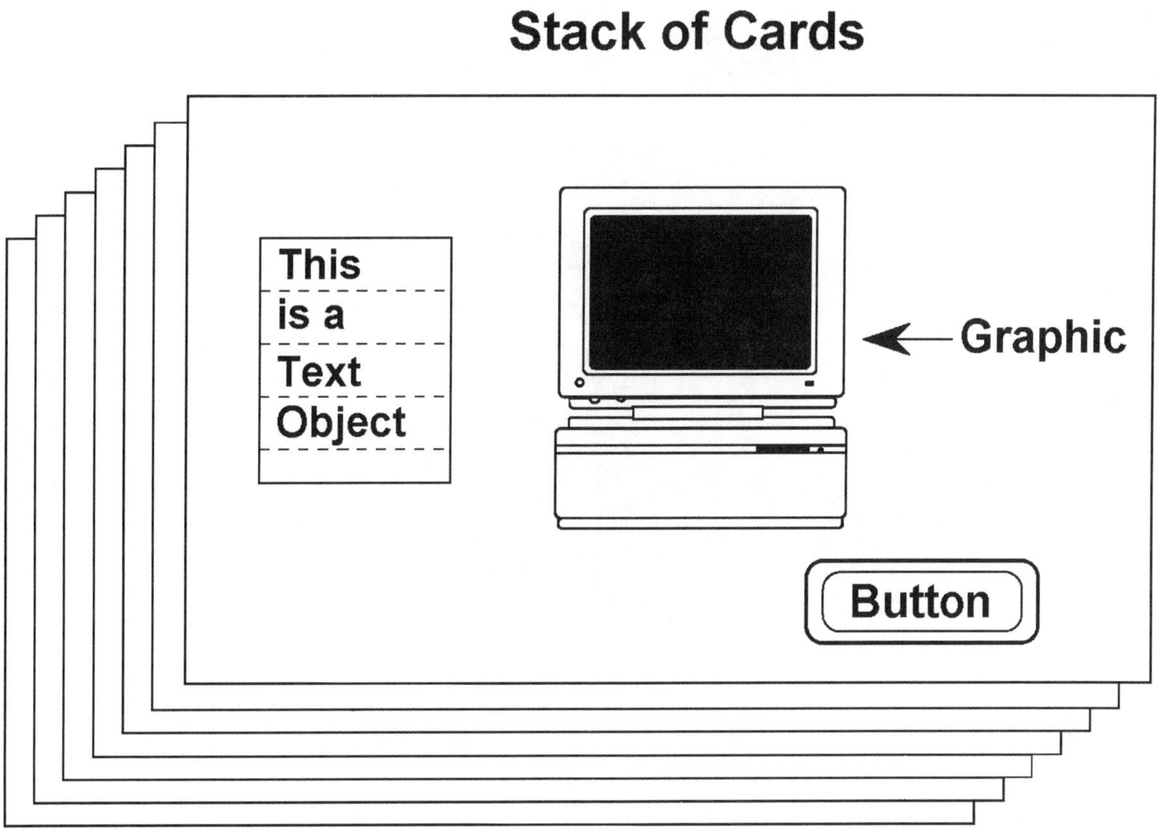

Stack of Cards

This is a Text Object

Graphic

Button

Figure 6.4 Structure of HyperStudio

- *NotesPages.* NotesPages will print each slide at the top of a page with notes on the bottom of the page. The students may want to print NotesPages with additional information if they are doing a class presentation.
- *Handouts.* Handouts of the presentation can be printed with two, four, or six miniature slides per page. The handouts are a great way to provide a hard copy of the presentation for an audience, with less expense for copying.
- *Outline View.* The Outline View printout provides the text outline of the presentation.

Overview of HyperStudio®

HyperStudio® (by Roger Wagner Publishing) is a very popular hypermedia program because it is inexpensive, easy to use, and runs on both Macintosh and Windows computers. The basic structure of HyperStudio consists of stacks and cards (a file is referred to as a *stack*, and a computer screen is called a *card*). Each card can contain text items, buttons, and graphics (see fig. 6.4).

Text objects are similar to miniature word processing blocks and are designed to contain text of various styles and sizes. *Buttons* are designated areas of the screens that can initiate an action, such as moving (branching) to another card, playing an audio file, or accessing a segment on a videodisc. Graphics can be created with paint tools within the

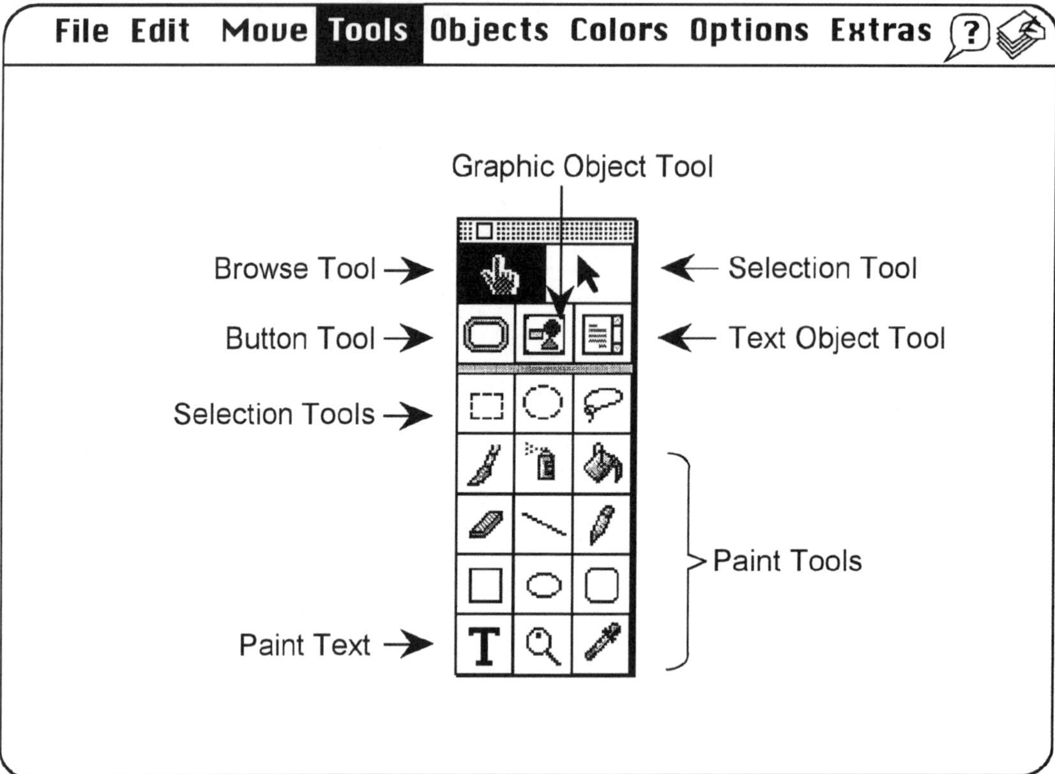

Figure 6.5 HyperStudio toolbox

hypermedia program, or they can be imported from clip art or other graphics programs.

With HyperStudio, a series of pull-down menus and dialog windows are used to develop the applications. HyperStudio is an impressive package that provides built-in links to videodisc, CD-Audio, digital movies, and digitized audio. Animation tools, Web tools, and testing functions that can track correct and incorrect answers are also available.

Developing a HyperStudio Program

The best way to understand the unique structure of HyperStudio is to create a small stack. The following procedure covers the basic steps for creating a stack with two cards.

Step 1. Start a New Stack

After HyperStudio is installed, click twice on the HyperStudio program icon to open HyperStudio. There are two ways to create a new stack: You can click on the "New Stack" button, or you can use the File pull-down menu and select "New Stack." A blank card will appear on the screen.

Step 2. Create a Graphic

A relatively powerful graphics program is embedded in HyperStudio. When the Tools menu is selected, the toolbox appears (see fig. 6.5). Except for the top two rows, most of the tools are paint tools. For example, there are shape tools for circles and rectangles, and there are drawing tools for lines and paintbrushes.

The Tools menu in HyperStudio is a "tear-off" menu. This means that the tools can be moved to another part of the screen, and they will remain in view for easy use. To move the tools, click on Tools and hold

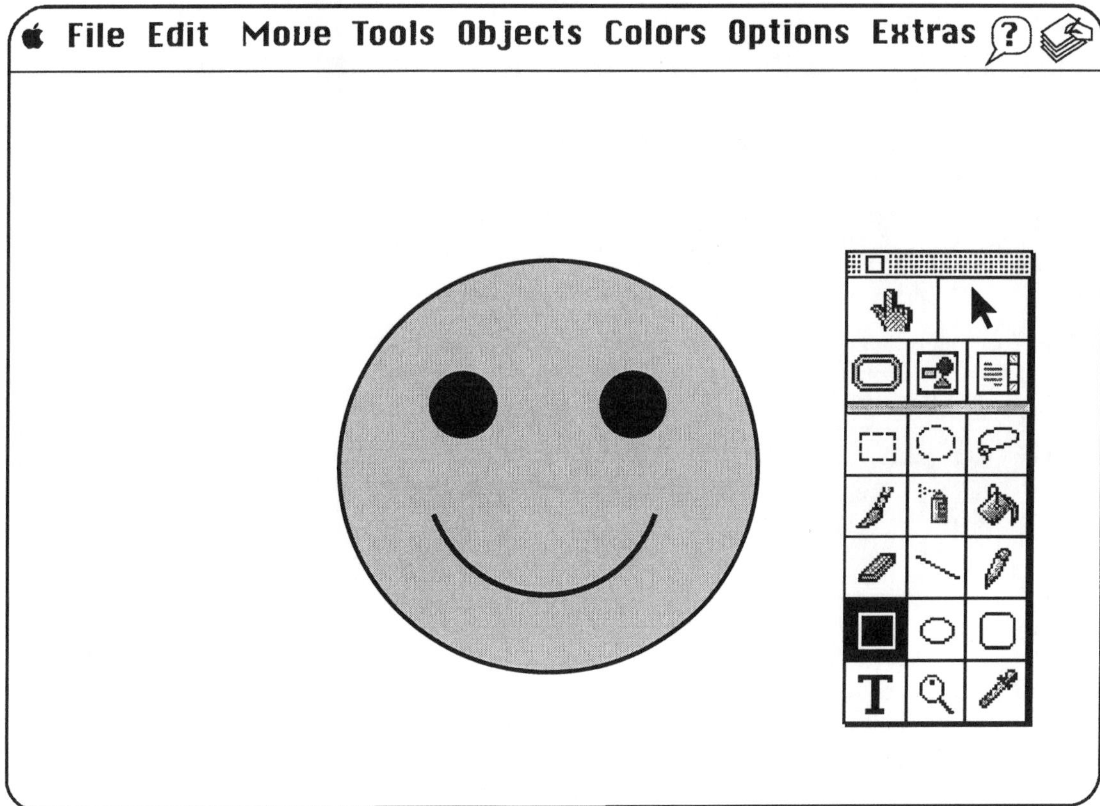

Figure 6.6 Sample graphic in HyperStudio

the mouse button down while dragging the tools to another part of the screen. After the tools are on the screen, use the circle and the paint tools to create a graphic of a smiley face, and use the paint bucket to fill color (from the Colors menu) into the circle (see fig. 6.6).

Step 3. Create a Text Object

HyperStudio uses the term *Text Object* to refer to an area on the screen that acts like a mini-word processor. These areas have text word wrap and can be edited and resized. On the Objects menu, select "Add a Text Object," and a dotted rectangle will show up in the center of the screen. This rectangle is the area designated for your text. When you are satisfied with the size and location of the rectangle, click anywhere on the screen outside of the rectangle. At this point, a Text Appearance box will appear. This dialog window allows you to name the field and set many of its attributes, such as text color, background color, and style (see fig. 6.7). After the attributes are set, click "OK" to return to the card. The final step is to enter the text in the field. For this example, type the text "Have a Nice Day!"

Step 4. Create Another Card

The next step is to create the second card in the stack. Choose "Edit...New Card" in the menu bar and a new blank card will appear. You can create your own graphics or you can import one of the graphic backgrounds provided with HyperStudio. To include the background illustrated in figure 6.8, choose "Import Background" from the File menu. An information box will appear. Locate the "HS Art folder" and

File Edit Move Tools Objects Colors Options Extras

Untitled - Card 1

Text Appearance

Text

HyperStudio Sample Text

Get File...

Background

Actions...

Name: Untitled

Draw scroll bar

Read only

Scrollable

Draw frame

Cancel

Style...

OK

Figure 6.7 Text item dialog box

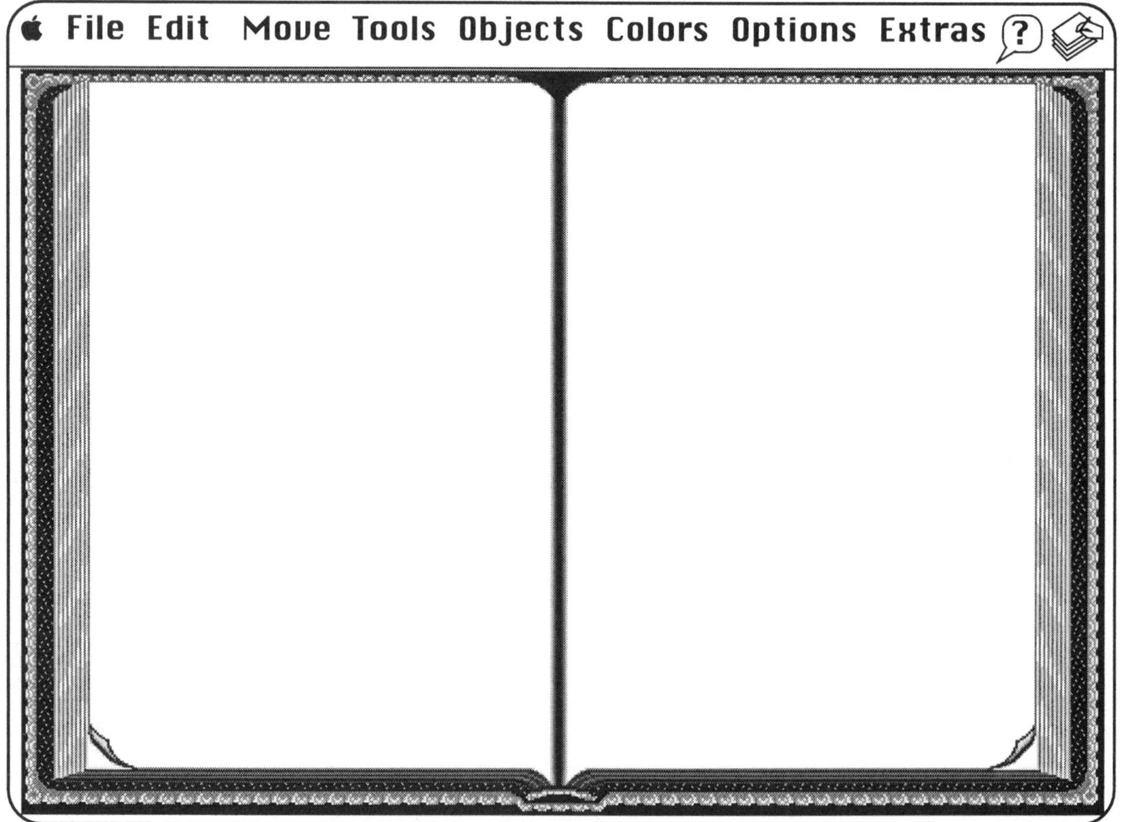

Figure 6.8 Importing a graphic background on a new card

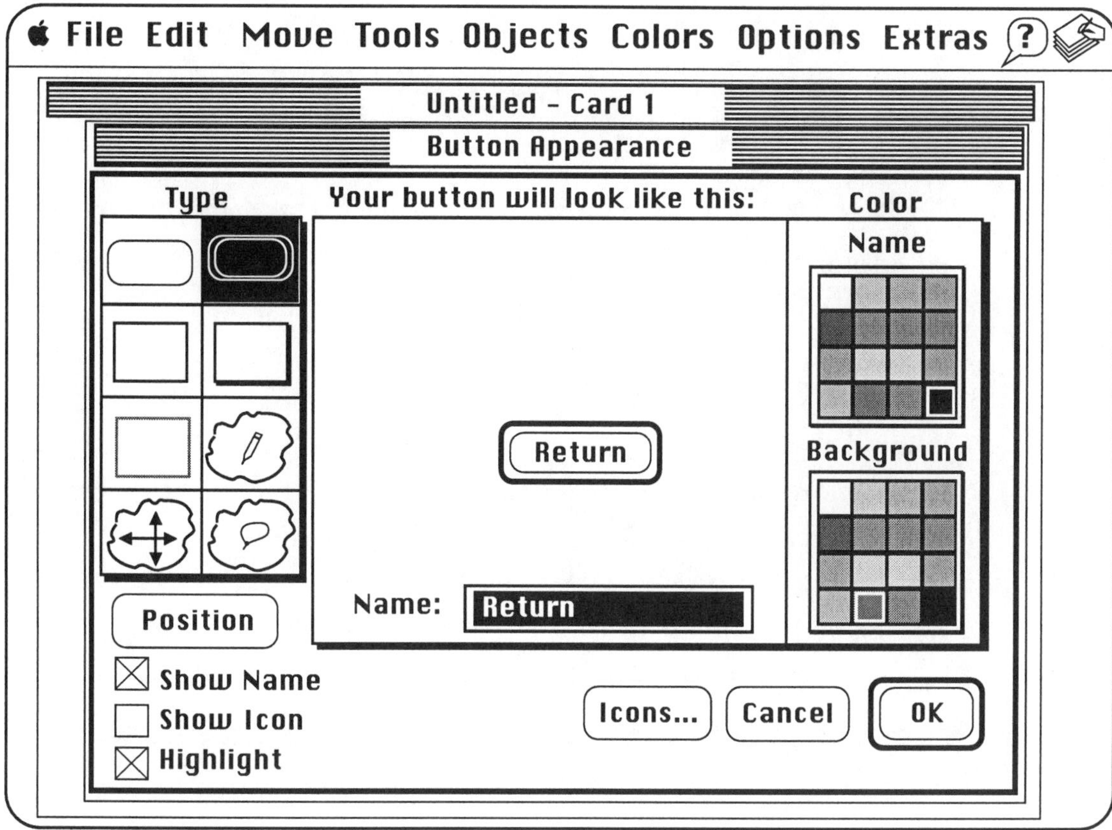

Figure 6.9 Button attribute window

scroll down until you find "Book" and click "Open." The graphic will be imported into your card.

Step 5. Create a Button

Buttons are used to initiate actions such as branching to another card or playing audio files. For example, to allow the user to return to the first card from the second card, a "Return" button can be added to the second card. The procedure is very similar to creating a text item:

- Choose "Add a Button" from the Objects menu.
- Name the button "Return" and select button type and color in the window (see fig. 6.9). Click on "OK."
- Move the button to the lower right corner, and click anwhere on the screen outside of the button.
- A Button Actions window will appear (see fig. 6.10).
- Select "Previous Card" for Places To Go.
- A dialog box with many transitions will appear. Select a transition and click "OK."
- Select "Play a sound..." for Things To Do. After you click "Done," you will see a cassette-type audio recording interface. Speak into the microphone to record a file, or select a sound provided by HyperStudio. Click on "OK" when you are finished.
- Click on "Done" to close the Button Actions window.

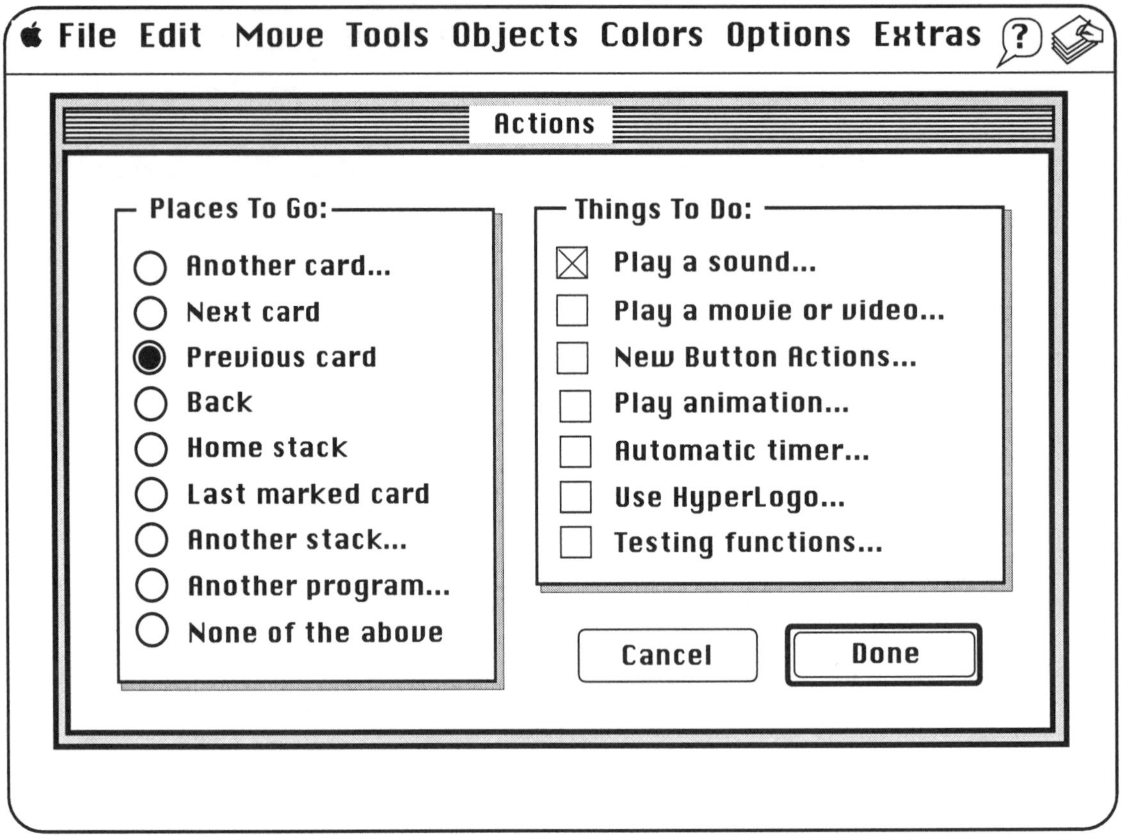

Figure 6.10 Button Actions window

Step 6. Pilot Test the Program

A valuable feature included with HyperStudio is the Player file, which can be used to run a stack without using the HyperStudio program. Students can distribute their stacks with a copy of the HyperStudio Player and pilot test their programs even if HyperStudio is not loaded on all of the computers.

Step 7. Print a Stack

If a printout is desired, HyperStudio will print cards in various sizes, from one to four cards per page depending on the size. These printouts can be very handy for distributing a hard-copy version of the projects.

Overview of HTML

Access to the Internet and World Wide Web is becoming more and more common for schools. This access provides a new environment for publishing multimedia projects. With a simple word processor, students can easily create Web pages that can be viewed by people throughout the world. Even if a school is not connected to the Internet, it is possible for students to use Web technology to publish documents that are available on intranets or stand-alone computers.

All Web pages are derived from text files that are interpreted and displayed by Web browsers (such as Netscape or Internet Explorer). For example, when the text file displayed in figure 6.11 is displayed through a browser, the student will see the Web page illustrated in figure 6.12.

The text files used in Web documents adhere to a specific format called the *HyperText Markup Language* or HTML. HTML files use *tags* (words embedded between the < and > characters) to define how

```
<HTML>
<HEAD>
<TITLE>Geography Home Page <TITLE></HEAD>
<BODY>
<IMG SRC = "geo.gif">
<BR>
<H2>This page provides links relevant to Freshman Geography</H2>
<P>
Click to see a <A HREF = "CA.mov">movie about Central America </A>
<BR>
<HR>
<UL>
<LI><A HREF = "http://www.geo.gov/">Geography sites</A>
<LI><A HREF = "http://www.chs.edu/assign/">Assignments</A>
<LI><A HREF = "http://www.chs.edu/reports/">Student reports</A>
</UL>
<HR>
</BODY>
</HTML>
```

Figure 6.11 Web page

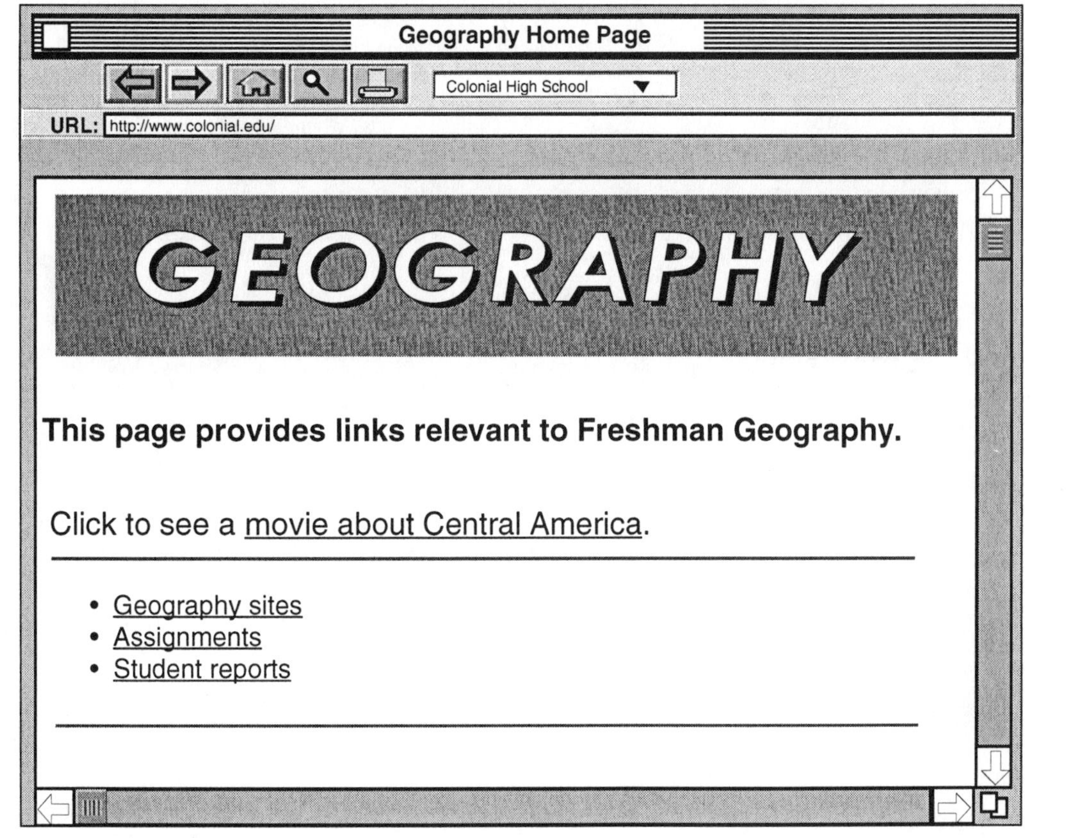

Figure 6.12 Web page

	Tag	Definition
Essential Parts	<HTML> <HEAD> <TITLE>...</TITLE> </HEAD> <BODY>...</BODY> </HTML>	These tags represent the template or "skeleton" of an HTML document. HTML tags identify the beginning and ending of the document; HEAD tags contain the TITLE tags, which identify the page's bookmark name; and BODY tags contain the text, pictures, headings, etc., of the document.
Formatting Text: Headings	<H1>...</H1> <H2>...</H2> <H3>...</H3> <H4>...</H4> <H5>...</H5> <H6>...</H6>	HTML has six levels of headings that are displayed in bolder and separate type than the regular body text. Level 1 is the largest heading; Level 6 is the smallest heading.
Formatting Text: Physical Styles	<B>...</B> <I>...</I> <U>...</U> <TT>...</TT>	Physical style tags tell browsers how to display text. For example, text within the tags <B>...</B> will be **boldface**; text within the tags <I>...</I> will be *italicized*; text within the tags <U>...</U> will be underlined; and text within the tags <TT>...</TT> will be a `typewriter font.`
Formatting Text: Paragraphs	<PRE>...</PRE> <P>...</P> 	A variety of tags are used to format paragraphs. <PRE>...</PRE> displays text with its original carriage returns and spacing (preformat); <P>...</P> identifies a paragraph; and inserts a carriage return. does not have an ending tag.
Making Lists	<UL> <LI>first item <LI>second item <LI>third item </UL>	<UL>...</UL> creates an unordered list. <LI> tags are placed within the <UL> and </UL> tags to identify each item in the list. Ordered lists that display numbers are created by using <OL> and </OL> instead of <UL> and </UL>. <LI> tags are placed within the <OL> and </OL> tags, also.
Displaying an Image	<IMG SRC = "image.gif" ALT = "alternative text"> <HR>	Place the name of the image in "image.gif" and "alternative text." <HR> displays a horizontal line.
Creating Hyperlinks	<A HREF = "http://whereto.dom"> location</A> <A HREF = "MAILTO:name@my.domain">e-mail address</A>	Place the location's address in "http://whereto.dom" and link information in "location." The MAILTO link sends an e-mail message.
Playing Movies and Sounds	<A HREF="file_name"> instructions</A>	Place the name of the sound or movie in "file_name" and directions (such as "click here") in "instructions."

Table 6.1 HTML quick reference guide

information is formatted on the screen. For example, in the line <B>This is bold.</B>, the first tag, turns the bold attribute on, and the second one (the one with the /B) turns the bold attribute off. A few common style tags are illustrated in table 6.1.

About 50 different tags are commonly used for HTML. Some define the styles of the text, some are used to embed audio or video links, and others format the bullets, colors, and similar elements. There are excellent tutorials online at http://www.webreference.com/html/tutorials.html.

Developing an HTML program

Creating a Web page by using the HTML language may appear to be intimidating, but many elementary school students are developing Web documents every day. In many cases, they learn a few basic HTML tags, and then gradually expand their vocabulary as they become more experienced. In other cases, they do not learn HTML at all; instead, they use a Web page creation program that allows them to create Web documents without typing in the command codes. There are several choices for development tools for Web pages, including simple text editors (such as SimpleText or NotePad), HTML editors, Web page creation programs, and HTML converters.

Text Editors

One of the least expensive methods for creating Web pages is to use the free text editors that come with a computer, such as *SimpleText* or *TeachText* on a Macintosh and *NotePad* on a Windows machine. An advantage of creating HTML in these simple text editors is that they automatically save the files in ASCII or text-only format—exactly the format needed for the final files.

To create HTML files in a text editor, you must type in all of the required codes, save the file with an .htm or .html extension, and then test the file by displaying it through a Web browser. If you have a word processor, such as Microsoft Word or WordPerfect, you can also use them to create the HTML files. Just remember to save the files as ASCII or text-only (with an .htm or .html extension) before testing them with a Web browser.

HTML Editors

To simplify the process, there are HTML editor programs. Many of these programs are available free of charge on the Internet and can be downloaded for classroom use (see the appendix at the end of this chapter). These editors enter many of the required codes and will add tags specified in the menu bars. You can select most of the options, such as bold, bullets, and so on, from the menu bar and the codes will be entered into the document automatically. For example, you might type "This is My Home Page" at the top of the screen, then highlight it and select Title in the menu bar. The <TITLE> and </TITLE> tags will be inserted automatically before and after the text.

The advantage of using HTML editors is that they simplify the tedious task of typing tags, and the number of typographical errors is thereby decreased significantly. Also, because the tags are added automatically, you are less likely to forget to add the ending tag in a pair.

Page Creation Programs

It is no longer a requirement to know HTML to create Web pages. Several programs are available that provide users with a *WYSIWYG* (what you see is what you get) environment. Some of the most popular programs at present are PageMill by Adobe, HomePage by Claris, FrontPage by Microsoft, and Navigator Gold by Netscape.

These programs allow users to type text on their Web pages just as they would in a word processing program. Styles such as bold are added by highlighting the text and selecting a style on the menu bar. Users do not see the HTML code; it is generated "behind the scenes" and will be interpreted by the Web browser. It is possible to insert graphics, include lists, create tables, and insert forms with these programs as well.

Some page creation programs must be purchased. For example, PageMill lists at about $100. Other programs are available at no charge. The latest version of Netscape (which is free to educators) contains a feature that will create Web pages. Internet Explorer 4.0 (by Microsoft) has a similar feature.

Attribute	Presentation	Hypermedia	Web Pages
Ease of use	High	Medium	Medium
Cost	Low	Medium	Low
Amount of interactivity	Low	High	Medium
Amount of multimedia	High	High	Low
Player for delivery	Free	Free	N/A
Audience distribution	Local	Local	Worldwide

Table 6.2 Comparison of authoring tools

HTML Converters

HTML has become so popular that many of the standard word processing programs, spreadsheets, presentation programs, and desktop publishing tools include an HTML converter. For example, in Office 97 by Microsoft, you can save PowerPoint, Word, Excel, or Access files in HTML. Hypermedia projects created with programs such as HyperStudio and Digital Chisel can also be converted to Web documents.

With HTML converters, the program will do the best it can to determine the correct format for the text you have entered. These programs offer a very fast way to create HTML documents from existing text. Although you may need to go in and add links or modify some of the code, they are a great way to get started on large, text-intensive projects.

Selecting an Authoring Tool

Each of the authoring tools described in this chapter offers features that are useful for student-created multimedia projects. The following guidelines may help in determining which type of tool is best for a particular situation.

- Use presentation or hypermedia tools if a large amount of audio and video is incorporated into the project. The bandwidth (speed) of the Internet is a major constraint in the amount of audio and video that can be added to Web pages.
- If cost is a factor, presentation programs or Web pages may be the least expensive. Presentation programs such as PowerPoint can be purchased by schools at minimal cost; Web pages can be created in text editors or HTML editors that are free.
- For maximum interactivity, hypermedia programs are the best. Hypermedia programs are designed to contain hyperlinks to graphics and media elements. In addition, they usually contain question formats and scoring techniques.
- For ease of use, presentation tools are the best. In many cases, it may be wise to have students complete their first multimedia projects with a presentation tool. See table 6.2 for a comparison of the authoring tools presented in this chapter.

Guidelines for Managing the Authoring Process

Using the group's flowchart, storyboards, and media elements, program authors work with their teammates to construct the multimedia project (see ch. 3 for scheduling computer time). When students have completed their projects, student groups should review each other's projects for spelling, grammatical, and punctuation errors; inconsistencies; clarity; and mechanical or software problems (see The Bug Stops Here blackline master in ch. 7). These findings should be returned to the developers and any necessary changes made before a group submits its project for final evaluation. While students are waiting to have their project reviewed by another group, the students can continue to work on other related, noncomputer assignments, outline their project presentation to the class, or begin writing a final report of their group's progress and accomplishments.

Summary

The final step in the development process is to combine the text, graphics, and media elements with an authoring tool. There are many alternatives on the market. This chapter focused on three inexpensive options for schools: PowerPoint, HyperStudio, and HTML. As you are planning the curriculum tools for your classroom, consider these tools and others that will allow your students to produce and deliver their products in a timely fashion.

Appendix

HTML Tutorials and Information on the Web

A Beginners Guide to HTML: http://www.ncsa.uiuc.edu/General/Internet/WWW/HTMLPrimer.html

An Interactive Tutorial for Beginners: http://www.davesite.com/webstation/html/

An Introduction to HTML: http://www.ucc.ie/~pflynn/books/ch7-8.html

Bare Bones Guide to HTML: http://werbach.com/barebones/

Webreference Tutorials: http://www.webreference.com/html/tutorials.html

Writing HTML: http://www.mcli.dist.maricopa.edu/tut/

HTML Editors and Information on the Web

Hotdog: http://www.sausage.com/dogindex.htm

HTML Editor for Macintosh: http://dragon.acadiau.ca/~giles/HTML_Editor/Documentation.html

Web Designer Help Desk: http://web.canlink.com/helpdesk/mac.html

Webedit: http://www.sandiego.com/webedit/

Webreference Editors: http://www.webreference.com/html/editors.html

HTML Converters and Information on the Web

HTML Converters: http://www.w3.org/pub/WWW/Tools/Filters.html

Converters To and From HTML: http://union.ncsa.uiuc.edu/HyperNews/get/www/html/converters.html

Browser Information on the Web

Internet Explorer Information Center: http://www.barkers.org/ie/index.html

Microsoft Internet Explorer: http://www.microsoft.com/

Netscape: http://home.netscape.com/

Yahoo Browser Information: http://www.yahoo.com/Computers_and_Internet/Software/Internet/World_Wide_Web/Browsers/

Authoring Information on the Web

Multimedia and Authoring Resources on the Internet: http://www.library.nwu.edu/media/resources/multimedia.html

Multimedia Authoring Systems FAQ: http://www.tiac.net/users/jasiglar/MMASFAQ.HTML#Q.15

Yahoo Hypermedia Information: http://www.yahoo.com/Computers_and_Internet/Multimedia/Hypermedia/

Hypermedia and Presentation Programs

Action!
Macromedia
600 Townsend Street
San Francisco, CA 94103
800-288-4797

Adobe Persuasion
Adobe Systems
345 Park Avenue
San Jose, CA 95110
800-833-6687

Astound!
Gold Disk, Inc.
3160 West Bayshore Road
Palo Alto, CA 94303
800-465-3375

Authorware Academic
Prentice Hall
113 Sylvan Avenue, Route 9W
Englewood Cliffs, NJ 07632
800-887-9998

Authorware Professional
Macromedia Inc.
600 Townsend Street, #408
San Francisco, CA 94103
800-945-4061

Compel
Asymetrix Corp.
110 110th Avenue NE
Bellevue, WA 98004
800-448-6543

Digital Chisel
Pierian Spring Software
5200 SW Macadam Avenue, Suite 250
Portland, OR 97201
800-472-8578

Director
Macromedia Inc.
600 Townsend Street, #408
San Francisco, CA 94103
800-945-4061

Freelance Graphics
Lotus Development Corp.
400 River Park Drive
North Reading, MA 01864
800-343-5414

Harvard Graphics for Windows
Software Publishing Corp.
P.O. Box 4772
Crawfordsville, IN 47933
800-234-2500

HyperBook
Gold Disk, Inc.
385 Van Ness, Suite 110
Torrance, CA 90501
800-465-3375

HyperCard
Apple Computer, Inc.
One Infinite Loop
Cupertino, CA 95014
800-767-2775

HyperScreen
Scholastic Software
P.O. Box 7502
Jefferson City, MO 65102
800-541-5513

HyperStudio
Roger Wagner Publishers
1050 Pioneer Way, Suite P
El Cajon, CA 92020
800-421-6526

HyperWriter
Ntergaid
60 Commerce Park
Milford, CT 06460
800-254-9737

Media Text
Wings for Learning
1600 Green Hills Road
Scotts Valley, CA 95067
800-321-7511

Multimedia Workshop
Davidson & Associates
P.O. Box 2961
Torrance, CA 90509
800-545-7677

Persuasion
Aldus Corp.
1585 Charleston Road
Mountain View, CA 94039
800-833-6687

PowerPoint
Microsoft Corp.
One Microsoft Way
Redmond, WA 98052
800-426-9400

StoryWorks
Teachers' Idea and Information Exchange
P.O. Box 6229
Lincoln, NE 68505
402-483-6987

SuperCard
Allegiant Technologies, Inc.
6496 Weathers Place
San Diego, CA 92121
800-255-8258

SuperLink
Washington Computer Services
2601 North Shore Road
Bellingham, WA 98226
206-734-8248

ToolBook
Asymetrix Corp.
110 110th Avenue NE
Bellevue, WA 98004
800-448-6543

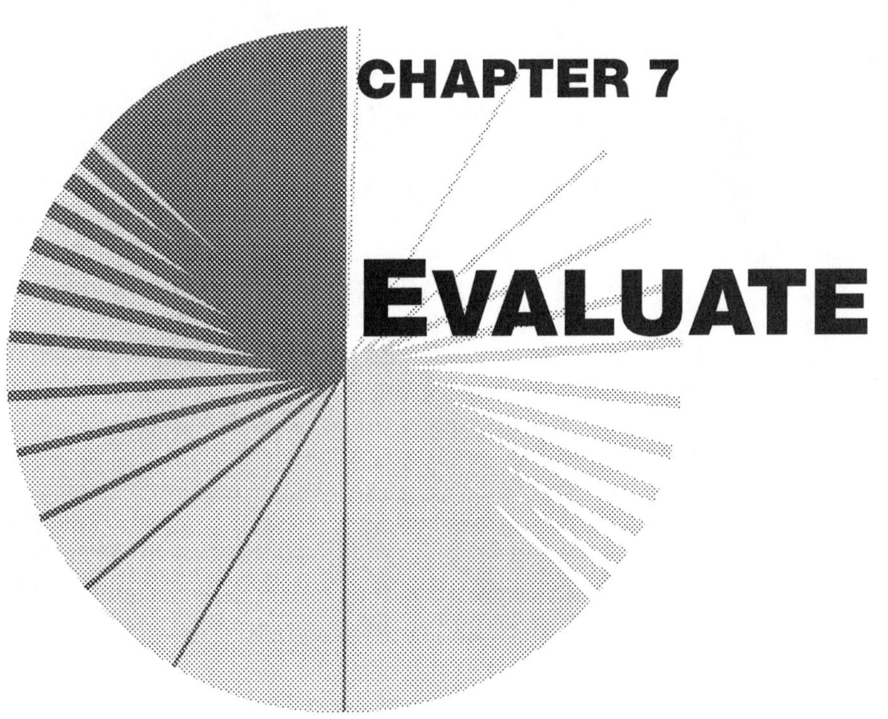

CHAPTER 7

EVALUATE

A Scenario

Ms. Higgs, the school's resource specialist, distributed a coloring book picture to each of the fourth-grade students and asked them to color it. She collected the pictures at the end of the period. The next day, she randomly redistributed the colored pictures to the fourth-grade students and explained that they were going to help her grade them. Ms. Higgs asked the students what would count as an "A" picture, a "B" picture, and so on. The students discussed their different ideas, and then Ms. Higgs explained the concept of a rubric. She told the students that this was how teachers evaluated their work.

The students decided how many points should be given for the different samples of colored pictures. For example, someone who colored all of the picture with realistic colors and stayed within the lines would get a 5—the highest score. Pictures would be given a lower score based on how well the colorers stayed in the lines, if the picture was complete, and so on. This information was placed in a rubric for everyone to see.

The pictures were evaluated by the students, collected, and returned to the students who had colored them. Following this lesson, many students commented that they would have done a better job if they had known they were going to be graded on their coloring. Students had the opportunity to discuss why they did or did not do their best job.

Overview

This simple example demonstrates the importance of making students aware of the criteria that will determine their grade. Check sheets and rubrics are two ways that students can assess their progress and evaluate their efforts. Unfortunately, many students will not put forth much effort unless the criteria for their performance are brought to their attention. Rubrics let students know what is expected of them. They serve as a grade contract. Based on the expectations outlined on a rubric, students can plan their time accordingly. For example, if video is not a requirement for a multimedia project, students should not spend time incorporating it into their project unless they have extra time on their hands. Rubrics can help students set their priorities and better manage their projects, as well as help teachers assess students' progress throughout the development of the multimedia projects.

Poor learning experiences can be avoided through well-planned and frequently assessed projects. Formative assessment provides constructive feedback at each phase of the DDD-E process. Without it, students may encounter unnecessary obstacles, extra work, frustration, unfinished products, and fragmented learning. Ongoing assessment helps educators teach for understanding and ensures that students are ready to move on to the next step of a project. This chapter defines several assessment techniques and their relationship to multimedia projects. In addition, this chapter provides rubrics for each phase of the DDD-E process. Topics include:

- Alternative assessment techniques
  - — The role of multimedia in alternative assessment
- Assessment strategies
  - — Using rubrics
  - — Additional rubric options
- Designing a rubric
  - — Clarifying rubric evaluations
- Assigning grades

Alternative Assessment Techniques

There are a variety of ways to evaluate students' learning. For years, schools have used standardized tests, but critics claim that standardized tests measure how well a student learns without considering whether the student can apply what was learned. Wiggins states that "the proof of a person's capacity is found in their ability to perform or produce, not in their ability to answer on cue" (Bruder 1993, 22). He further asserts that traditional tests tend to reveal only if the student can recall, recognize, or plug in what was learned out of context (Wiggins 1990).

Alternative assessment is assessment in some form other than the true/false, multiple-choice, matching, and fill-in-the-blank responses often associated with standardized tests. Performance-based assessment, authentic assessment, and portfolio assessment are forms of alternative assessment. Many of these terms overlap and are used interchangeably. They are defined as follows.

Performance-based assessment. Performance-based assessment requires teachers to evaluate a student's skill by asking the student to create an answer or product that demonstrates his or her knowledge or skills.

Authentic assessment. The goal of authentic assessment is to involve students in activities that better represent what they are likely to face as professionals. Authentic assessment includes performance tests, observations, interviews, exhibitions, and portfolios. The context, purpose, audience, and constraints of the task *must* connect to real-world situations and problems. For example, students might be asked to identify the chemical composition of a given solution by conducting various analyses, or they might take samples from local rivers and lakes and identify pollutants. Both tasks would be performance-based, but the latter would be considered authentic because it involves and addresses a real-world problem.

Portfolio assessment. Portfolios show growth over time, focusing on a student's progress rather than on a finished product. It is a systematic collection of a student's best work, records of observation, test results, and the like.

Based on the needs of the learner, alternative assessment techniques have the advantage of providing teachers and parents with directly observable products and clear evidence of students' performance. Assessment results are both meaningful and useful for improving instruction. The Virginia Education Association (1992) offers the following guidelines and recommendations for introducing alternative techniques in the classroom:

- Start small and begin by following someone else's example.
- Develop clear rubrics for judging students' products and performances. Past student products and performances can be used to create assessment rubrics and standards for the class.
- Be prepared to accept that developing and evaluating alternative assessments and their rubrics may require more time than expected.
- Plan assessment alongside instruction, not as an afterthought.
- If possible, work with a partner and share ideas and concerns.
- Collect examples of alternative assessments and activities and modify them for your students.
- Make expectations clear and assign a high value (grade) to the assessment.
- Expect to learn by trial and error. The best assessments are created over time with repeated use.
- Include peer assessment techniques. This can enhance students' evaluation skills and accountability.
- Don't give up! If at first you do not succeed, ask yourself what worked, what needs modification, what you should do differently, how the students responded, if the end results justify the time spent, and what the students learned.

The Role of Multimedia in Alternative Assessment

The creation of multimedia projects provides ample opportunities for performance-based assessment, authentic assessment, and portfolio assessment. Table 7.1 identifies project ideas for each of these assessment techniques. Evaluating students on their performance places greater emphasis on comprehension, critical thinking, reasoning, problem solving, and metacognitive processes (Linn, Baker, and Dunbar 1991).

Assessment Technique	Relationship to Multimedia Projects
Performance-Based Assessment	Multimedia projects can be used to demonstrate students' proficiency in specific computer skills, as well as serve as a forum for demonstrating and presenting the students' knowledge and skills. For example, using a variety of media elements, students may create a project that demonstrates their knowledge of the water cycle, different body systems, or plate tectonics.
Authentic Assessment	Multimedia projects may be designed to support classroom presentations, similar to what students are likely to face as professionals. In addition, students may create projects that are designed to gather data for analysis (such as a Web page that collects information from users).
Portfolio Assessment	A multimedia database can be designed to house digitized samples of a student's work. This includes stories, poetry, artwork, math papers, handwriting samples, etc. Items may be entered into the computer by keyboard, a scanner, or from a digital camera. Students may also create multimedia résumés.

Table 7.1 Multimedia project ideas for various assessment techniques

In addition to evaluating students on the final outcome of their performance, it is important to assess students' progress through each step of the DDD-E process. To create successful multimedia projects, assessment must be ongoing. It begins with the DECIDE process and ends with an evaluation of the final product.

Assessment Strategies

Checklists or rubrics can be designed to guide students through each step of their project, and daily journals (see ch. 3) can assist teachers with diagnosing each group's progress, problem-solving skills, and social skills. Rubrics help students know what is expected, leaving the teacher more time to advise and assist with specific questions.

Using Rubrics

A list of evaluation criteria and standards for the assigned multimedia project should be given to the students at the onset of their projects. Rubrics ensure that the students and teacher understand how the project will be evaluated. Students know what is expected of them and may put more effort into their projects because of it.

Rubrics can be designed to address each step of the DDD-E process and the desired outcome or focus of the multimedia projects. Steps include:

- DECIDE—Brainstorming and researching
- DESIGN—Planning and designing
- DEVELOP—Gathering and creating media
- EVALUATE—Evaluating final projects

Figure 7.1 depicts the evaluation stages of the DDD-E process. Note that daily journals are reviewed by the teacher on a daily basis to ensure the groups' progress and to help the teacher facilitate instruction. With the exception of the daily journal, each item in figure 7.1 is included as a blackline master at the end of this chapter. The daily journal entry sheet is in chapter 3. Additional checklists can be found in chapter 4.

DECIDE. Assessment begins with the groups' original idea and their ability to define the major sections of their reports, as well as how these sections relate to each other. Students should be able to articulate their research question, explain why it is important, and discuss how they intend to pursue it. Following the students' initial research, the

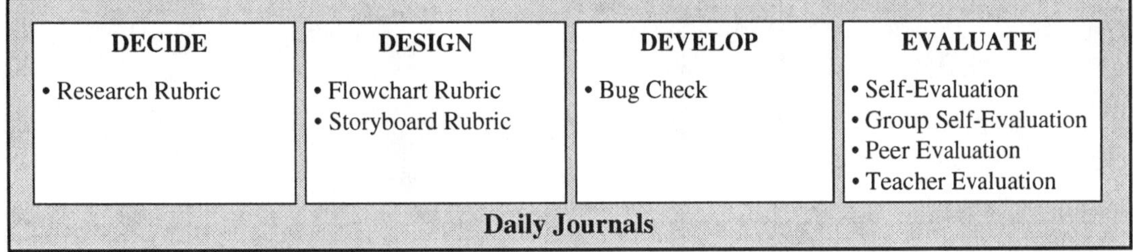

DECIDE
• Research Rubric
DESIGN
• Flowchart Rubric
• Storyboard Rubric
DEVELOP
• Bug Check
EVALUATE
• Self-Evaluation
• Group Self-Evaluation
• Peer Evaluation
• Teacher Evaluation
Daily Journals

Figure 7.1 Evaluation stages of the DDD-E process

Research Rubric

	1 inc.	2 poor	3 fair	4 good	5 excellent
Research questions are stated clearly.					
The research answers support the stated questions.					
A variety of reputable resources are used.					
The researched information is accurate.					
The bibliographical information is correct.					
Brainstorm (or KWL Knowledge Chart) is complete.					
	Total ______				

Figure 7.2 Sample research rubric

Flowchart Rubric

	1 inc.	2 poor	3 fair	4 good	5 excellent
The flowchart's structure is appropriate for the project.					
Branching is complete and clearly depicted.					
Each element of the flowchart is labeled.					
Correct symbols are used.					
The flowchart is easy to follow.					
	Total ______				

Figure 7.3 Sample flowchart rubric

teacher may decide to collect, review, and discuss each groups' brainstorming or KWL Knowledge Chart (see ch. 3), as well as their research findings. Teachers can check the accuracy of the information, ensure that students are using a variety of resources, and verify that the students are addressing the stated questions (see fig. 7.2).

Design. After their research has been verified, students need to map and define their ideas through flowcharts. After reviewing the flowcharts, the teacher should meet with each group to discuss the anticipated links, sequences, and section relationships identified in their flowcharts. Assessment may be based on the flowchart's structure, links, clarity, symbols, and labels (see fig. 7.3).

Storyboard production can begin after the flowcharts have been approved. Storyboards help students plan how their computer screens will look and relate to each other. Students should make their storyboards as clear and complete as possible. This allows the teacher to

Storyboard Rubric

	1 inc.	2 poor	3 fair	4 good	5 excellent
The required screens are included (title, credit, main menu, directions, etc.).					
Forward, back, and other links are indicated and described.					
The content is factual, interesting, and easy to understand.					
The layout design is consistent and clear.					
The required media elements are included and described.					
The storyboards include font information for text boxes and titles.					
Background and transition information is provided.					
	Total ______				

Figure 7.4 Sample storyboard rubric

The Bug Stops Here

Name of group being reviewed: ______

Project title: ______

Reviewed by: ______

Spelling Corrections

Word	Page	Word	Page

Punctuation and Grammar Corrections

Problem	Page	Problem	Page

Link and Media Corrections

Problem	Page	Problem	Page

List design and content comments on back.

Figure 7.5 Sample debugging form

provide guidance before the students invest a great amount of time in the final production phase. Teachers may want to provide students with a list of design guidelines (see ch. 4). Figure 7.4 shows a sample storyboard evaluation form. The final production phase takes place on the computer after the groups' storyboards have been approved.

DEVELOP. In the DEVELOP phase, students construct their final product to meet the standards and criteria set at the beginning of the assignment. Before students submit their projects for final evaluation, projects should go through a review and debugging phase. This is best performed by their peers. Students can check each other's projects to see if they meet the required criteria, as well as check for programming, spelling, and punctuation errors (see fig. 7.5).

EVALUATE. Self-, peer, and teacher evaluations occur after the projects are complete. These evaluations provide students with multiple levels of feedback. Self-evaluation encourages students to reflect on what they learned as well as how it was learned. In addition, it provides students with the opportunity to elaborate on what went well and what they might have done differently. Peer evaluation offers students another audience for their projects. It allows students to measure the extent to which they were able to successfully explain their work and ideas to their peers. In addition, peer evaluations allow students to practice their evaluation skills, provide ideas and constructive feedback, and help each other with the projects. Peer evaluations may also be used within groups to evaluate each member's cooperative efforts. (See Group Self-Evalution blackline master at the end of this chapter.) Teacher assessment provides ongoing support and guidance, as well as

Content Rubric					
	1 inc.	2 poor	3 fair	4 good	5 excellent
The content begins with an introduction.					
The content states the main ideas.					
The content provides accurate supporting evidence.					
The information is presented in a meaningful way.					
The authors explain the concepts in their own words.					
The content ends with a conclusion.					
The content shows depth of understanding.					
	Total ______				

Figure 7.6 Sample content rubric

Mechanics Rubric					
	1 inc.	2 poor	3 fair	4 good	5 excellent
The group proofread the project for spelling errors.					
The group proofread the project for punctuation and grammatical errors.					
The group tested all of the project's links.					
The group included the required elements in the project.					
The group ensured that all of the media elements worked (audio, animations, etc.).					
	Total ______				

Figure 7.7 Sample mechanics rubric

a final evaluation of the project. The teacher's evaluation should reflect the criteria established during the beginning stages of the project.

The final evaluation of the project may be based on one or more of the following: content learning, tool skills, design skills (see Additional Rubric Options section), as well as media appropriateness, social skills, or self-reflection—depending on the purpose of the project. The depth and scope of the evaluation should be consistent with the age and ability level of the students. Sample evaluation forms are reproduced at the end of this chapter.

Additional Rubric Options

Depending on the goal of the project and the ability level of the students, teachers may wish to employ multiple rubrics to evaluate various outcomes. For example, a content rubric may be used to evaluate the students' understanding of a particular topic. A content rubric may contain the following elements: begins with an introduction, states the main ideas, provides accurate supporting evidence, chunks and presents information in a meaningful way, explains concepts in students' own words, ends with a conclusion, shows a depth of understanding (see fig. 7.6).

A mechanics rubric (fig. 7.7) may review spelling, grammatical, and punctuation errors; defective links; inoperative media (e.g., video or audio clips); use of required tools; read-only text; and whether students incorporated specific elements into their project (e.g., title card, credits, bibliography, animation, etc.).

A design rubric (fig. 7.8) may critique the clarity and consistency of the layout, purpose of the media and navigation options, contrast

Design Rubric					
	1 inc.	2 poor	3 fair	4 good	5 excellent
The layout is clear and consistent.					
Graphics and other media elements are meaningful and add to the project.					
The project matches the storyboard instructions.					
The text is easy to read and contrasts with the background.					
Navigation buttons are easy to understand.					
Feedback is consistent and appropriate.					
					Total ______

Figure 7.8 Sample design rubric

Presentation Rubric					
	1	2	3	4	5
The presenter(s) spoke clearly and in a loud enough voice.					
The presenter(s) was dressed appropriately.					
The presenter(s) presented him/herself in a professional manner.					
The presenter(s) was organized.					
The presenter(s) captured and held my attention.					
The presentation was informative.					
1 = strongly disagree 2 = disagree 3 = somewhat agree 4 = agree 5 = strongly agree					Total ______

Figure 7.9 Sample presentation rubric

between text and background, readability of text (including fonts, sizes, colors, and styles), types of feedback, and the like.

A presentation rubric (fig. 7.9) may provide students with feedback on their speaking skills, appearance, organization, persuasiveness, ability to capture and hold the audience's attention, and so on. In addition to presentation projects, a presentation rubric may be used to evaluate students' class presentations of hypermedia or Web projects. Teachers may randomly select audience members to evaluate the presenters, or they provide presentation evaluations to everyone. Ratings may be averaged or totalled for a final score.

One or more of these rubrics may be provided to the students and attached to the teacher's final evaluation form to aid in the summative evaluation of the students' projects. Blackline masters of these rubrics appear at the end of this chapter.

Designing a Rubric

When designing a rubric, consider the age and ability level of the students, as well as the desired learning outcomes. Encourage student input. This allows students to work toward individual goals and to create their own learning experiences. Keep rubrics short, simple, and to the point. Categorize topic areas or provide separate rubrics for each area, depending on the sophistication of the multimedia project. For beginning projects, focus on only a few outcomes.

A five-point scale can be used to evaluate learning outcomes: 1 = incomplete, 2 = poor, 3 = fair, 4 = good, and 5 = excellent or 1 = strongly disagree, 2 = disagree, 3 = somewhat agree, 4 = agree, and 5 = strongly agree. If possible, space should be provided to indicate

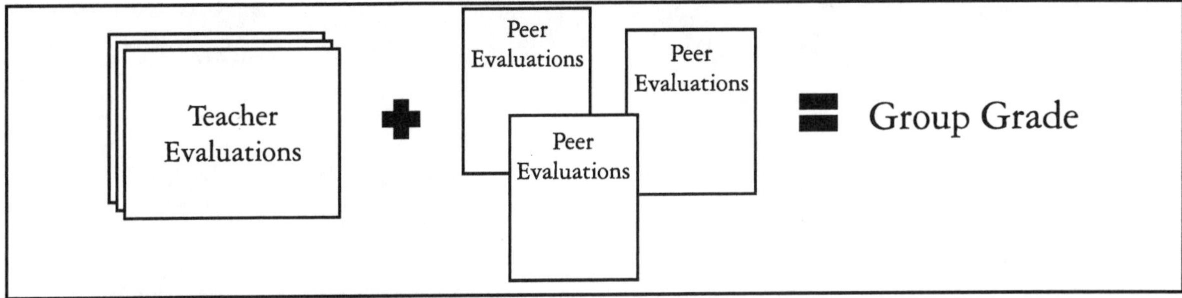

Figure 7.10 Assigning group grades

evidence or explanation of each rating. For example, if a group receives a rating of 2 for depth of knowledge, a comment may be made that they did not provide the necessary number of examples. For younger students, rubrics should be as simple as possible and include pictorial forms of evaluation. For example, a happy face would indicate a great job (see the Primary MM Rubric blackline master).

Clarifying Rubric Evaluations

To ensure that students understand rubric ratings, review several existing multimedia projects. These may be teacher-created for demonstration purposes, samples included with the multimedia program, projects from previous classes, or examples downloaded from the Internet. Review projects that are comparable to your students' ability levels. Encourage students to discuss what they like and dislike about the projects, the projects' strengths and weaknesses, and what they might do to make the project better. Decide what determines an excellent rating, a good rating, and so on. This allows students to begin their projects with a set of clear and consistent guidelines by which they will be evaluated. Review sample projects before the DESIGN stage.

Assigning Grades

Groups may receive a grade based on the combined and averaged scores of the teacher and peer evaluations (see fig. 7.10). Sample teacher and peer evaluation forms appear at the end of this chapter.

Teacher evaluation forms may include an overall rating of a group's journal entries and bibliography information, as well as the average rating of the group's storyboard rubric, design rubric, content rubric, and mechanics rubric. For example, using the sample teacher evaluation form located at the end of this chapter, a group may have averaged a rating of 4 on their storyboards, design, content, and mechanics, and the teacher may have rated the group's journal entries and bibliography information as excellent (see fig. 7.11). The teacher's evaluation equals 26 points, or an average score of 4.3.

Teachers may choose to insert their own categories for final evaluation. A blank teacher evaluation form is included at the end of this chapter.

Using the Peer Evaluation blackline master, students can evaluate each other's projects. The sample form available at the end of this chapter provides space for students to comment on a project's content and design. It also asks that students rate the project on a scale of 1 to 5. Teachers can evaluate the students' comments and weight them

Teacher Evaluation	1 inc.	2 poor	3 fair	4 good	5 excellent
Storyboards (see Storyboard Rubric)				X	
Design (see Design Rubric)				X	
Content (see Content Rubric)				X	
Mechanics (see Mechanics Rubric)				X	
Daily journal entries					X
Bibliographical information					X
Good job! You effectively organized your project and demonstrated excellent teamwork! You averaged 4.3 on your project.				Total	26

Figure 7.11 Sample teacher evaluation form

Final Grades	1 inc.	2 poor	3 fair	4 good	5 excellent
Group Self-Evaluations					
Self-Evaluation					
Peer Evaluations				4.3	
Teacher Evaluation				4.3	
Group Grade 4.3			Individual Grade ______		

Figure 7.12 Final grade sheet with two transferred scores

appropriately, transferring the students' average rating to the final grades evaluation form (see Final Grades Blackline master).

For example, if three groups evaluated a project, and groups one and two gave the project a 4 and group three gave the project a 5, the average score transferred to the final grades sheet would be 4.3. Figure 7.12 shows the final grade sheet with transferred scores from the teacher's evaluation and average peer evaluation. In this example, the group grade equals 4.3, the average of the teacher and peer evaluations. The letter grade depends upon the teacher's grading scale.

Individual grades may be based on the combined and averaged scores of students' self-assessment, the group's self-evaluations, and the group grade (see fig. 7.13). This ensures individual accountability within groups. Sample self-evaluation and group self-evaluation forms appear at the end of this chapter.

Using the Self-Evaluation blackline master, students reflect on what they learned. The teacher uses the student's comments to rate the evaluation on a scale of 1 to 5 and adds his or her rationale for the score on the back of the evaluation. For example, if a student is specific and notably reflective on each of the questions, the teacher may score the evaluation a 5. This score is transferred to the final grade sheet.

The Group Self-Evaluation blackline master provides group members with the opportunity to rate the participation and contributions of their teammates, as well as themselves. The average score of each student is transferred to his or her final grade sheet. For example, if

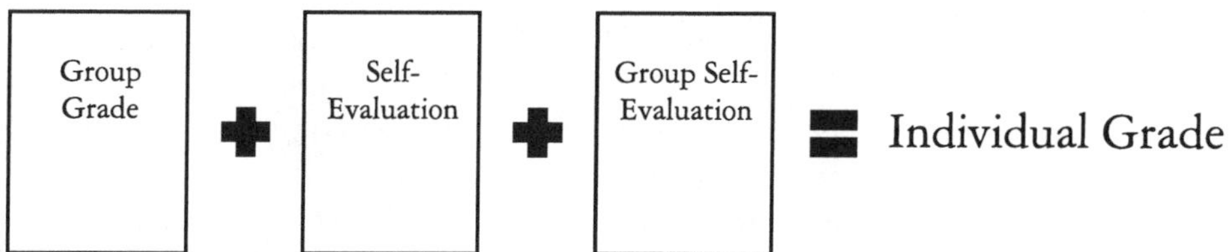

Figure 7.13 Assigning an individual grade

Final Grades					
	1 inc.	2 poor	3 fair	4 good	5 excellent
Group Self-Evaluations				4.8	
Self-Evaluation					5
Peer Evaluations				4.3	
Teacher Evaluation				4.3	
Group Grade 4.3			Individual Grade 4.7		

Figure 7.14 Final grade sheet with transferred scores

Nawang received ratings of 5, 5, and 4 from his teammates and rated himself a 5, his average group self-evaluation score would be 4.8. The average of the self-evaluation, group self-evaluation, and group grade determine an individual's final grade. In figure 7.14, the self-evaluation and group self-evaluation scores have been transferred to the final grade sheet, along with the scores from figure 7.12. The final individual grade equals 4.7: the average of the group grade (4.3), the group self-evaluation (4.8), and the self-evaluation (5). Again, the letter grade depends upon the teacher's grading scale.

Teachers are encouraged to make their own evaluation forms designed to meet the needs and ability levels of their students. This chapter provides several examples of various rubrics; teachers may pick and choose those that are applicable to their students and multimedia projects. Additional forms for specific projects are included in chapters 8, 9, and 10.

Summary

The multifaceted nature of multimedia project development encourages multiple steps of assessment. Assessment is ongoing and determines whether a group is ready to proceed to the next stage of development. In the DECIDE stage, students should be able to articulate their research question, explain why it is important, and discuss how they intend to pursue it. Next, they should demonstrate their ability to gather, organize, and synthesize information through brainstorming activities and research. In the DESIGN stage, students need to display how they intend to map and link their ideas together. In addition to examining the project flowcharts, students can explain the anticipated links, sequences, and section relationships identified in their flowcharts with the teacher. Afterwards, students can begin producing their project's storyboards. The completed set is assessed by the teacher before the students continue to the DEVELOP stage. The DEVELOP stage includes review and debugging by the students' peers. Final projects include self-, peer, and teacher evaluations. Daily journal entries (see ch. 3) that assess the group's progress and ability to work together can be collected and submitted with the groups' final projects. Groups may receive a grade based on the combined scores of the teacher and peer evaluations, and a final individual grade may be based on students' self-assessment, group self-evaluations, and group grade. Rubrics ensure that both students and teacher understand how each step of the project will be evaluated.

Blackline Masters

This chapter includes an assortment of blackline masters designed to assist teachers and students in reviewing and evaluating multimedia projects. Blackline masters include:

- Research Rubric—used in the DECIDE phase to ensure that students are ready to move on to the DESIGN phase
- Flowchart Rubric—a form used to evaluate a group's flowchart before the students proceed to the storyboard stage of the DESIGN phase
- Storyboard Rubric—a final evaluation form for a group's storyboards; a storyboard checklist is provided in chapter 4
- The Bug Stops Here—a review sheet used to help students debug projects during the DEVELOP phase, before the projects are submitted for final evaluation
- Self-Evaluation—one way in which students can reflect on their participation and learning at the end of a multimedia assignment
- Peer Evaluation—one way in which student groups can evaluate other groups' work
- Group Self-Evaluation—a sample of how students may evaluate their own group's performance
- Teacher Evaluation (blank)—a template for creating your own evaluation categories

- Content Rubric—a sample rubric for evaluating the content of a project
- Mechanics Rubric—a sample rubric for evaluating the spelling, grammar, and punctuation of a project
- Design Rubric—a sample rubric for evaluating a project's design
- Presentation Rubric—a sample rubric for evaluating project presentations
- Primary MM Rubric—a simple rubric designed for young children
- Final Grades—an accumulating score sheet for determining an individual's final grade, as well as a group grade

References

Bruder, I. January 1993. Alternative assessment: Putting technology to the test. *Electronic Learning* 22–29.

Linn, R. L., E. L. Baker, and S. B. Dunbar. 1991. Complex, performance-based assessment: Expectations and validation criteria. *Educational Researcher* 20(8): 15–21.

Virginia Education Association. 1992. Recommendations for teachers. *ERIC Clearinghouse of Assessment and Evaluation.* [On-line]. Available: gopher://vmsgopher.cua.edu: 70/00gopher_root_eric_ae%3A%5B_alt%5D_rectea.txt

Wiggins, G. 1990. *The case for authentic assessment.* (Report no. TM-016-142). Washington, DC: American Institute for Research. (ERIC Document Reproduction Service No. ED 328 611)

Research Rubric

	1 inc.	2 poor	3 fair	4 good	5 excellent
Research questions are stated clearly.					
The research answers support the stated questions.					
A variety of reputable resources are used.					
The researched information is accurate.					
The bibliographical information is correct.					
Brainstorm (or KWL Knowledge Chart) is complete.					
	Total ______				

Flowchart Rubric

	1 inc.	2 poor	3 fair	4 good	5 excellent
The flowchart's structure is appropriate for the project.					
Branching is complete and clearly depicted.					
Each element of the flowchart is labeled.					
Correct symbols are used.					
The flowchart is easy to follow.					
					Total ______

Storyboard Rubric

	1 inc.	2 poor	3 fair	4 good	5 excellent
The required screens are included (title, credit, main menu, directions, etc.).					
Forward, back, and other links are indicated and described.					
The content is factual, interesting, and easy to understand.					
The layout design is consistent and clear.					
The required media elements are included and described.					
The storyboards include font information for text boxes and titles.					
Background and transition information is provided.					
					Total ______

The Bug Stops Here

Name of group being reviewed: ______________________

Project title: ______________________

Reviewed by: ______________________

Spelling Corrections

Word	Page	Word	Page

Punctuation and Grammar Corrections

Problem	Page	Problem	Page

Link and Media Corrections

Problem	Page	Problem	Page

List design and content comments on back.

Self-Evaluation

Name of group: ______________________________

Project title: ______________________________

Group member: ______________________________

How did you contribute to the project?

What did you learn about your topic in the process of developing this project?

What did you learn about multimedia development in the process of developing this project?

What did you learn about yourself in the process of developing this project?

Teacher's Rating: ______________ (Comments on back)

Peer Evaluation

Name of group being reviewed: ____________________

Project title: ____________________

Reviewed by: ____________________

Content

What did you learn about this topic that you did not know before?

In terms of content, what are the strengths of this project?

How might the presentation of information be improved?

Design

What are the strengths in the design of this project?

What improvements in the design would you suggest?

On a scale of 1 to 5 (5 being the highest),
how would you rate this project? ____________

Group Self-Evaluation

Name of group being reviewed: ____________________

Project title: ____________________

Group member: ____________________

What were your group's strengths?

What were your group's weaknesses?

What are some of the things that you learned about working with others?

What would you do better the next time your group works together?

On the back of this form, list yourself and your group members. Rate yourself and each of your group members' level of participation in the project. 1 = not enough, 2 = fair, 3 = a lot, 4 = did most of the work. Explain your ratings.

Teacher Evaluation

	1 inc.	2 poor	3 fair	4 good	5 excellent
Storyboards (see Storyboard Rubric)					
Design (see Design Rubric)					
Content (see Content Rubric)					
Mechanics (see Mechanics Rubric)					
Daily journal entries					
Bibliographical information					
					Total ______

Teacher Evaluation (continued)

(insert your own categories)	1 inc.	2 poor	3 fair	4 good	5 excellent
	Total ______				

Content Rubric

	1 inc.	2 poor	3 fair	4 good	5 excellent
The content begins with an introduction.					
The content states the main ideas.					
The content provides accurate supporting evidence.					
The information is presented in a meaningful way.					
The authors explain the concepts in their own words.					
The content ends with a conclusion.					
The content shows depth of understanding.					
	Total ______				

Mechanics Rubric

	1 inc.	2 poor	3 fair	4 good	5 excellent
The group proofread the project for spelling errors.					
The group proofread the project for punctuation and grammatical errors.					
The group tested all of the project's links.					
The group included the required elements in the project.					
The group ensured that all of the media elements worked (audio, animations, etc.).					
	Total ______				

Design Rubric

	1 inc.	2 poor	3 fair	4 good	5 excellent
The layout is clear and consistent.					
Graphics and other media elements are meaningful and add to the project.					
The project matches the storyboard instructions.					
The text is easy to read and contrasts with the background.					
Navigation buttons are easy to understand.					
Feedback is consistent and appropriate.					
	Total ______				

Presentation Rubric

	1	2	3	4	5
The presenter(s) spoke clearly and in a loud enough voice.					
The presenter(s) was dressed appropriately.					
The presenter(s) presented him/herself in a professional manner.					
The presenter(s) was organized.					
The presenter(s) captured and held my attention.					
The presentation was informative.					
1 = strongly disagree 2 = disagree 3 = somewhat agree 4 = agree 5 = strongly agree					Total ______

Primary MM Rubric

The project starts with a title screen.

Directions are provided.

The information is correct.

There are no spelling or punctuation errors.

___ pictures were used.

___ sounds were used.

The screens are linked together so the project makes sense.

Final Grades

	1 inc.	2 poor	3 fair	4 good	5 excellent
Group Self-Evaluations					
Self-Evaluation					
Peer Evaluations					
Teacher Evaluation					

Group Grade ______ Individual Grade ______

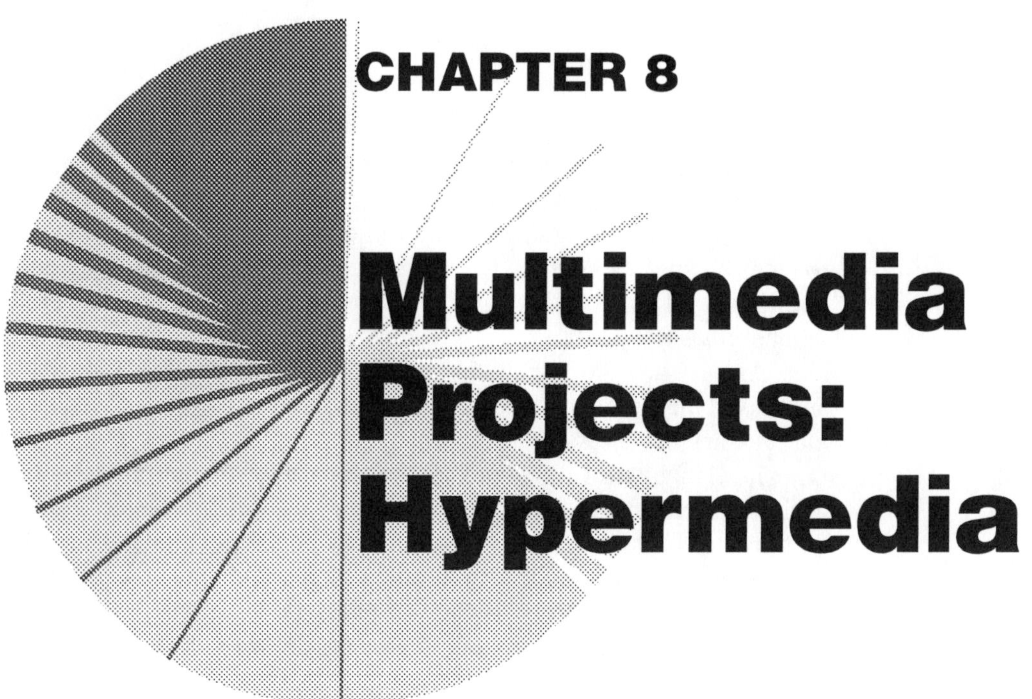

CHAPTER 8

Multimedia Projects: Hypermedia

A Scenario

Martin, Diane, Connie, and John enjoyed working together on multimedia projects because they each felt they had something to contribute to the project. Martin created most of the graphics, Diane oversaw the design of the flowcharts and storyboards, Connie organized and edited the text, and John put all of the project's pieces together using the assigned authoring tool. Each student took pride in teaching teammates his or her own specific skills, and they all tutored each other throughout the design and development of the project. In addition to design and development skills, the multimedia projects focused on a variety of subject areas. Connie dreaded the thought of creating a stack that focused on mathematics, but John was quick to remind her that they all had different strengths and would support each other through the project. He recalled the multimedia project that involved interviewing members of the community, and how awkward and misplaced he had felt. He had been glad his teammates were there to support and encourage him. Thanks to them and that project, he now feels a lot more comfortable conducting interviews.

Mr. Thompson read similar comments from other students as he reviewed their class journals. Their comments and reflections confirmed his decision to incorporate multimedia projects throughout his curriculum. The students' teamwork and social growth were encouraging, and they continued to perform well, if not better, academically. By integrating multimedia projects throughout the curriculum, Mr. Thompson allowed his students to share their strengths in subject areas as well as in multimedia production.

Overview

Ideas for multimedia projects are endless, limited only by the imagination of teachers and students. Multimedia projects can be integrated across the curriculum, and they can help students share their knowledge in a variety of ways. In addition, multimedia projects may be designed to focus on specific student skills (e.g., learning how to use a particular authoring tool), selected media formats (e.g., animation), or social skills (cooperative learning).

As with any other curricular unit, planning is an essential part of successful multimedia projects. In addition, limited computer resources may require educators to facilitate several activities at once. This idea is not new; many educators find themselves managing multiple activities in the classroom on a daily basis. For example, during a social studies unit on the Gold Rush, some students may be panning for gold, others may be working on a model of a mining camp, some may be working on written reports, and more may be weighing and evaluating the value of gold nuggets. During multimedia projects, the only difference is that some students may be working on computers while others are working on noncomputer related activities. The computer provides the students with yet another mode of learning—one that provides new insights into organizing, synthesizing, evaluating, and presenting information. This chapter presents several ideas for multimedia projects that can be created with hypermedia tools such as HyperStudio, HyperCard, Digital Chisel, and others. A lesson description, the DDD-E process, and ideas for concurrent activities are provided for each project.

Sample Projects

The following projects address various areas of the curriculum and can be created with most authoring tools. Students should be familiar with the chosen tool before engaging in the multimedia project. The sample projects are designed for classrooms with 4 computers and 32 students; however, adjustments can be made to meet other conditions. Design teams consist of 4 students and periods consist of 60 minutes. See chapter 3 for computer scheduling options.

All About Me

Lesson Description: This project is designed for beginners, to provide them with the opportunity to focus on planning, design issues, and the authoring tool. The content of the stack is information about the students. Each student team creates an eight-card stack consisting of the following cards: title, information, main menu, student 1, student 2, student 3, student 4, and a credits card. All About Me blackline masters are provided at the end of this chapter.

Decide. Assign student teams as described in previous chapters. As a class, brainstorm what makes people interesting, what information students might find in an autobiography, and other related questions. Generate a class list of 10 items (e.g., name, date and place of birth, hobbies, favorite books, etc.) from the brainstorm. Assign each student the responsibility of providing information about himself or herself for each of the 10 items.

Design. The next period, provide student teams with a copy of a flowchart (see the All About Me: Flowchart blackline master). Discuss the flowchart's layout and how the cards will be connected. Next, distribute copies of the All About Me: Storyboard Templates (see the blackline masters at the end of this chapter). Explain how the students should complete the storyboards, and how they will use the storyboards to create the computer screens of their multimedia projects. Discuss design issues (contrasting background and text, consistency, etc.) and, if possible, demonstrate sample All About Me stacks. These sample stacks may be created by the teacher or be projects from previous classes. Use the stacks to show good and bad examples of design, and let the students discuss what they observe. For example, a bad example might have navigation icons in inconsistent places on the screens, unreadable text, links that do not work, and spelling mistakes. Following the class discussion, provide students with a list of design guidelines (see ch. 4) and a checklist of expectations (see All About Me: Project Checklist blackline master). During the next period, students work on their team's storyboards, including the storyboards about themselves. Each self storyboard should contain a paragraph describing the 10 items that the student has answered about himself or herself. Teams' storyboards should be assessed and approved by the teacher before students are allowed to work on the computers. Students can keep track of their progress by using the journal entry forms discussed in chapter 3.

Develop. After the students' storyboards have been approved, teams take turns at the computer stations. If teams are not working on the computers or on their storyboards, students can be:

- Reading an autobiography or biography of a famous person of their choice and working with a Venn diagram to compare differences and similarities between the person they are reading about and themselves
- Creating a self-portrait using pastels, papier-mâché, clay, or other medium
- Creating a 3D, life-size body cutout of themselves using two sheets of butcher paper and paper scrap stuffing
- Using a life-size cutout of a member of their team to study and illustrate the skeletal system, muscles, and so on
- Researching, gathering, and organizing information for a class newspaper or magazine that describes what occurred during the year most students were born
- Researching information about their place and date of birth, hobbies, or the like, for a possible extension activity that adds more cards to their stack

As students complete their multimedia projects, another team reviews the stack for problems or errors (see ch. 7). The corrected stack, along with the group and self-evaluations and journal entries, is submitted to the teacher. It may take students four to six periods to finish their stack.

Evaluate. In addition to the teacher's evaluation, peers may be asked to evaluate each other's projects (see the All About Me: Teacher Evaluation and All About Me: Peer Evaluation blackline masters). The students receive a group grade based on the teacher and peer evaluations. Students receive an individual grade based on their group, self-, and intragroup evaluations. The two grades can be averaged for a final score.

Pollution Solution

Lesson Description: This project focuses on the students' ability to research, synthesize, and present information about the hazards of pollution. Students are required to use a variety of media formats to help them emphasize the importance of finding solutions to pollution. For example, they may incorporate digitized photographs and video segments into their stacks to illustrate the outcomes of pollution or animations that illustrate a recycling process.

Decide. Assign student teams as described in previous chapters. As a class, brainstorm what students already know about pollution and what they want to learn about pollution (see the KWL Knowledge Chart in ch. 3). For example, they may know that pollution is harmful, but they may not know the extensive effects of pollution on the environment, what regulations are in effect to help stop pollution, what causes smog, how and what items are recycled, the dirtiest cities in the world, and steps they can take to help stop pollution. Assign or have each group select a different topic to research. Distribute and explain the Brain-Storm activity sheet and the Bibliography sheet (see ch. 3). Before groups brainstorm and begin research about their specific topic, stipulate that groups need to incorporate photos, video segments, or animations to illustrate their points. Ask the students why pictures are important when discussing a topic like pollution. Discuss (or demonstrate) how a picture of dead fish in a river has a stronger impact on people than the text "dead fish in a river" has by itself.

Design. Students may take two or three class periods to research their specific topic. As students are finishing their research, discuss the concept of flowcharts and storyboards. Students need to examine their research findings and organize the information by chunks and meaningful links. Students may want to use index cards to create and manipulate a rough draft of their flowchart and storyboard ideas. Discuss the design issues explained in chapter 4. View sample stacks that contain video, animations, and photographs and have students discuss what makes the stacks effective or ineffective. Provide groups with a list of design guidelines, a storyboard template (see ch. 4), and the journal entry form, project checklist, and bibliography sheet available in chapters 3 and 4. Explain each form. In addition, provide groups with the storyboard, design, content, and mechanics rubrics available in chapter 7. Groups should keep these forms in a binder. Multiple copies of the journal entry form and the bibliography form should also be available. Students may take three to five class periods to complete their flowchart and storyboards.

Develop. After the students' flowchart and storyboards have been approved, teams take turns at the computer stations (see ch. 3 for a computer schedule). If teams are not working on the computers or on their storyboards, students can be:

- Creating a brochure that lists local recycling centers and ways that people can help stop pollution
- Writing and illustrating a creative story, performing a skit, or creating an audio story (with sound effects and music) about a

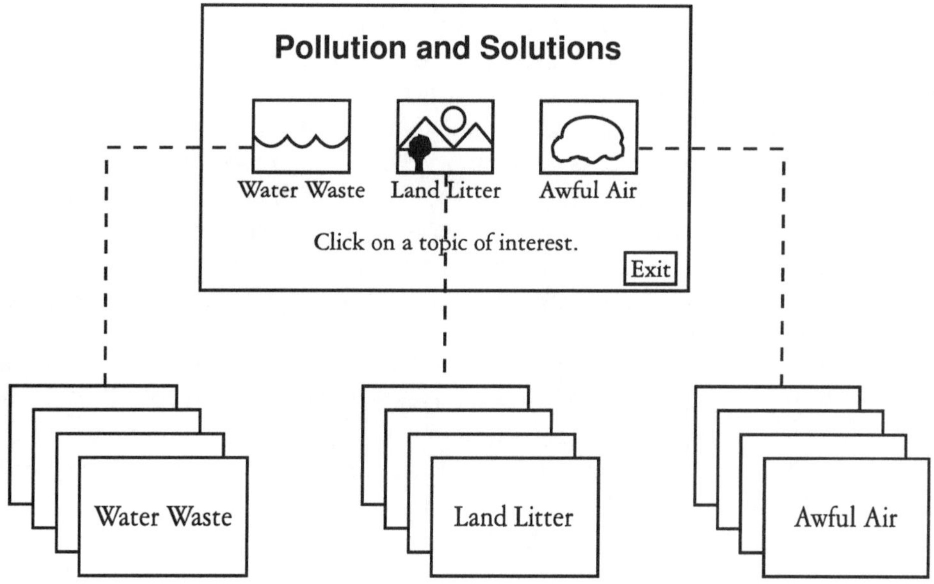

Figure 8.1 Link student stacks to a main menu

superhero who helps prevent pollution, a boy (or girl) who always threw trash on the ground until the ground fought back, a container's question as to whether there is life after trash, and other ideas

- Working on a classroom mural of the trash collected from the school yard
- Creating and videotaping a show where the students demonstrate or create products made from other things, such as bird feeders made from pinecones, peanut butter, and bird seed
- Writing a poem or song about pollution
- Creating and solving math problems related to money earned by recycling
- Developing quiz questions about their stack for other students

As students complete their multimedia projects, another team reviews the stack for problems or errors (see ch. 7). The corrected stack, along with the project's rubrics, group and self-evaluations, bibliography sheets, and journal entries, is submitted to the teacher.

Evaluate. Following the teacher's evaluation of the projects, peers need to evaluate each other's projects, too (see ch. 7). The students receive a group grade based on the teacher and peer evaluations. Students receive an individual grade based on their group, self-, and intragroup evaluations.

When the grading is complete, a main menu can be developed that links the projects together (see fig. 8.1). Students can view the entire multimedia presentation and answer each other's quiz questions for additional content evaluation. The remaining column on the KWL Knowledge Chart can now be completed.

Community Concerns

Lesson Description: This project focuses on the students' ability to develop and issue a survey, organize and interpret the collected information, discuss issues with members of the community, and participate in an authentic learning experience. Students are required to research and address community concerns by reading the local newspaper, watching the local news, and interacting with members of the community. Findings are presented in a multimedia project. Authentic learning experiences are the result of conducting interviews, making video recordings and audio tracks of community members, and compiling the data.

Decide. Assign student teams as described in previous chapters. As a class, discuss the concept of a community and what issues their community may be facing. Topics may include the homeless, curfews, the elderly, crime, education, and other concerns. Assign or have each group select a different topic to research. Explain that their research should include local newspaper articles and television news, as well as interviews with members of the community. Distribute the BrainStorm activity sheet (see ch. 3) to assist students in organizing the possibilities of their topic. During the next two or three class periods, discuss how to construct a survey and, if possible, distribute sample surveys. Students should think about questions that are important to their particular topic. For example, students researching the concerns of the elderly may ask the elderly questions regarding health care, social security, transportation, recreation services, and family concerns. This student group may contrast and compare answers they receive from the elderly with answers they receive from other age groups. During the interviews, students should ask permission to record, video, or photograph the person being interviewed. All of the data are accumulated, synthesized, and evaluated. Students can keep track of their sources using the Bibliography sheet in chapter 3. Surveys should be approved by the teacher before students begin their interviews. Provide the students with an additional week to conduct the interviews and finalize the results.

Design. Discuss the concept of flowcharts and storyboards. Students need to examine their research findings and organize the information by chunks and meaningful links. Students may want to use index cards to create and manipulate a rough draft of their flowchart and storyboard ideas. Discuss the design issues explained in chapter 4. View sample stacks that contain audio tracks, video, and photographs, and have students discuss what makes the stacks effective or ineffective. Provide groups with a list of design guidelines, a storyboard template (see ch. 4), and the journal entry form and project checklist available in chapters 3 and 4. Explain each form. In addition, provide groups with the storyboard, design, content, and mechanics rubrics available in chapter 7. Groups should keep these forms in a binder. Multiple copies of the journal entry form and the bibliography form should be available. Students may take three to five class periods to complete their flowchart and storyboards. Remind students to complete daily journal entries (see ch. 3).

Develop. After the students' flowchart and storyboards have been approved, teams take turns at the computer stations. If teams are not working on the computers or on their storyboards, students can be:

- Proposing a club or fund-raising campaign that supports their specific topic
- Developing quiz questions about their stack for other students
- Working on a class model of their community
- Creating a travel brochure about the benefits of their community
- Writing letters to their local congresspersons about their findings and concerns
- Composing letters to other classes in other communities, encouraging them to conduct the same surveys and share their results (e-mail or regular mail)
- Researching and constructing models or pictures of historical places, events, or people tied to their community
- Creating an interesting facts or trivia game about their community to play with other students

As students complete their multimedia projects, another team reviews the stack for problems or errors (see ch. 7). The corrected stack, along with the project's rubrics, group and self-evaluations, bibliography sheets, and journal entries, is submitted to the teacher.

Evaluate. Students may choose to share their projects with local community members. Peers and teachers can also evaluate the projects. Students may receive a group grade based on the average score of their peer, teacher, and community evaluations. Individual grades are calculated by the group grade, self-, and intragroup evaluations.

All That Jazz

Lesson Description: This project focuses on the students' ability to research, synthesize, and present information about different styles of music. Students are required to incorporate audio clips of a select music style into their stacks to help teach other students about music. For example, students creating a stack about ragtime could include audio clips of *The Entertainer* and the *Maple Leaf Rag* while discussing the contributions and history of Scott Joplin. Each team chooses or is assigned a specific music style and generates a multimedia stack that reports at least certain assigned information about that style. Educators may choose to impose a specific layout and style for student storyboards and flowcharts; hence, the stacks will contain the same topics and can be connected at the end of the project.

Decide. Assign student teams as described in previous chapters. As a class, generate a list of different types of music (e.g., rock and roll, ragtime, classical, jazz, country-western, etc.). Discuss what students already know about certain types of music and what they would like to learn about the types of music (see the KWL Knowledge Chart in ch. 3). For example, they may know that Elvis Presley is considered the King of Rock and Roll, that Beethoven wrote classical music, and that ragtime was popular during the 1920s. Students may want to learn the origins

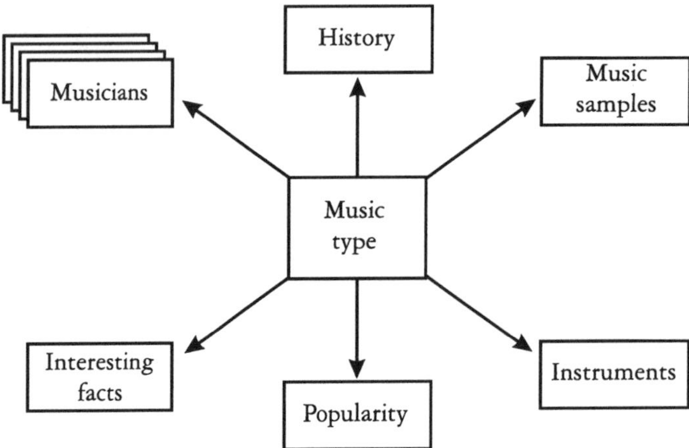

Figure 8.2 Sample flowchart

of country music or find out more about New Age music. In addition to the students' topics of interest, ask students to research the following information: the music's history and peak(s) of popularity; at least three musicians and their history and contribution to the music style; and additional music titles and interesting facts. Randomly assign or let students choose a music style from the list. Distribute the BrainStorm activity sheet from chapter 3. To adhere to a specific project format, explain that each group's BrainStorm sheet should contain the following information: the music type should be placed in the Main Idea bubble and Related Idea bubbles should contain music history, musicians, music titles, and interesting facts. Students can create additional Related Idea bubbles for other topics. Branches from the Related Idea bubbles will contain more specific information about the topic. Provide students with three to five periods of research time, reminding them that audio clips are required for the project. Assist students with their research by bringing in a variety of music recordings on CD, cassettes, albums, or audio clips.

Design. As students are finishing their research, discuss the concept of flowcharts and storyboards. As a class, discuss how the gathered information might best be organized, chunked, and linked together. Create a flowchart for everyone to follow (see fig. 8.2).

Next, discuss the design issues explained in chapter 4. View sample stacks that contain music clips and have students discuss what makes the stacks effective or ineffective. Discuss storyboard designs and decide on a standard layout for everyone to use. Distribute the journal entry form and project checklist available in chapters 3 and 4. Explain each form. In addition, provide groups with the storyboard, design, content, and mechanics rubrics available in chapter 7. Students may take three to five class periods to complete their flowchart and storyboards.

Develop. After the students' flowchart and storyboards have been approved, teams take turns at the computer stations. If teams are not working on the computers or on their storyboards, students can be:

- Writing a persuasive report for a future debate explaining why their music style is the best
- Developing quiz questions about their stack for other students
- Developing a board game about the life of a composer
- Reading a biography of a composer and designing a diorama depicting and explaining an important event in the composer's life
- Learning and interpreting the lyrics to a particular song
- Creating a water-color or acrylic painting that depicts the mood or feelings associated with a particular piece of music
- Learning to play a music selection
- Creating a composition of their own

As students complete their multimedia projects, another team reviews the stack for problems or errors (see ch. 7). The corrected stack, along with the project's rubrics, group and self-evaluations, bibliography sheets, and journal entries, is submitted to the teacher.

EVALUATE. Both students and teachers evaluate the projects. The students receive a group grade based on the teacher and peer evaluations. Students receive an individual grade based on their group, self-, and intragroup evaluations. When the grading is complete, a main menu can be developed that links the projects together. The remaining column on the KWL Knowledge Chart can now be completed.

Sherlock Stack: A Problem-Solving Adventure

Lesson Description: This project focuses on the students' ability to solve problems, research, and develop interdependent clues to produce a multimedia stack that demonstrates their processing skills. In addition, graphics and pop-up text boxes can be required components of the stack. Students are required to create a mystery that is solved by finding and deciphering the various clues within the stack. For example, a group may use the theme of a haunted house and tell the story of how the only way out of the house is to enter the correct combination into the passageway door. Throughout the stack, students create mathematical and logic problems that will assist users in determining the correct code. For example, in the first room of the house, the following clue could be discovered when users click on a ghost (see fig. 8.3):

> It happened on a scary night,
> One I know was full of fright;
> Yet Joey Jones, as calm as could be,
> Said, "Divide 800 by the answer in three."

A text box may appear or the clue may be recorded audio, or both. Room three's clue might appear when users click on a book (see fig. 8.4):

> Weary travelers visit here;
> Guess how many times a year?
> (7 * 8) – (10 + 21)

By combining the clues in rooms one and three, the answer to room one is 32. Room six's clue may indicate that this is the first number in the

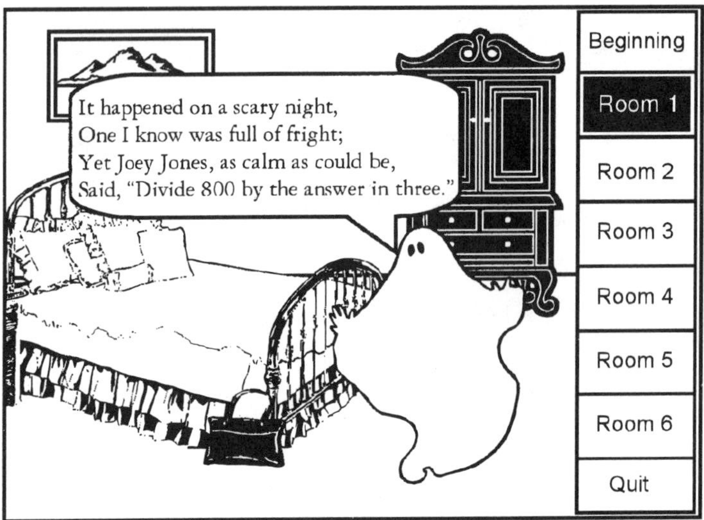

Figure 8.3 Sample screen design for room one

Figure 8.4 Sample screen design for room three

combination. For example, upon visiting room six, the users may find the following scrawled on the wall (see fig. 8.5):

Room 1 = 1st number to combination

Stacks can be made much more complex and sophisticated by integrating current areas of study, incorporating outside research into the answers to the clues, making answers to clues dependent on more than one other clue, and incorporating different media that become part of the clues. To begin, limit students to six clues in the puzzle.

Decide. Assign student teams as described in previous chapters. As a class, discuss the different strategies students use when solving a math problem, as well as the basic problem-solving steps: (1) understanding the problem, (2) devising a plan, (3) carrying out the plan, and

Figure 8.5 Sample screen design for room six

(4) looking back. Discuss the importance of gathering all information before coming to a conclusion about a problem. Illustrate this by distributing one puzzle clue to each different student group (see the Introductory Puzzle blackline master at the end of this chapter). Ask the students if they can solve the puzzle. Obviously, they cannot, because they each hold only one piece to the puzzle. Randomly select groups to read their puzzle pieces aloud, while everyone else takes notes. Inquire whether students can solve the puzzle after each clue. Note that some clues may not make any sense until other clues are read, and that some clues are interdependent (they rely on other clues for additional information). Some clues may have to be repeated. After all of the clues are read, discuss the answer and how students arrived at it. Reflect on the interdependent puzzle pieces and the importance of gathering and understanding all the clues.

Explain that students are going to create a multimedia stack based on the puzzle example. Their stack should contain a theme (e.g., a haunted house, a pirate's treasure, outer space, the jungle, etc.) and their clues should be hidden (pop-up text boxes) or part of the graphic environment. Users should experience traveling from room to room or place to place.

Let student teams brainstorm about a specific theme and a mystery to go along with it. For example, using an outer space theme, the story might involve the crash of a spaceship on an unknown planet; the clues might spell the name of the planet or give its position from the sun. Or, using a pirate theme, the story might involve the location of a buried treasure; the clues could provide the x and y coordinates to a location on a treasure map. After a theme and a story have been decided, students can discuss the solution to their mystery and create clues that users will need to solve the mystery. Remind students to make some of their clues interdependent. Provide students with two or three periods to complete this first step.

Design. Once student teams have finished their puzzles, review the concepts of flowcharts and storyboards. Each clue should have its own storyboard and the flowchart should show the navigation possibilities throughout the stack. Clue cards may be linked to a central location, be accessible from every clue card, or found attached to another clue card. Discuss the design issues explained in chapter 4. If possible, view sample problem-solving stacks for additional design ideas. Provide groups with a list of design guidelines, a storyboard template (see ch. 4), and the journal entry form and project checklist available in chapters 3 and 4. Explain each form. In addition, provide groups with the storyboard, design, and mechanics rubrics available in chapter 7 and the puzzle rubric blackline master at the end of this chapter. Groups should keep these forms in a binder and complete daily journal entries.

Develop. After the students' flowchart and storyboards have been approved, teams take turns at the computer stations. If teams are not working on the computers or on their storyboards, students can be:

- Working on problem-solving puzzles provided by the teacher or brought in by other students
- Creating a record-keeping sheet for users to keep track of their notes as they attempt to solve their completed Sherlock stack
- Researching and contributing to a class book on mathematical magic tricks
- Reading and acting out a mystery on video
- Playing problem-solving games like Master Mind and chess
- Researching and reporting on famous (fictional or nonfictional) detectives
- Writing a mystery and creating puppets for its production

As students complete their multimedia projects, another team reviews the stack for problems or errors (see ch. 7). The corrected stack, along with the project's rubrics, group and self-evaluations (see ch. 7), and journal entries, is submitted to the teacher. Provide the students with at least 10 class periods on the computer to finish a 10-card stack, especially because some of the students will spend their development time creating and researching different pictures for their stack's theme. Clip art libraries should be made available to the students.

Evaluate. Following the teacher's evaluation of the project, peers need to evaluate each other's projects, too (see ch. 7), remembering that specific content may or may not be an integral part of the project. Emphasis should be placed on the clarity of information, sophistication of the puzzle, use of graphics, and overall design. For alternative evaluation forms, see the puzzle rubric and Peer Puzzle Evaluation blackline masters at the end of this chapter. Each Sherlock stack should be shared and solved by the different groups.

Summary

The possibilities for multimedia stacks are endless, and emphasis on student learning outcomes can be placed in a variety of areas. This chapter presented sample multimedia projects that focus on different areas of the curriculum and learning outcomes. It also provided a variety of ongoing activities for students not working on computers. Extension activities for the projects presented in this chapter include sharing projects over the Internet, with the school and community, and at local conferences. In addition, projects may be recorded to CD-ROMs for student distribution and archive purposes.

Blackline Masters

This chapter contains variations of several blackline masters presented in other chapters. This provides teachers with additional ideas for creating their own checklists and evaluation forms that are specific to the students projects and ability levels. Specific forms have been designed for the All About Me and Sherlock stacks. References are also made to the checklists and evaluation forms in other chapters. Blackline masters in this chapter include:

- All About Me: Flowchart—a flowchart for All About Me projects
- All About Me: Storyboard Template—an alternative storyboard layout
- All About Me: Project Checklist—a specific checklist for All About Me projects
- All About Me: Teacher Evaluation—a simplified evaluation sheet for All About Me projects
- All About Me: Peer Evaluation—a specific evaluation sheet for All About Me projects
- Introductory Puzzle—a story problem containing independent clues
- Puzzle Rubric—one way of evaluating problem-solving adventure stacks
- Peer Puzzle Evaluation—an alternative peer evaluation form for problem-solving adventures

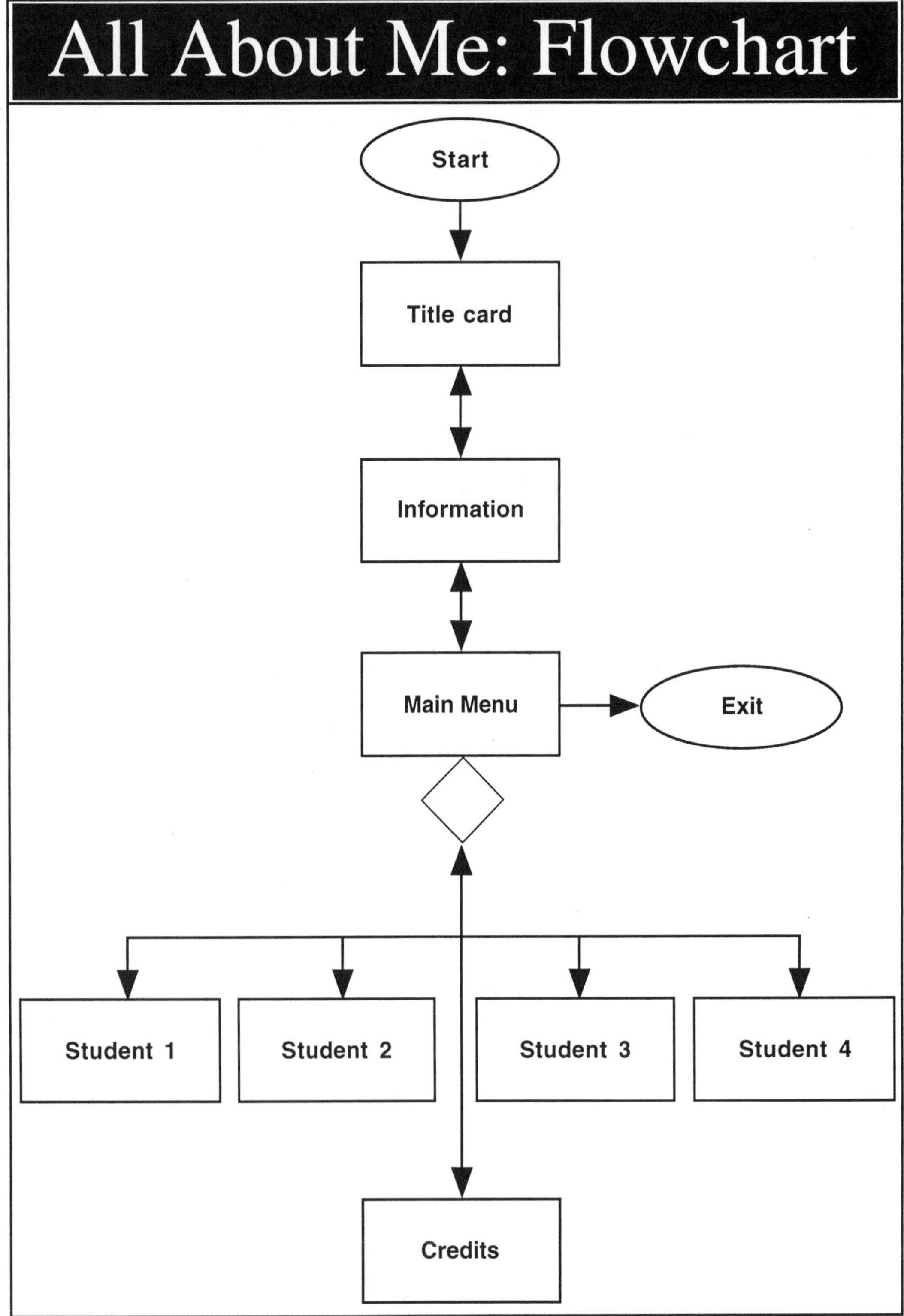
All About Me: Flowchart
Start
Title card
Information
Main Menu
Exit
Student 1
Student 2
Student 3
Student 4
Credits

All About Me: Storyboard Template

Background: ____________________

Border: ____________________

Pictures: ____________________

	Font	Size	Style	Justification	Color
Title					
Text					

Button	Go to	Transition	Other

All About Me: Project Checklist

Team Name ____________________

Before developing your project at the computer, complete the following:

☐ Flowchart ☐ Storyboards

Make sure your project has:

☐ A minimum of _____ pages (or cards).

☐ A maximum of _____ pages (or cards).

☐ A Title page (or card).

☐ An Information page (or card).

☐ A Main Menu.

☐ A page (or card) with a paragraph description for each member in your group.

☐ A Credits page (or card).

☐ Appropriate navigation options.

☐ Text that is easy to read and is accurate.

☐ Complete sentences with correct punctuation, grammar, and spelling.

☐ The assigned media requirements:

_____ Clip art

_____ Original drawings (use of paint tools)

_____ Audio

☐ Other: ____________________

All About Me: Teacher Evaluation

	1 inc.	2 poor	3 fair	4 good	5 excellent
Students' project matches their flowchart and storyboards.					
Project contains paragraphs about each team member.					
Content is free of spelling, grammar, and punctuation errors.					
Assigned media elements have been successfully incorporated into the project.					
Navigation buttons function correctly.					
Students followed design guidelines presented in class.					
Students kept daily journal entries.					
	Total ______				

All About Me: Peer Evaluation

Name of group being reviewed: ______________________________

Project title: ______________________________

Reviewed by: ______________________________

What are the strengths of this stack?

How might the presentation of information be improved?

What improvements in the design would you suggest?

On a scale of 1 to 5 (5 being the highest), how would you rate this project? Why?

Introductory Puzzle

Help Mr. Alfonzo calculate the average number of pages read in one week by a group of his students: Fred, Ethel, Lucy, Ricky, Wilma, and Betty.

Both Fred and Ethel read two books with 70 pages each. In addition, Fred read a 20-page book about frogs.

Lucy read the same frog book as Fred, the same cat book as Barney, and half of the dog book that Ricky read.

Ricky read a 20-page book about dogs.

Barney read a 60-page book about cats and two 30-page books.

Both Wilma and Betty read the same books as Ethel.

Answer: 115 pages. [Fred: (2x70) + 20 = 160; Ethel: 2x70 = 140; Lucy: 20 + 60 + (20÷2) = 90; Ricky: 20; Wilma: 140; Betty: 140] Divide total pages by 6.

Extension Activities:

- Calculate each student's average number of pages read in one week.
- Determine the range, mode, and medium of the group. Compare and contrast this to the group mean.
- Track and calculate the average number of pages read in one week by individuals and the class. Compare this with other classes and age groups.
- Create a bar graph that illustrates the favorite genre of the class. Compare this with other classes and age groups.

Puzzle Rubric

	1 inc.	2 poor	3 fair	4 good	5 excellent
The project presented users with the goal(s) and objectives of the puzzle.					
The group used interdependent clues.					
The group included all of the information necessary to solve the puzzle.					
The puzzle challenged the user's thinking skills (it was not overly simplistic).					
It was easy to navigate through the puzzle.					
The design of the project was appealing.					
	Total ______				

Peer Puzzle Evaluation

Name of group being reviewed: ______________________________

Project title: ______________________________

Reviewed by: ______________________________

What are the strengths of this stack?

How might the presentation of information be improved?

Explain why you were able or unable to solve the puzzle.

On a scale of 1 to 5 (5 being the highest), how would you rate this project? Explain your answer.

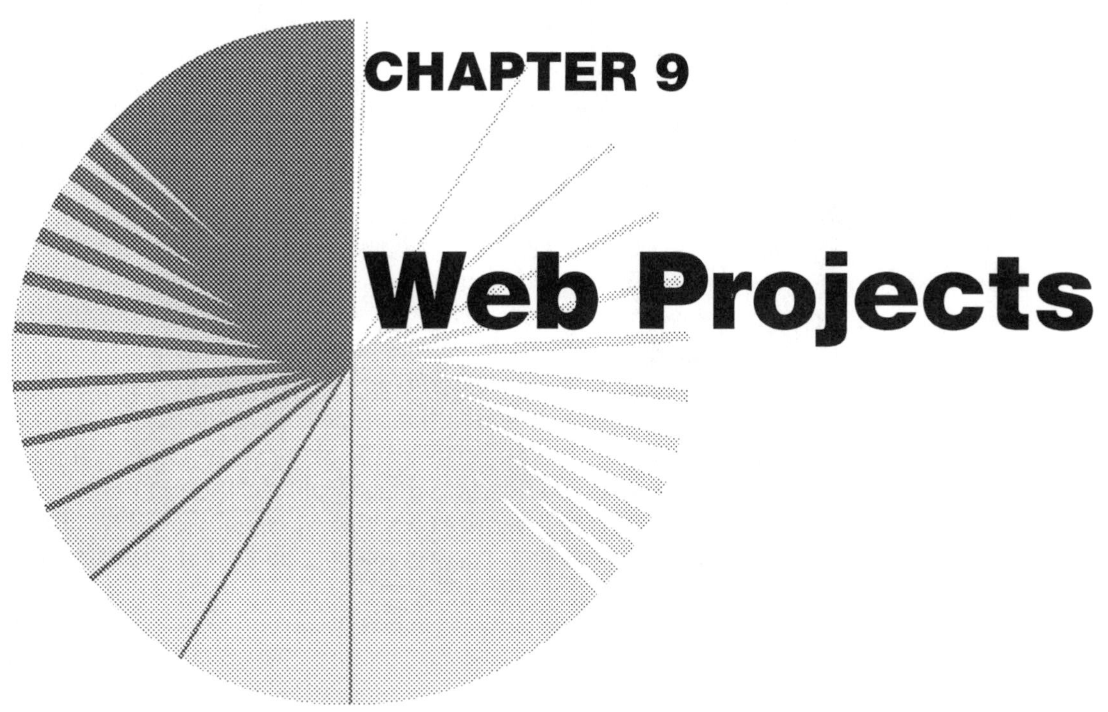

CHAPTER 9

Web Projects

A Scenario

The students in Mr. Little's class had been using the Web to gather information all year. They found it particularly helpful during the research phase of their multimedia projects. It seemed that there was up-to-date information on just about everything on the Web! For the next multimedia project, Mr. Little wanted his students to use the Web to deliver their projects. This time, their final products would be available to others all over the world.

The first step was to learn a little HTML (the language of the Web). Mr. Little showed his students some sites on the Web that provided HTML tutorials, and they found that it was very easy to learn a few of the commands and to type them into the text editor. Even linking to other Web pages and graphics was very easy.

As the students worked through the DDD-E process, they were glad that they understood the basics of design and evaluation. Although they worked hard on all of their projects throughout the year, this one seemed even more important, because it would have a worldwide audience.

When the students finished their projects, they added their school's e-mail address for feedback in the footer of each page. The excitement they felt when messages started coming in from all over the world was overwhelming!

Overview

The World Wide Web is a powerful resource for K-12 education. Never before has the educational community had such an inexpensive, easily accessible method of communicating and distributing information. It opens doors to multicultural education, establishes real-world learning experiences, promotes higher order thinking skills, and helps increase motivation and writing skills (Barron and Ivers 1996).

The Web offers a wonderful environment for students to create and publish multimedia projects. These projects may be placed on an intranet (for internal viewing only), or they can be placed on the Internet (for the whole world to see). In either case, the development of the projects serves worthwhile learning objectives and challenges the students to share their projects with others.

There are many reasons for students to create Web pages and Web sites. In addition to sharing their artwork and stories with other schools, students can collect data for original research projects and produce reports that are linked to authentic, dynamic information sources. They can also post school news for the community; establish on-line homework assignment centers; create subject guides with links to the Internet; or produce interactive lessons.

The projects outlined in this chapter are examples of school-based activities that involve Web-based development. The first project centers around a personal home page for students. In this project, they can concentrate on the development process rather than on obtaining the content. The second project (School Newsletter) and third project (Our Town) require that the students interact with others to acquire the information needed.

The Web is also a great place for students to publish reports on a variety of topics that they can share. By creating a Web-based report, they can include links to many of the resources available at other sites. The "Sailing the Internet with Magellan" project is an example of a report that incorporates many sites, but also includes original material developed by student groups to synthesize the information.

The final project in this chapter focuses on creating instructional materials to be distributed on the Web. Similar to interactions designed in hypermedia programs, students can provide information on a Web page and then embed questions to test the knowledge of the users. The complexity of the interactions and the design may vary tremendously. Some of the instructional Web sites listed in table 9.2 can provide further examples.

Sample Projects for Web-Based Development

The following projects can be created with tools ranging from simple text editors (such as NotePad or SimpleText) to sophisticated Web creation programs (such as FrontPage or PageMill). Teachers should choose the most appropriate tool for their students and ensure that their students are familiar with the tool before engaging in the project (see ch. 6 for more information on Web authoring tools).

The sample projects can be designed and developed by individual students or by groups of up to six students. In all cases, it is important to maintain a thorough review cycle before uploading the pages, particularly if they will be accessible through the Internet and the Web.

My Personal Home Page

Lesson Description: This project challenges students to create a personal home page that focuses on their interests. It is an appropriate introductory project for students because they can focus on the development process rather than having to research a new topic.

Figure 9.1 My Personal Home Page sample

The content of the project is personal information about the students' interests. A word of caution: If the projects will be accessible on the Internet (as opposed to an intranet), you must caution the students about providing personal contact information. In most cases, it is not wise to include a student's picture, home address, phone number, or any other information that someone could use to contact the student. Instead, recommend that the students focus on their interests and their projects, such as artwork they have created, songs they have composed, or Web sites they like to visit (see fig. 9.1).

Decide. Begin the assignment by explaining to the students why some personal information should not be included in Web pages. Emphasize that Web pages are open to millions of people on the Internet, and that it is important for students to protect their privacy. Explain that placing their pictures and home addresses on the Web would be similar to "talking to strangers," or handing out flyers with personal information at the shopping mall.

Continue the discussion by brainstorming the types of information that students might want to share on their personal pages. Ask each group to generate at least 20 ideas of possible content items. Share these items with the class and develop a list of potential topics for the pages. Items could include: sports activities, stories or research papers the students have written, original artwork or music, information about their pets, links to favorite Web sites, class projects, community information, vacation stories, and so on.

Design. Begin the design process by showing the students examples of good and poor Web page design. Discuss general design issues (such as contrasting colors, chunking information, etc.) and design issues that are specific to the Web. Remind the students that bandwidth (speed) is a major consideration for Web pages, so they must try to make their graphics as small (in file size) as possible and include audio or video only when it is essential. Following the discussion, provide students with a list of design guidelines for the Web (see the Web Design Guidelines blackline master included with this chapter).

During the next work period, students should develop their flowcharts and storyboards for the project. Flowcharts are particularly important because of the number of hyperlinks on most Web pages. Remind the students to provide an easy-to-use structure for their pages. Also, they should provide information about links so that users will understand where they are branching and why. A storyboard template is provided at the end of chapter 4 for Web projects. It should be modified as necessary to reflect the particular components involved in specific projects.

Develop. After the students' storyboards have been approved, students can begin producing the media elements for their projects. There are many ways to produce the HTML required for Web pages (see ch. 5 for more information). Demonstrate the tools that are available for your students. If students are not working on the computers or on their storyboards, they can be:

- Conducting research about their ancestry
- Drawing pictures that they can scan into the computer for graphics on their pages
- Taking pictures of their school or classrooms
- Gathering information about Web sites from books and magazines
- Researching their hobbies or areas of interest

As students complete their pages, another team should review the pages for consistency, ease of use, and operational errors. The corrected pages, along with the project's rubrics, group and self-evaluations (see ch. 7), and journal entries, are submitted to the teacher. All Web pages should be thoroughly reviewed by the teacher or other adults prior to being uploaded to a Web server.

Evaluate. In addition to the teacher's evaluation and the peer evaluations, students should be encouraged to solicit feedback from others via an e-mail address on the Web page. Student projects can be linked to a central class menu from which others can access the personal pages. Explain that upkeep and maintenance are important issues for Web pages. Plan to revisit the project a couple of weeks later and allow time for the students to check their external links to see if they are still active.

School Newsletter

Lesson Description: The School Newsletter project is an extension of the Personal Home Pages, in that it includes information about the entire student body rather than just individual students. This project is ideal

Site	Address
Classroom Connect: ClassroomWeb	http://www.classroom.net/classweb/
Hot List of K-12 Schools on Net	http://www.sendit.nodak.edu/k12/
K-12+ Servers	http://www.tenet.edu/education/main.html
KidPub	http://www.kidpub.org/kidpub
Web66 Schools Registry	http://web66.coled.umn.edu/Schools.html
Yahoo K-12 Schools	http://www.yahoo.com/Regional/Countries/United_States/Education/K_12/

Table 9.1 School Web sites

for student groups. Each group can be assigned one particular aspect of student life, such as sports, clubs, drama, scheduling, faculty profiles, upcoming events, and so on.

The on-line school newsletter can serve as a supplement to a print newsletter, or it can be developed completely separately. If the students are in a journalism course, or if the school newspaper is interested in establishing an on-line presence, the project can serve as an extension and integration of other school activities. If there is already an on-line newspaper at your school, this project can have a narrower focus, such as a class newsletter rather than a school newsletter.

Decide. As a class, brainstorm potential topics that could be included in an on-line newsletter. Allow time for the students to investigate resources available at the school, such as statistics for sports, electronic files of school history, photographs, or other archival information.

Assign student teams that will focus on one particular aspect of student life. Allow plenty of time for the students to review other school Web sites and investigate the format of other on-line newspapers. Ask them to visit the sites listed in table 9.1, which provide links to K-12 schools on the Web.

Design. Discuss the overall flow of the lesson with the entire class. Emphasize the need for a consistent interface for the entire on-line newsletter, as well as the need for each section to be unique. Discuss navigation options and whether the project should incorporate frames or tables. Do the students need basic banners or icons to appear on each page? Can they incorporate the school colors or the school mascot? How can they assure that each student group receives equal exposure?

Remind the students that they must be careful not to include personal information (such as photos or home addresses) about individual students. Also, emphasize the need to involve the school's administrators in the review cycle.

Develop. After the students' flowchart and storyboards have been approved, teams take turns at the computer stations (see ch. 3). Other activities that the students can work on include:

- Reviewing hard-copy newsletters from the school
- Interviewing administrators, teachers, and students for the newsletter
- Taking pictures of the school and community
- Reviewing films from sports events for possible inclusion in the project

- Recording greetings, speeches, and other narratives for the project
- Experimenting with alternate ways to display the statistics

EVALUATE. As students complete their portion of the on-line newsletter, another team reviews the pages for problems or errors. Be sure to include as many administrators, teachers, coaches, and students as possible in the review cycle. All content that relates to a particular club or organization should be authorized by the club's president and faculty sponsor before being uploaded to the Internet or intranet.

Our Town

Lesson Description: This project focuses on research, interactions with community members, and students' ability to organize and interpret collected information. Students are required to create a Web site for the community that includes links to local interest groups, information of interest to tourists, and documents related to community concerns. If possible, the project should include local field trips to collect photographs, video, and audio samples that reflect the flavor of the community and focus on its unique attributes.

DECIDE. As a class, discuss the community and possible topics for a Web site. Brainstorm in small groups to generate as many ideas as possible for consideration. Allow students time to search on the Web for sites within the local area that already have Web pages. Discuss criteria for links that should be established. For example, should the school link only to nonprofit institutions? Should the project include local churches? Are there sites at each of the local schools? What might a potential tourist want to find out about the community?

After the students have compiled a list of existing sites, have the class brainstorm about the pieces (pages) that are missing. For example, if a local tourist attraction does not have a Web page, should the class produce one for it? If some churches have Web pages and others do not, should the students create a list of churches with contact information?

As the students conduct their field research, they should ask permission to record, video, or photograph anyone whom they want to include on the Web page. If existing graphics are used, they should seek permission to scan the images. Students can keep track of their sources using the Bibliography sheet in chapter 3. At frequent intervals, review the entire project with the class, ensuring that it does not grow too large.

DESIGN. Allow time for the students to review the design of other community Web sites. They should note the elements included, the HTML features used, and the transfer time required. Each group should work with the agreed-upon templates so that navigation is consistent from one part of the program to another. Be sure that all links to other sites include information that is appropriate for all family members.

DEVELOP. Teams can alternate between data collection and media production and the creation of their Web pages. The focus should be on community involvement and focus. If a team is waiting for a computer, team members can be:

- Creating a travel brochure for tourists
- Researching the history of the town

- Interviewing senior community members about the evolution of the community
- Taking pictures of community groups and historical sites
- Recording unique sounds and videos of the community
- Interviewing the mayor or other elected officials

EVALUATE. As students complete their Web pages, the projects should be reviewed by the teacher, other students, the community members who were involved, and the administration. It is very important that each page be thoroughly reviewed before it is uploaded to the Internet. In addition, the copyright releases for all media elements should be documented and filed for future reference.

Sailing Through the Internet: A Research Project About Ferdinand Magellan

Lesson Description: This research project encourages students to use resources on the Internet as integral parts of the report. The project requires that students locate relevant information on the Internet about a particular topic. They must also integrate the resources into a report with links at appropriate places throughout the report. Before assigning such a project, teachers should conduct Internet searches to verify that appropriate material exists for the topic areas assigned. It is also recommended that Internet filters (such as Net Nanny) be used to prevent students from accessing inappropriate information as they conduct their searches. The example focuses on a report on Ferdinand Magellan (see fig. 9.2). Other relevant topics might be the rain forest, medical research, a U.S. president, well-known authors or musicians, or an historical topic.

DECIDE. Provide an overview of the project's goals. Assign teams and allow the students to select a topic from a prepared list. If the topic is exploration, the topic list may include Ferdinand Magellan, Christopher Columbus, Ponce de León, Marco Polo, and others. As a class, brainstorm what students already know about the explorer and what they need to know (see the KWL Knowledge Chart in ch. 3). For example, they may know that these persons are famous explorers, but not know the exact dates or routes of their explorations. Next, have the students speculate about the information they might find about the explorers on the Web. They can also speculate about how the information was added to the Internet and by whom. For example, if the research centers around contemporary artists, they may have developed their own personal home pages. If the research centers around a historical character (such as Magellan), someone else must have been responsible for creating the resource.

As students conduct their searches, emphasize that they must attempt to ascertain the validity and accuracy of the content. Ask them to fill out a Fact or Fiction sheet (see the blackline master at the end of this chapter) when they are analyzing the reliability of the sources.

DESIGN. Students may take two or three class periods researching their specific topic, depending on the number of Internet connections available for student use. If connections are limited, require the students to print potential sites (along with the URL) so that they can read and evaluate the information off-line.

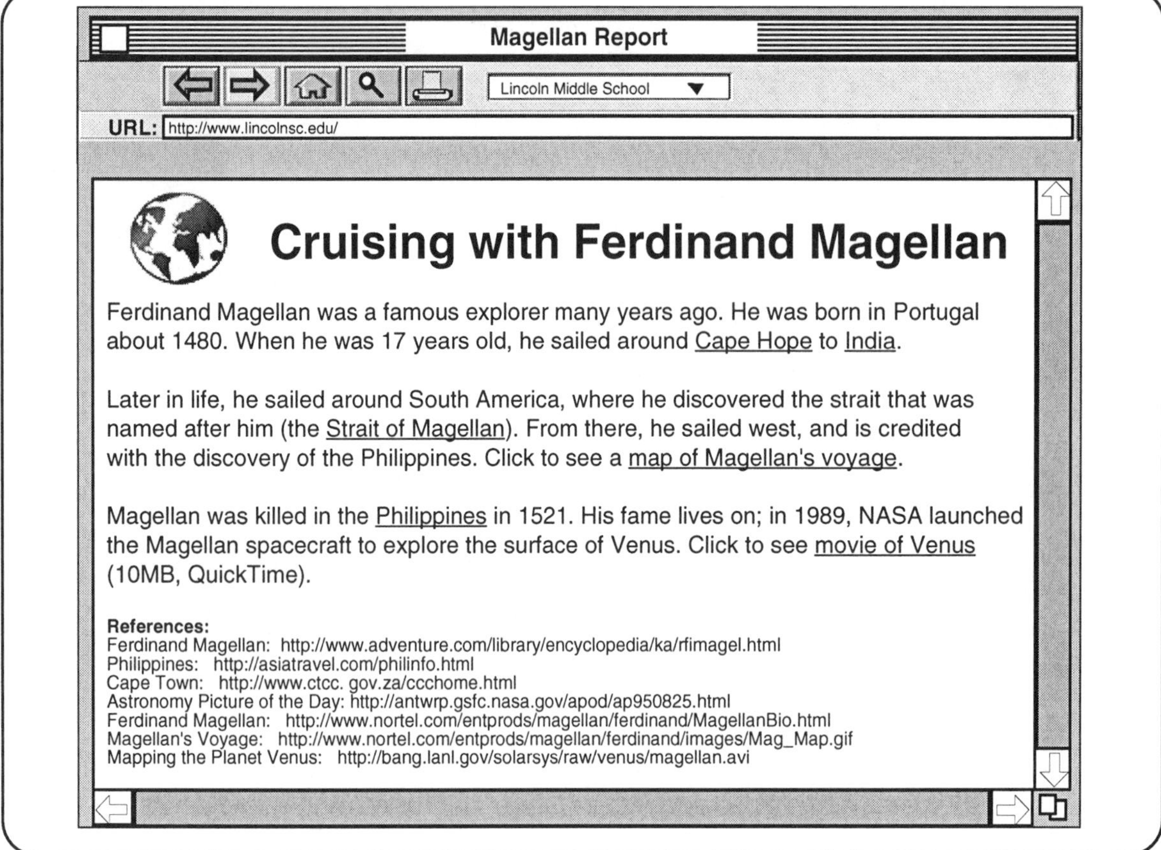

Figure 9.2 Ferdinand Magellan report

As students complete their research, they should write the reports, linking to the Web at appropriate places. Flowcharts and storyboards are extremely important to help students map out their ideas and provide a structure for their reports.

Discuss the use of media elements in the projects. Point out that graphics may be slow to load through the Web. Students should incorporate only graphics that are pertinent to the project (such as a map of exploration). Provide copies of the Web design guidelines and a storyboard template.

Remind students of copyright restrictions. Publishing on the Web is different from producing a multimedia project that will be used only within the classroom. All graphics, music, text, and video should be original or should be part of the public domain. If students locate a graphic or other media elements on the Web, they should read the copyright statements to make sure that they can place that element on a Web page that will be accessible through the Internet.

Develop. After the students' flowchart and storyboards have been approved, teams take turns at the computer stations (see ch. 3 for a computer schedule). If teams are not working on the computers or on their storyboards, students can be:

- Conducting research about the topic in textbooks, videos, and encyclopedias to continue to verify the content found on the Web

- Building a model of Magellan's ship with paper or cardboard
- Charting Magellan's journeys on a contemporary world map
- Writing a comparison of Magellan's journey to that of John Glenn

As students complete their Web-based reports, another group reviews the report. If some of the links do not work, the reviewers should note them so that they can be corrected. If possible, student review teams should also note any graphics or media elements that take too long to download. The content of the report should be original and should access other resources as supporting documentation.

Evaluate. Follow the general procedure for project evaluations (teacher evaluation, peer evaluation, etc.). If the projects are going to be uploaded to a Web server (and therefore accessible throughout the world), an additional review/revision cycle may be necessary. After the teacher has noted changes, students should revise the content as necessary before uploading the projects to the server. All class reports can be linked via a class page that explains the project and the parameters.

A Lesson in Life

Lesson Description: After your students master the basics of designing and developing a Web site with HTML and other tools, they can focus on more advanced interactions on the Web. There are various programs and techniques that can produce interactions, from simple HTML links to Java, JavaScript, and ActiveX programs. Some authoring tools, including HyperStudio and Authorware, also have plug-ins that allow these programs to run on the Web.

This project focuses on the students' ability to design a lesson that teaches about a concept they are currently studying. Interactions should be included whereby users can test their knowledge of the subject and receive meaningful feedback.

Decide. Before beginning the project, demonstrate several Web sites that are designed to deliver instruction. Table 9.2 provides many examples of on-line courses. Prior to the demonstrations, review the sites and show the students examples based on student age, site content, and programming expertise required.

Assign student teams as described in previous chapters. As a class, generate a list of possible topics about life that could be taught on the Internet. The topics could include such areas as AIDS, life management skills, health, sex education, reproduction, air quality, and so on. Allow plenty of time for the students to generate possible topics and areas of investigation.

Demonstrate techniques for incorporating interaction on the Web. Discuss the advantages of delivering Web-based education, including access to a worldwide audience, ease of distribution, and ease of updates and maintenance. Allow the students to work through several sites on the Internet that deliver instruction.

Design. After each group has selected or been assigned a topic, the groups can begin developing the flowcharts and storyboards. Most of this project should take place within a confined set of Web pages, without branches to external sites. Caution the students to carefully flowchart the lesson so that there are no endless loops or frustrating branches.

Site	Address	Content
Sticky Situations	http://www.iconos.com	Glue and adhesives
Draw and Color with Uncle Fred	http://www.unclefred.com	Lessons in drawing cartoons
Anatomy of an Eye	http://www.netscape.com/comprod/products/navigator/version_2.0/frames/eye/index.html	Tutorial about eyes
Gamelan	http://www.gamelan.com	Educational programs using Java
HTML Tutorial	http://www.coedu.usf.edu/inst_tech/publications/html/	Interactive HTML primer
Teacher's Guide to the Holocaust	http://fcit.coedu.usf.edu/holocaust/	Resources for Holocaust education
New Technologies	http://www.coedu.usf.edu/inst_tech/publications	Tutorial on videodiscs, CD-ROM, QuickTime, Photo-CD
School Networks	http://fcit.coedu.usf.edu/network/	Tutorial on installing a school network
Newton's Apple	http://ericir.syr.edu/Projects/Newton/	Antibiotics, brain, electricity, floods, gravity, earthquakes, etc.
Netscape Frames	http://www.newbie.net/frames	Advanced features in Netscape
Tutorial Gateway	http://www.civeng.carleton.ca/~nholtz/tut/doc/doc.html	Instructions for creating interactive lessons on the World Wide Web

Table 9.2 Instructional sites on the Web

After the storyboards are complete, the teacher should review them carefully to make sure the content is chunked and presented in a logical manner. Students should be encouraged to create short pages that are easy to navigate.

Develop. After the students' flowchart and storyboards have been approved, teams take turns at the computer stations. If teams are not working at a computer, they can be involved in the following activities:

- Reviewing books and articles about the latest developments in Web authoring tools
- Creating a brochure or other advertisement that discusses the benefits of their project
- Taking pictures or drawing graphics that can be incorporated into their lesson
- Developing off-line support materials for the project

Evaluate. Following the reviews and evaluations by the teacher and peers, the students should be encouraged to pilot test their programs with other classes. The classes may be within the same school or located elsewhere in the world. After the program has been thoroughly tested, it can be uploaded to the Internet. Students should be encouraged to include e-mail feedback forms on the program to solicit responses from other students and teachers who implement the lesson.

Summary

The possibilities for multimedia projects on the Web include informational pages, instructional sites, and worldwide research. This chapter presented sample Web projects focusing on students, schools, local communities, and instruction. As the Web continues to proliferate in our homes and schools, the development of Web-based programs will become an increasingly important tool for students.

Blackline Masters

The Web is an invaluable resource for sharing and researching information. This chapter described several activities and two blackline masters for assisting students with their Web projects. Blackline masters in this chapter include:

- Web Design Guidelines—a list of guidelines specific to Web projects
- Fact or Fiction—a means to records and analyze information on the Web

References

Barron, A., and K. Ivers. 1996. *The Internet and instruction: Activities and ideas.* Englewood, CO: Libraries Unlimited, Inc.

Web Design Guidelines

The following guidelines can help to make your Web pages more user-friendly for the visitors to your site.

General

Carefully plan your pages before you create them.
Place a descriptive title on the top of all pages.
Include the date of the last revision on the pages.
Limit the length of Web pages to three screens.
Test the pages with several different browsers and computers.
Check all pages for correct spelling and grammar.

Graphics

Make sure the graphics are relevant to the page.
Limit the file size of the graphics to less than 30K each.
Limit the number of graphics on each page.
Use GIF graphics for line drawings and simple graphics.
Use JPG graphics for photographs.
Limit the width of graphics to less than 470 pixels.

Text

Make sure there is high contrast between background and text.
Limit the length of text lines.
Include blank space between paragraphs.
Limit the use of blinking text.

Media: Audio and Video

Use audio and video only when necessary.
Include information about audio and video file sizes.
Include information about format (wav, avi, quicktime, etc.)

Fact or Fiction

Because anyone can create a Web page, it is important to try to determine if the information presented there is true or not. Fill out this form for Web sites that you are including in your project.

Web Site #1

Title of Site ______________________________

Address (URL) ______________________________

Author ______________________________

Date last modified ______________________________

Clues that help to determine if the information is Fact or Fiction

____

Web Site #2

Title of Site ______________________________

Address (URL) ______________________________

Author ______________________________

Date last modified ______________________________

Clues that help to determine if the information is Fact or Fiction

____

Web Site #3

Title of Site ______________________________

Address (URL) ______________________________

Author ______________________________

Date last modified ______________________________

Clues that help to determine if the information is Fact or Fiction

____

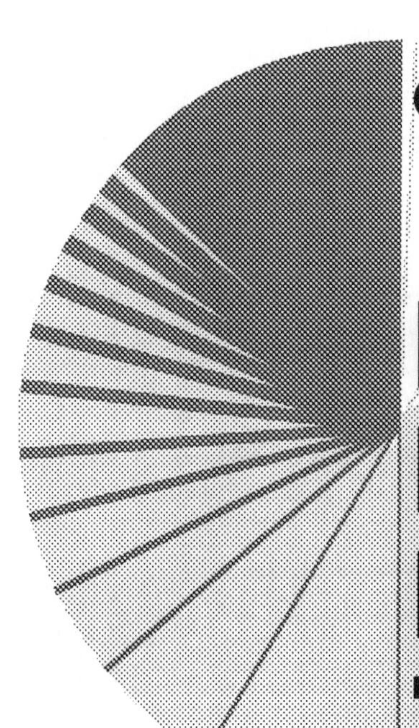

CHAPTER 10

Multimedia Projects: Presentation Tools

A Scenario

The students in Mrs. Lu's class were about to give their class presentations on famous persons in history. Mrs. Lu had placed the students into groups of four and let each group decide on a famous person. Students were to be graded on their group skills, organization and presentation skills, and ability to speak in front of an audience. Mrs. Lu had provided student groups with the appropriate rubrics when the assignment was introduced and had explained the purpose of the groups' daily journal entries. The students spent two weeks researching and organizing information for their presentations. Now they were ready to present their research using PowerPoint, a presentation tool that Mrs. Lu had received through a grant from Microsoft.

Patsy, Marilyn, Scott, and Sarah were the first presenters. Patsy and Marilyn had had little experience speaking in front of a group, but Scott and Sarah had assured them that they would do well. They had practiced together several times before today's big event. Both Patsy and Marilyn appreciated the opportunity to use a presentation program to assist them with their parts of the presentation. The bulleted text helped them to organize their thoughts, and the graphics, animation, and video segments seemed to make the presentation much more interesting than just standing up in front of the class and talking.

Scott started the group's presentation. Music captured the audience's attention and the title of the project dissolved in: "The Secret of Houdini." The group had decided to research and present the life of the famous magician, Harry Houdini. Not only did they think the audience would find Houdini interesting, but Scott and Sarah's hobby was magic. Sarah had been performing at children's birthday parties since she was 10 years old, and Scott worked part-time in his dad's magic and costume shop. Patsy and Marilyn were intrigued with the idea and knew some great media effects to tie into the theme of magic.

Marilyn followed Scott. She used the presentation screens to help her focus and explain how Houdini rose to stardom. The presentation screens included a video segment and photographs of Houdini's daring escapes. Marilyn felt confident about her part of the presentation. She appreciated the support of her teammates and the presentation tool.

Patsy followed Marilyn. She had helped the team design animations to illustrate how Houdini exposed psychic frauds. The group continued to captivate the audience. Sarah concluded the presentation, and the group took its well-deserved applause.

Mrs. Lu applauded the group as well, and she commended the students' teamwork, content presentation, and speaking skills. Patsy, Marilyn, Scott, and Sarah all beamed with contentment, even as they attributed their success to planning and practice. Patsy and Marilyn breathed deep sighs of relief, but they now felt confident that they could speak effectively in front of a group.

Overview

Designing and presenting multimedia projects provide students with invaluable real-world learning experiences; presentation and public speaking skills are necessary in many occupations. Students learn to work together, apply their research skills, plan and organize content, select appropriate media and layouts, and deliver professional-looking presentations.

Although professional-looking presentations can be created with authoring and Web tools, there are several tools on the market especially designed for creating large group presentations. These include Microsoft PowerPoint, Adobe Persuasion, and Action by Macromedia (see ch. 6). Some integrated packages, such as the later versions of Microsoft Works, also have slide show options for creating presentations. Most presentation programs give the option of using predesigned templates. Some programs also have "wizards" or other guides that prompt users through the design process.

This chapter presents several ideas for multimedia projects that can be created with presentation tools. A lesson description, the DDD-E process, and ideas for concurrent activities are provided for each project.

Sample Projects

The following projects can be created with most presentation tools. Teachers should choose the most appropriate tool for their students and ensure that their students are familiar with the tool before engaging in the project. The sample projects describe classrooms with 4 computers and 32 students; however, adjustments can be made to meet other conditions. Design teams consist of 4 students. See chapter 3 for computer scheduling options.

Persuasive Officials

Lesson Description: The goal of this lesson is to engage upper-grade students in persuasive speaking. Each group of students is assigned a different form of government. As part of their research assignment, student groups must try to persuade classmates that their assigned government is the best. For example, students researching democracy would create a presentation highlighting what they believe are its benefits. Audience members would have the chance to ask questions and debate the presented issues. Other topics for persuasive speaking include school rules, laws, and so on. For younger students, children may try to persuade one another of Goldilock's guilt or innocence in trespassing, the best pet, and so forth.

DECIDE. As a class, inquire what students know about the different forms of government that exist in the world (use the KWL Knowledge Chart in ch. 3). Ask students what they know about their own government and what makes it different from others. Complete the second column of the KWL Knowledge Chart by asking students what they would like to know about the different forms of government.

Introduce the project by assigning students to teams as described in previous chapters. Explain that groups will randomly choose a form of government to study and share with the class. As part of the assignment, explain that they will be required to present an overview and the benefits of their form of government via a presentation tool. Continue to explain that the purpose of the presentation is to persuade classmates that their form of government is the best. Groups must be prepared to answer questions and to debate the presented issues. As a group, design an evaluation form for the presentation. For an example, see the Persuasive Presentation Evaluation blackline master at the end of this chapter.

Provide student groups with the opportunity to brainstorm and research topics about their form of government. Check their progress and Bibliography sheets (see ch. 3) before letting them move on to the DESIGN phase.

DESIGN. After the students' research has been approved, provide class time for the creation of flowcharts and storyboards. To expedite the process, teachers may provide the students with a standardized template (see fig. 10.1). A limit of 15 screens could be imposed, if desired. Remind students of the purpose of bulleted text and the printout options available in the presentation tool.

DEVELOP. After the students' flowchart and storyboards have been approved, teams take turns at the computer stations (see ch. 3 for a computer schedule). If teams are not working on the computers or on their storyboards, students can be:

- Conducting additional research about their form of government
- Locating and charting where in the world their form of government exists
- Creating a travel brochure to a place with their form of government
- Comparing and contrasting their assigned form of government with other governments

Team members should review and practice their presentation before presenting it to the class.

EVALUATE. Teachers and students use the evaluation form created during the DECIDE phase of the project. Students may be evaluated on the effectiveness of their presentation, the organization and structure of their presentation, the content and accuracy of their presentation,

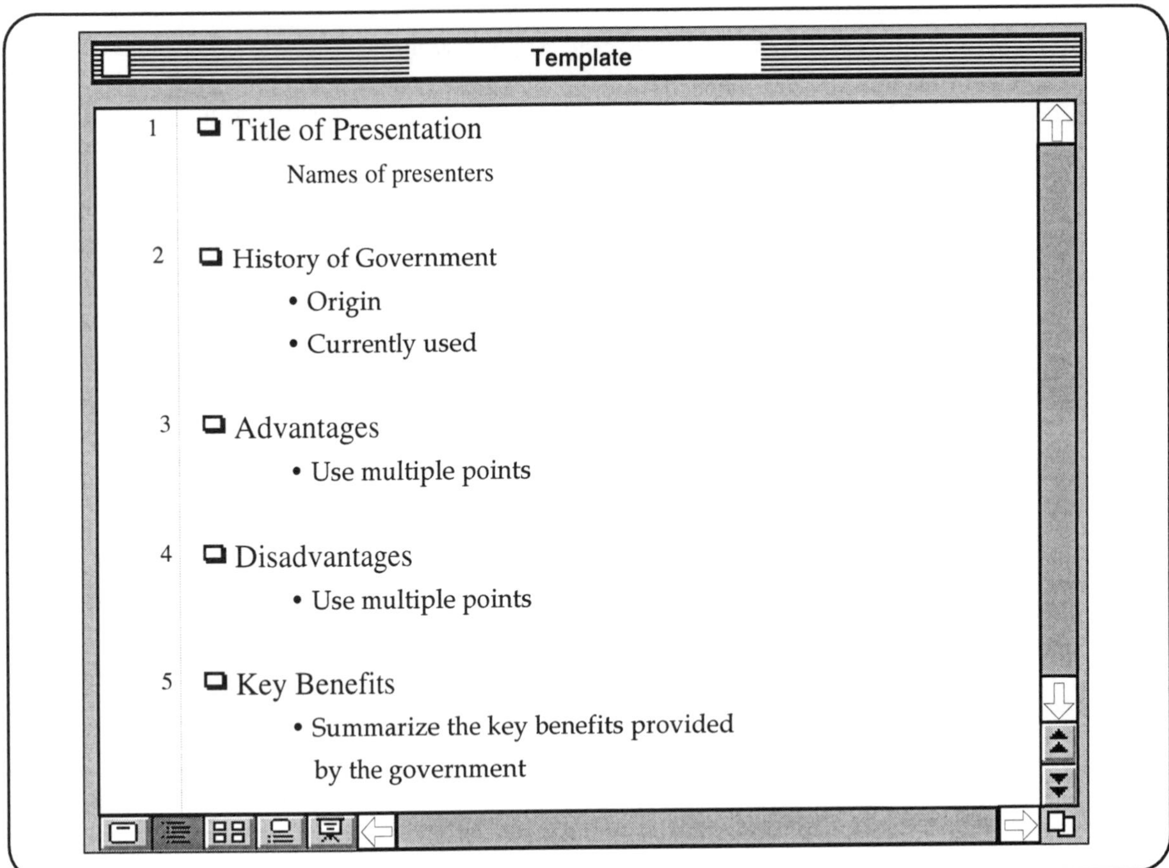

Figure 10.1 Sample template

their speaking skills, and so on. The evaluations are collected and averaged by the teacher. Students may also choose to conduct self- and intragroup evaluations (see ch. 7).

Famous People in History

Lesson Description: The goal of this lesson is to engage students in an informative presentation about a famous person in history. Student groups have the opportunity to choose a famous person and to share their findings with the class. Media elements can be added to the presentations to highlight certain aspects of the famous person. For example, if students choose to do a presentation on Scott Joplin, music can be added to demonstrate his work. Or, if Neil Armstrong were chosen, students might opt to include an audio segment of his first words on the moon. In any case, the goal of the presentation should be to inform viewers about a particular person in history. Presentations should be clear, well-organized, and interesting.

Decide. Assign student teams as described in previous chapters. Ask what makes a person famous. Students may discuss current celebrities. Ask them what makes these people different from others, or debate whether they are really different. Discuss how celebrities or famous people of today compare with famous people of yesterday. Inquire what made people in history famous.

Following this discussion, groups decide on a famous historical person to research and present to the class. Ensure that each group chooses a different person. After their selection is approved, students conduct research on the person they have chosen. Evaluate their research before letting students continue the DESIGN phase.

DESIGN. Students need to examine their research findings and organize the information for their presentation. Make sure students understand the importance of flowcharts and storyboards. Provide groups with a list of design guidelines, a presentation storyboard template (see ch. 4), and the journal entry form and project checklist. Explain each form. In addition, provide groups with the storyboard, design, content, and mechanics rubrics available in chapter 7. Groups should keep these forms in a binder. Multiple copies of the journal entry form and the bibliography form should be available. Remind students of the purpose of bulleted text and the printout options available in the presentation tool (see ch. 6). Teachers may choose to set a minimum and maximum number of screens in the presentation.

DEVELOP. After the students' flowchart and storyboards have been approved, teams take turns at the computer stations. If teams are not working on the computers or on their storyboards, students can be:

- Creating a Venn diagram that compares the life of their famous person to their own lives
- Designing a booklet about the career of their famous person
- Drawing a portrait of their famous person
- Creating a timeline of their famous person's life

EVALUATE. Peers and the teacher can evaluate group presentations by using the Content, Mechanics, and Presentation rubrics in chapter 7. The students receive a group grade based on combined scores. Students receive an individual grade based on their group, self-, and intragroup evaluations.

Scientific Follow-Up

Lesson Description: The goal of this lesson is to engage students in the reporting of their scientific findings, providing them with a real-world experience.

Following small-group science experiments, organize student groups into design teams to present their findings to the full class. Inquire how they think such presentations might relate to real life. Discuss the importance and purpose of presentations in the business world, in the scientific community, and in education.

DECIDE. In the DECIDE phase, student groups must decide how best to represent and discuss their findings by reexaming their data and methods. Students should organize their ideas with a planning sheet (see ch. 4) before continuing to the DESIGN phase.

DESIGN. Depending on the experiment, students may want to incorporate a variety of media (e.g., charts, photos, animations, etc.) into their presentations to illustrate their methods and findings (see fig. 10.2).

Make sure students understand the importance of flowcharts and storyboards. Provide groups with a list of design guidelines, a presentation storyboard template (see ch. 4), and the journal entry form and project checklist available in chapters 3 and 4. Explain each form. In addition, provide groups with the storyboard, presentation design, content, and mechanics rubrics available in chapter 7. Remind students

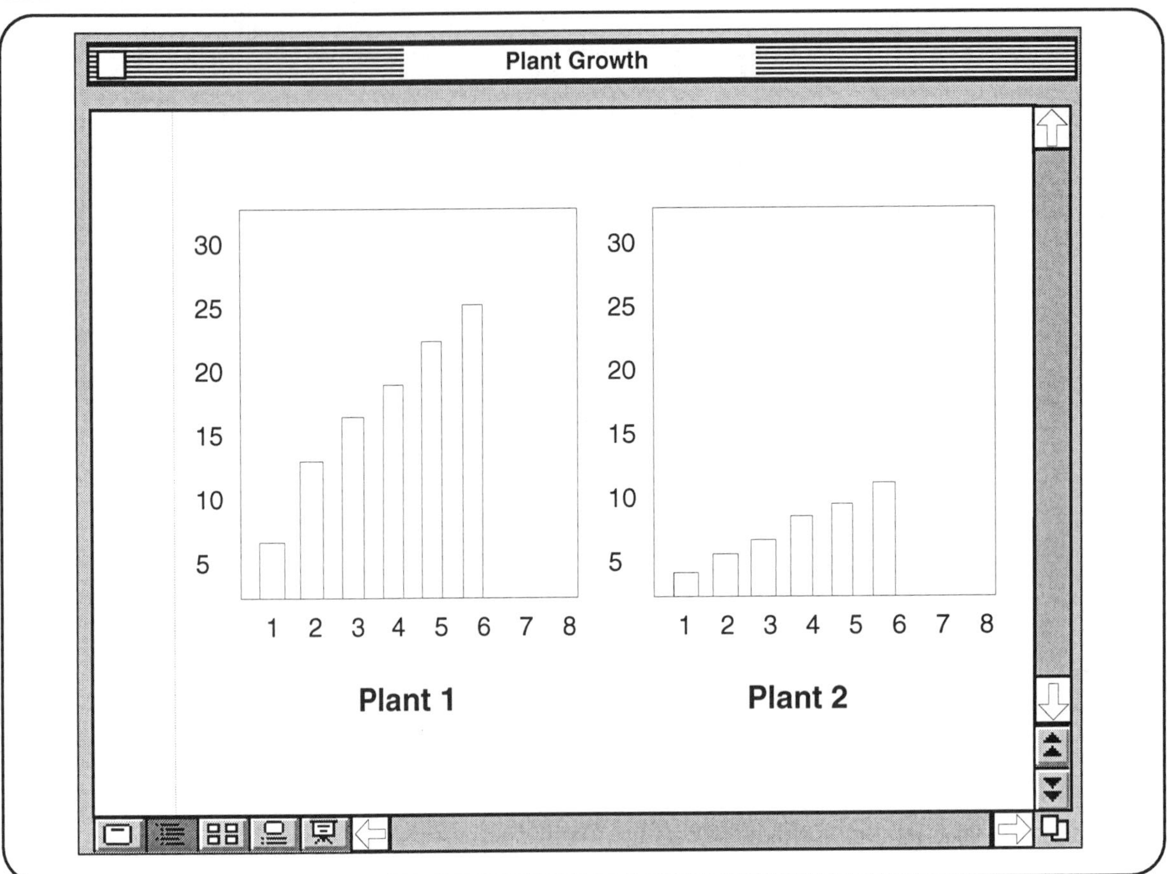

Figure 10.2 Chart example

of the purpose of bulleted text and the printout options available in the presentation tool (see ch. 6). Teachers may choose to set a minimum and maximum number of screens in the presentation.

Develop. After the students' flowchart and storyboards have been approved, teams take turns at the computer stations (see ch. 3 for a computer schedule). If teams are not working on the computers or on their storyboards, students can be:

- Conducting further research on their scientific investigation
- Conducting a similar experiment and comparing the results
- Creating a newsletter about the implications of their experiment

Evaluate. Peers and the teacher can evaluate group presentations (see ch. 7). The students receive a group grade based on the teacher and peer evaluations. Students receive an individual grade based on their self- and intragroup evaluations. The two grades can be averaged for a final score (see Final Grades in ch. 7).

How To

Lesson Description: The goal of this lesson is to encourage students to teach each other how to do something. The are many advantages of using a presentation tool for instruction: Step-by-step instructions can be bulleted; enlarged photographs can show procedures close up; video and animation can show a sequence of events; and learners can be provided with screen-by-screen handouts to assist them in the learning process.

Decide. Assign student teams as described in previous chapters. Introduce the project, explaining that the goal of the presentation is to teach their classmates how to do something. Discuss different strategies for communicating how to do something. Discuss the advantages of different media elements. Following the discussion, let groups decide on something to teach. Next, students should brainstorm different ways to teach the procedure to the class.

Design. When students are ready to move on to the Design phase, make sure they understand the importance of flowcharts and storyboards. Discuss the design issues explained in chapter 4 and, if possible, show the students sample "how-to" presentations. Again, review the significance of certain media elements. Once the students' flowchart and storyboards are approved, they can begin developing their presentations.

Develop. After the students' flowchart and storyboards have been approved, teams take turns at the computer stations. If teams are not working on the computers or on their storyboards, students can be:

- Conducting further research on their how-to activity
- Practicing their presentation through their storyboards
- Researching and evaluating how-to books
- Creating a how-to commercial

Evaluate. How-to presentations may be evaluated by the rubrics in chapter 7 or by a customized rubric designed by the class. For an example, see the How-to Evaluation blackline master at the end of this chapter.

Summary

In addition to planning and organizational skills, presentation tools provide students with the opportunity to practice speaking in front of a group and conveying their ideas verbally. Presentation tools can help support a presenter's train of thought, as well as provide visual cues for learners. Creating and delivering presentations through presentation tools provides students with valuable real-world learning experiences.

Blackline Masters

Presentation projects provide students with opportunities to practice their speaking and presentation skills. This chapter includes additional evaluation forms for assessing specific student projects. Blackline masters in this chapter include:

- Persuasive Presentation Evaluation—a rubric designed to rate the presenter's ability to persuade his or her audience
- How-to Evaluation—a rubric designed to rate the presenter's ability to teach members of the audience a procedure

Persuasive Presentation Evaluation

	1	2	3	4	5
The presenter(s) spoke clearly and in a loud enough voice.					
The presenter(s) was organized.					
The presenter(s) supported his/her opinion with interesting facts.					
The presenter(s) considered other opinions and provided a compelling reason why the audience should consider his/her opinion instead.					
The presenter(s) captured and held the audience's attention.					
The presenter(s) changed my opinion.					
1 = strongly disagree 2 = disagree 3 = somewhat agree 4 = agree 5 = strongly agree					Total ______

How-to Evaluation

	1	2	3	4	5
The presenter(s) spoke clearly and in a loud enough voice.					
The presenter(s) provided step-by-step directions.					
The directions given by the presenter(s) were clear.					
The presenter(s) used a variety of instructional approaches, such as pictures, different strategies, helpful hints, and so on.					
The presenter(s) captured and held the audience's attention.					
I was able to learn from the presenter(s).					
1 = strongly disagree 2 = disagree 3 = somewhat agree 4 = agree 5 = strongly agree					
	Total ______				

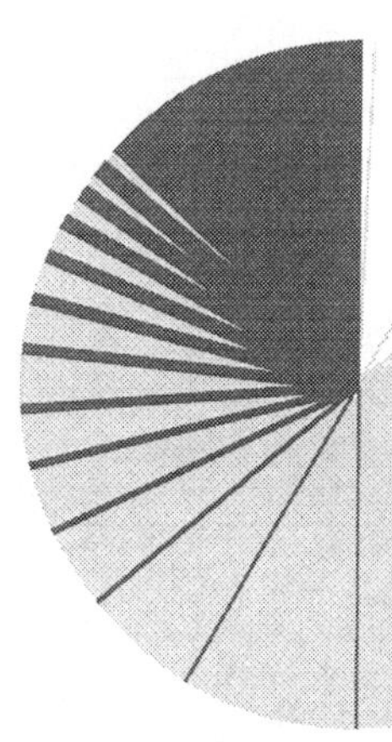

GLOSSARY

alternative assessment. A form of assessment other than the true/false, multiple-choice, matching, and fill-in-the-blank responses that are often associated with standardized tests. Performance-based assessment, authentic assessment, and portfolio assessment are forms of alternative assessment.

.AU. A common audio format for files that are linked to World Wide Web pages. These files will play on Macintosh, Windows, or UNIX computers.

authentic assessment. A method of evaluating a student's performance based on observations, performance tests, interviews, exhibitions, or portfolios. The context, purpose, audience, and constraints of the task must connect to real-world situations and problems.

authoring system. A computer program designed specifically to create computer-based instruction.

bitmapped image. A computer image that consists of individual dots or picture elements (pixels).

bits per second (bps). A common method of measuring the speed of a modem. Modems range in speed from 2,400 bps to over 33,600 bps.

branch. To move from one location of a program to another. For example, if a button initiates a video file, it is said to *branch* to video.

bug. An error in a program.

button. An object or area of the screen used to initiate an action, such as a branch to another card.

capture. The process of collecting and saving text or image data.

card. The basic unit of HyperCard and HyperStudio, equivalent to one screen of information.

CD-audio (compact disc-audio). High-quality audio stored on a compact disc in a linear format. Each compact disc can store 74 minutes of sound with no degradation of quality during playback.

CD-ROM (compact disc-read only memory). A prerecorded, non-erasable optical storage disc that stores approximately 650MB of digital data.

clip art. Graphics that are commercially distributed for use in product development.

compression. Reduction of data for more efficient storage and transmission; saves disk space, but may also reduce the quality of the playback.

constructivism. The belief that learning takes place through the construction of knowledge.

cooperative learning. A way of structuring student-to-student interaction so that students are successful only if their group is successful. Students are held accountable for their individual learning, students receive specific instruction in the social skills necessary for the group to succeed, and students have the opportunity to discuss how well their group is working.

DDD-E. A model for the systematic design of multimedia projects, consisting of four phases: DECIDE, DESIGN, DEVELOP, and EVALUATE.

debug. The process of correcting problems (code, grammar, spelling, etc.) in a program.

dialog box. A window that asks a question or allows users to input information.

digital camera. A camera that records images in true digital form. The images are usually downloaded directly into a computer through its serial port.

digital recording. A method of recording in which samples of an original analog signal are encoded as bits and bytes.

digital video. Video that is stored in bits and bytes on a computer. It can be manipulated and displayed on a computer screen.

digitizing. The process of converting an analog signal into a digital signal.

disc. Usually refers to a videodisc or compact disc. Computer diskettes are generally referred to as *disks* (with a *k*), and videodiscs and other optical storage media are referred to as *discs* (with a *c*).

disk. *See* disc.

flowchart. A visual depiction of the sequence and structure of a program.

frame. One complete video picture.

frame rate. The number of video frames displayed each second.

full-motion video. Video frames displayed at 30 frames per second.

general MIDI. A MIDI standard that assigns each instrument a unique identification number.

group investigation. A cooperative group technique similar to the Jigsaw method except that students do not form "expert groups." Student teams give class presentations of findings.

hertz (Hz). Unit of measurement of frequency; numerically equal to cycles per second.

Home Stack. A special card that acts as an index to other cards in HyperStudio.

HTML (HyperText Markup Language). Coding language used to create hypertext documents to be posted on the Web. HTML code consists of embedded tags that specify how a block of text should appear, or that specify how a word is linked to another file on the Internet.

HTTP (HyperText Transfer Protocol). The protocol for moving hypertext files across the World Wide Web.

HyperCard. A hypermedia development program developed by Apple Computer.

hypermedia program. A software program that provides seamless access to text, graphics, audio, and video through multiple connected pathways.

HyperStudio. A hypermedia development program for Windows and Macintosh computers, developed by Roger Wagner Publishing, Inc.

icon. A symbol that provides a visual representation of an action or other information. An icon of an arrow is often used to denote directional movement in hypermedia.

image. A graphic, picture, or one frame of video.

Internet. A group of networks connecting governmental institutions, military branches, educational institutions, and commercial companies.

Internet service providers (ISPs). Organizations that provide connections to the Internet. They may be universities or private companies.

Jigsaw. A method of cooperative group learning that assigns each of its members a particular learning task. Team members meet with members of other groups to form "expert groups" to discuss and research their topic. Following research and discussion, the students return to their own teams and take turns teaching their teammates about their topic.

JPEG (Joint Photographic Experts Group). An organization that has developed an international standard for compression and decompression of still images.

kilohertz (kHz). Unit of measurement of frequency; equal to 1,000 hertz.

learning together. A method of cooperative group learning that incorporates heterogeneous student groups that work on a single assignment and receive rewards based on their group product.

link. A connection from one place or medium to another. For example, buttons contain the linking information between cards.

liquid crystal display (LCD) panel. A panel that connects to a computer to display the computer screen when the LCD panel is placed on top of an overhead projector.

MIDI (Musical Instrument Digital Interface). A standard for communicating musical information among computers and musical devices. *See also* general MIDI.

MPEG (Moving Picture Experts Group). Working parties for standardization of motion video compression. MPEG-1 is used for linear video movies on compact discs; MPEG-2 is designed for broadcast quality digital video, and MPEG-3 is being developed for high-definition TV.

multimedia. A type of program that combines more than one media type for dissemination of information. For example, a multimedia program may include text, audio, graphics, animation, and video.

objects. In hypermedia, generally refers to elements that are placed on the screen, such as buttons, fields, and graphics. Objects are components that can be manipulated and can contain links to other objects.

performance-based assessment. An assessment method whereby teachers evaluate a student's skill by asking the student to create an answer or product that demonstrates his or her knowledge or skills.

pixel. A single dot or point of an image on a computer screen. *Pixel* is a contraction of the words *picture element*.

portfolio assessment. An estimation of a student's abilities based on a systematic collection of the student's best work, records of observation, test results, and so on.

PowerPoint. A presentation program developed by Microsoft.

QuickTake. A digital camera marketed by Apple Computer.

QuickTime. A file format that allows computers to compress and play digitized video movies.

RealAudio. A compression and transfer technique that allows audio files to play over the Internet as they are transferring.

resolution. The number of dots or pixels that can be displayed on a computer screen. Higher resolutions create sharper images. Also, the sharpness or clarity of a computer screen. Displays with more lines and pixels of information have better resolution.

runtime. A file used to run a hypermedia stack. It can generally be distributed without charge.

sampling rate. The number of intervals per second used to capture a sound when it is digitized. Sampling rate affects sound quality; the higher the sampling rate, the better the sound quality.

scanner. A hardware peripheral that takes a picture of an item and transfers the image to a computer.

scripting language. A set of commands that are included in some icon- and menu-based development systems. The scripting language allows complex computer instructions to be created.

scripts. A series of commands written in a language embedded in a hypermedia program.

sequencer. A device that records MIDI events and data.

slide show (electronic). Computer screens designed in a sequence for projection purposes. Many hypermedia programs provide transitional effects for these sequences (such as dissolves or wipes).

sound module. A peripheral for MIDI that uses an electronic synthesizer to generate the sounds of musical instruments.

stack. A group of cards in the same HyperCard or HyperStudio file, usually based on the same theme.

storyboard. A visual representation of what will be placed on a computer screen. In addition, storyboards contain information that assist the programmer and the production specialists in the development of media components.

Student Teams Achievement Divisions (STAD). A cooperative group technique: Students learn something as a team, contribute to their team by improving their own past performance, and earn team rewards based on their improvements.

synthesizer. A musical instrument or device that generates sound electronically.

Team Assisted Individualization (TAI). A cooperative group technique that combines cooperative learning with individualized instruction. Students are placed into groups but work at their own pace and level.

Teams Games Tournament (TGT). A cooperative group technique similar to STAD except that weekly tournaments replace weekly quizzes. Homogeneous, three-member teams formed from the existing heterogeneous groups compete against similar ability groups to earn points for their regular, heterogeneous group.

text-to-speech synthesis. Sounds created by applying computer algorithms to text to produce spoken words.

Theory of Multiple Intelligences. A theory proposing that there are multiple ways of knowing, suggesting that people possess several different intelligences (musical, linguistic, etc.).

toolbox. The menu component in hypermedia programs that contains tools to create graphics.

transition. Visual effects, such as dissolves or wipes, that take place as a program moves from one image or screen of information to the next.

Uniform Resource Locator (URL). URLs are the exact location (address) of an Internet resource, such as a Web page, a Gopher site, or a newsgroup.

upload. The process of sending a complete file to the host computer.

vector image. A computer image constructed from graphic formulae. Images that are made up of lines, boxes, and circles (such as charts) usually are vector images.

.WAV. The extension (last three letters) for sound files saved in Microsoft wave format.

Web browser. A software program that can display Web pages in HTML.

window. An area on a computer screen that displays text, graphics, messages, or documents.

World Wide Web (WWW). Hypermedia-based Internet information system. Graphical user interfaces allow users to click a mouse on desired menu items, accessing text, sound, pictures, or even motion video from all over the world.

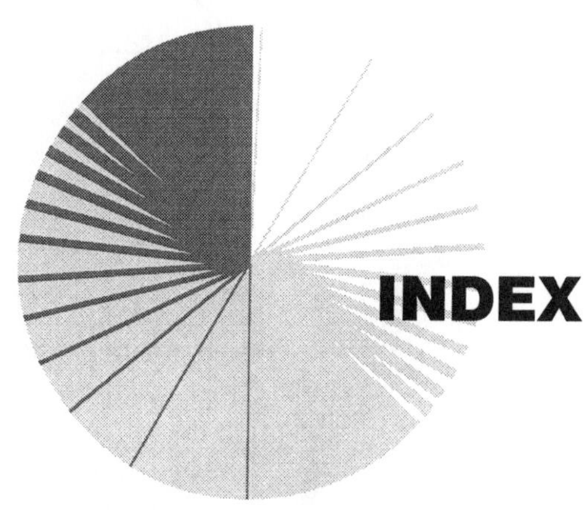

INDEX

Note: Page numbers ending in "f" refer to a figure on the cited page; page numbers ending in "t" refer to a table on the cited page.